I0760112

# HITLER'S COLLAPSE IN THE EAST

# HITLER'S COLLAPSE IN THE EAST

## A New Analysis of the Catastrophic Campaigns of 1944

DMITRY DEGTEV

FRONTLINE
BOOKS

First published in Great Britain in 2025 by
Frontline Books
An imprint of
Pen & Sword Books Ltd
Yorkshire – Philadelphia



ISBN 9781036140168



A CIP catalogue record for this book is available from the British Library.



Typeset by Lapiz Digital
Printed and bound in the UK by
CPI Group (UK) Ltd, Croydon, CR0 4YY.

The Publisher's authorised representative in the EU for product safety is Authorised Rep Compliance Ltd., Ground Floor, 71 Lower Baggot Street, Dublin D02 P593, Ireland.
www.arccompliance.com

For a complete list of Pen & Sword titles please contact

PEN & SWORD BOOKS LIMITED
47 Church Street, Barnsley, South Yorkshire, S70 2AS, England
E-mail: enquiries@pen-and-sword.co.uk
Website: www.pen-and-sword.co.uk
or
PEN AND SWORD BOOKS
1950 Lawrence Road, Havertown, PA 19083, USA
E-mail: uspen-and-sword@casematepublishers.com
Website: www.penandswordbooks.com

# CONTENTS

# LIST OF PLATES

# LIST OF MAPS

# INTRODUCTION

At the end of 1943, despite the great successes of the Red Army, Joseph Stalin still believed that victory in the war was not guaranteed. After the liberation of Kiev, he said: 'We have achieved a fundamental turning point in the war in favour of our country, and the war is now coming to a final denouement. But the Soviet people do not need to stop there, revel in their successes. Victory can be missed if complacency appears in our ranks. Victory is now close, but it will take a new strain of strength to win it.'

On the same day that Kiev was liberated, events dedicated to the twenty-sixth anniversary of the October Revolution were held in the city of Gorky.[1] The main event was the opening of the monument to Kuzma Minin on Sovetskaya Square. After several speeches at noon, the chairman of the City Council, Alexander Shulpin, pulled the red cloth from the 10m monument. 'The name of the great Nizhny Novgorod citizen became a battle banner for his descendants, which inspires them to heroic struggle against the Nazi invaders, to heroic work to strengthen the power of the Red Army,' the press wrote. In fact, this event had a significant and symbolic meaning. According to pre-war plans, a huge monument to Bolshevik Yakov Sverdlov was to be erected in place of Kuzma Minin, who in 1612 formed a new Russian army in Nizhny Novgorod that defeated Poland.

Soon after the outbreak of war with Germany, it became clear that the heroes of the revolution did not inspire Russians to great deeds. Then Stalin showed his characteristic flexibility, recalling the heroes of the past, pre-revolutionary eras: Prince Alexander Nevsky, field marshals Alexander Suvorov and Mikhail Kutuzov. And Sverdlov's place on the pedestal was taken by Minin, the Russian national hero of the seventeenth century. There were also big changes in the Red Army in 1943. The power of the sinister commissars was greatly reduced, and

1 Present-day Nizhny Novgorod.

the loyalty of the soldiers to the Bolshevik Party was no longer the main criterion for raising military ranks and awards. Stalin also returned the old-style military uniforms (with shoulder straps). The brutal repression was replaced by motivation in the form of rewards and bonuses.

Two days after the liberation of Kiev, the Supreme Soviet of the USSR established a new award (medal) Fame (Honour) of three degrees. Its statute was quite unusual. Unlike the previously existing awards and medals, which were awarded on the basis of rather abstract and generalised criteria (such as 'skilful leadership of a combat operation' or 'repeated displays of fearlessness in front of the enemy'), in this case the merits for which the award relied on were described in great detail. For example, it should have been awarded to someone who: while in a burning tank, continued to carry out a combat mission; to someone who damaged two tanks with fire from an anti-tank rifle; to someone who captured an enemy patrol post at night; to someone who shot down an aircraft with his personal weapon; to someone who, while on reconnaissance, extracted valuable information; to the one who captured an enemy banner in battle; to the one who captured an enemy officer; to the one who, being wounded, returned to the ranks after bandaging, etc. In addition, receiving the award of Fame guaranteed quite large benefits: a monthly payment of 5 to 15 rubles, an increase in the disability pension by 50 per cent, free education for children in schools and universities.

Later, this award was nicknamed 'soldier's'. The fact is that they were awarded only to ordinary soldiers and sergeants, and in the air force pilots only with the rank of second lieutenant. At the same time, if at the beginning of the war the awarding procedure was very complex and multilevel, and the lists were approved by the Supreme Council, after the capture of Kiev, the procedure was simplified as much as possible. Even platoon commanders had the authority to present the award of Fame of the III degree, and the decision was made by the commanders of divisions and corps. As a result, over a million people received this award for the remaining year and a half of the war, mostly ordinary soldiers. Stalin's style of command also changed a lot. Instead of the former total distrust and search for traitors, the Soviet leader began to rely more on a large cohort of his military leaders. Having previously reserved the right to make important strategic decisions, Stalin now gave the generals more freedom of action. And the newspapers constantly created a cult of Soviet marshals and generals, to whom poems were dedicated.

And what changes had taken place in the Third Reich? According to the testimony of people from Hitler's entourage, the catastrophic defeats suffered by the Wehrmacht in late summer and early autumn of 1943, as well as the unexpected exit of Italy from the war that coincided with them, had a strong effect on him. It turned out that the 'total war' declared after the Stalingrad collapse did not give the expected results. The 'miracle weapons', in which the Nazi leader constantly believed and with dreams of which he tried to revive faith in victory in his subordinates and allies, did not help either. The new Tiger and Panther heavy tanks did not have a noticeable impact on the course of the battles, and the production of promised other new equipment was constantly postponed. Under these conditions, Hitler seriously considered the possibility of negotiations, not with the British and Americans, but with the Soviet Union. 'The Führer would rather have gone to negotiations with Stalin,' Joseph Goebbels wrote in his diary. 'In these days of permanent crisis and incredible activity of our opponents, Hitler's confidants began to talk to him about plans to negotiate peace with one of these opponents. They tried to attract the Führer to their own side with their thoughts about such an agreement with Stalin,' wrote the Führer's adjutant Nicolaus von Below in his diary.

Hitler's entourage hoped that the loss of the capital of Ukraine would further convince him of the need to start negotiations. However, contrary to expectations, he, on the contrary, took the news of the capture of Kiev by the Russians with complete indifference. On 8 November, speaking in Munich to the 'old fighters' (veterans of the Nazi Party), shaking his fists, he shouted: 'Let this war go on as long as it pleases, Germany will never capitulate! Providence is on our side, and it will grant us victory!' After that, the Führer went to his Berghof residence in the Alps, where he quietly rested and breathed fresh air for a week. He blamed the loss of Kiev on another 'scapegoat', the list of whom since the defeat near Moscow had already reached several dozen generals and field marshals. This time, the 'culprit' turned out to be the commander of the 4th Panzer Army, Generaloberst Hermann Hoth. Hitler said that he was overworked, discouraged and failed in his job, therefore he needed to rest.

Instead of trusting generals and field marshals, there was now general suspicion, a search for traitors and those responsible for defeats. Hitler demanded that his subordinates hold all positions and cities at the front at all costs and not retreat a step. Now he constantly interfered with the command of the troops and trusted only those generals who fanatically followed his orders. In early January 1944, Hitler met with Field Marshal Erich von Manstein, commander of Army Group South. In response to suggestions to retreat from some positions, the Führer confessed to him that he pinned his main hopes on the collapse of the Allied coalition. He argued that the coalition was full of internal contradictions and was very fragile. The main thing was for his forces to bide their time. Therefore, he forbade Manstein from retreating and urged him to wait for a 'turning point in the war' …

Thanks to the huge amount of documents collected, the author has managed for the first time to completely reconstruct the course of battles during this dramatic period of the war. In Russia, it is known as the 'ten Stalin strikes'. Many of the events included in the book have never been described in historical literature either in Russia or in the West.

- The events are shown dynamically and consistently, restoring the chronology and creating a complete mosaic of the battle on the Eastern Front in 1944. The plans of the Soviet command, the true objectives of the operations and their results are analysed.
- The actions and tactics of all branches of the armed forces are described in detail: tanks, infantry, motorised infantry, artillery, cavalry. Is it true that the Russians had a huge superiority in tanks?
- Special attention is paid to the actions of the air force and their impact on the course of grandiose battles.
- The book answers topical questions: what efforts the Red Army made to support the Warsaw and Slovak uprisings. Could the Soviets have saved Warsaw and was Stalin really interested in an unsuccessful outcome of the uprising?
- Why was the Red Army unable to cross the Vistula River in 1944?
- What actually stopped the large-scale Soviet offensive in August–September 1944?
- What was the potato war and where did this strange term come from?
- How did the Russians learn to break through strong German defences and storm cities?
- What role did Armia Krajowa, the Ukrainian Rebel Army and other 'freedom warriors' play in these events?
- How did the Russians and Germans fight in pockets and how did their tactics differ?
- Finally, how did Hitler differ from Stalin?

Chapter 1

# JANUARY THUNDER

## Attacks in the fog

The Russians struck the first powerful blow in the Leningrad area. Fighting in this sector of the front began in autumn 1941. In September, Army Group North reached the outskirts of the huge city on the Gulf of Finland and the shore of Lake Ladoga. Hitler refused to storm Leningrad and decided to strangle it with a blockade. This venture led to huge civilian casualties (600,000 residents died of starvation), but did not shake the fanatical determination of the Russians to defend the enclave. For two and a half years, fierce battles were fought around Leningrad: the Soviets sought to break the blockade at any cost, and the Germans tried to prevent this. In fact, it was a senseless and bloody battle, distracting significant forces of the Wehrmacht and the Luftwaffe. By the beginning of 1944, the entire marshy lowland in the area of Leningrad and Lake Ladoga was a desert pitted with endless trenches and shell craters.

From the outskirts of Leningrad, the front line passed through the vast wastelands between the Mga railway station and the Volkhov River, along the Volkhov and Lovat rivers to a huge swampy area located west of the city of Velikiye Luki. The main strongholds on this line were the ancient Russian cities of Chudovo, Novgorod, Staraya Russa and Holm. The Germans were able to hold all these locations in 1942–43, despite constant attacks from the Red Army. And now Hitler was not going to give up these outposts without a fight. However, the situation had changed significantly by this time. In January 1943, the Soviets managed to push the Germans back from the southern shore of Lake Ladoga and they could now freely transfer their troops to Leningrad and to the Oranienbaum bridgehead – a large stretch of the Gulf of Finland coast that the Germans could not occupy in 1941. By the

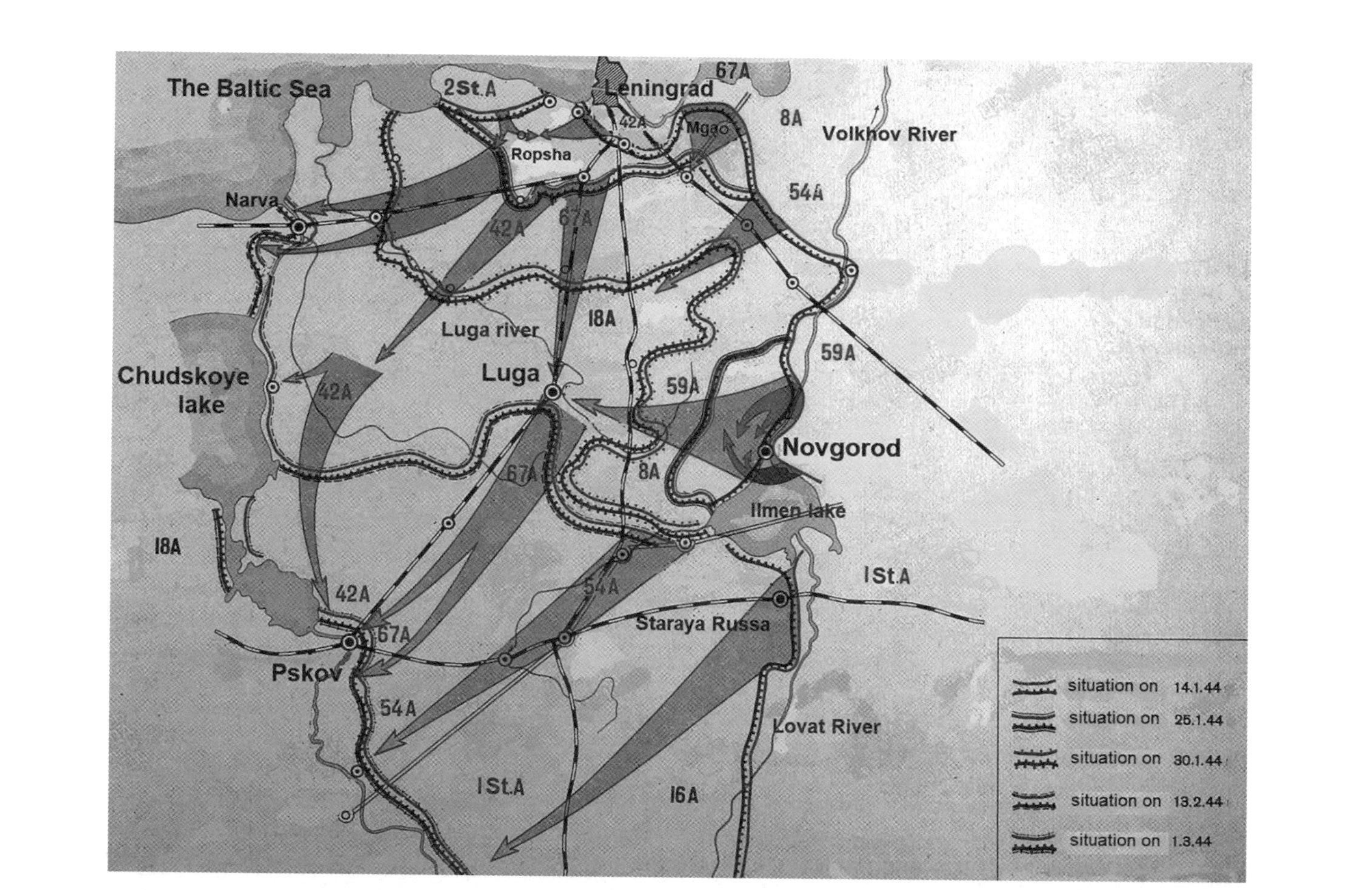

The Baltic Sea
2St.A
Leningrad
67A
42A
Mgao
8A
Volkhov River
Ropsha
Narva
54A
42A
67A
Luga river
18A
59A
Chudskoye
lake
42A
Luga
59A
Novgorod
67A
8A
Ilmen lake
18A
1St.A
54A
42A
67A
Staraya Russa
Pskov
54A
Lovat River
1St.A
16A
situation on 14.1.44
situation on 25.1.44
situation on 30.1.44
situation on 13.2.44
situation on 1.3.44

beginning of January 1944, the Leningrad Front (commander General Alexander Govorov) had thirty rifle divisions, three rifle brigades and four tank brigades, a total of about 400,000 soldiers and 600 tanks and self-propelled artillery pieces. There were about 500 aircraft in the 14th Air Army, the Baltic Fleet Air Force and the 7th Air Defence Fighter Corps. In addition, the Russians concentrated about 5,000 artillery pieces near Leningrad and prepared their ships stationed in the city for firing. Two cruisers and one battleship were supposed to support the offensive by firing directly from the Neva River.

The purpose of Operation January Thunder was the final lifting of the siege of Leningrad, the encirclement and defeat of the main forces of the German 18th Army, and the creation of conditions for the rapid liberation of the Baltic region.

The German troops in the Leningrad area were severely exhausted by continuous fighting, and they had not received sufficient reinforcements for a long time since this sector of the front was considered calm. In late December, two infantry divisions were selected from Army Group North and these withdrew to other sectors of the front. And in early January, the 1st Infantry Division – one of the oldest and best divisions of the Wehrmacht – was sent to Army Group South. The front line from the Baltic Sea to the Mga station was defended by nine infantry divisions, two Luftwaffe field divisions and two SS volunteer Panzergrenadier brigades. These units had almost no tanks, but only self-propelled artillery pieces (fewer than 100 pieces). The Luftwaffe forces in the sector of Army Group North were also severely weakened. There were only two fighters air groups (IV./JG54 and II./JG5, based at the airfields of Dno, Pleskau (Pskov) and Siverskaya), one Ju 87 air group (I./SG5) and one air group of light night bombers, armed with old Go 145s and He 46s.

The commander of Army Group North, Field Marshal Georg von Küchler, knew that the Soviets were preparing a powerful offensive against his troops. He was sure that it would not be possible to hold the stretched positions this time, and on 30 December he suggested to Hitler that he should retreat and withdraw to the straightened line of defence. But he received a predictably firm refusal.

On the morning of 14 January, thousands of shells of various calibres, including 180mm and 305mm shells fired from ships and railway artillery pieces, rained down on the German trenches. Then, in front of the German trenches in the area of the Oranienbaum bridgehead, a terrifying series of 109 powerful explosions rang out. It was the mines laid by Russian sappers that exploded, making wide passages in the German minefields. By early 1944, the Russians had already gained a lot of experience in overcoming German defensive positions. Since it was impossible to deactivate thousands of antipersonnel mines buried in the ground unnoticed, Russian sapper companies usually penetrated minefields in the dark, made narrow paths, and then buried explosive charges along them. Every night, dozens of sappers crawled into the minefield and went about their work. By morning they had masked the results of their labour and crawled away. It was dangerous and painstaking work, but afterwards it had a great effect. With the simultaneous detonation of many charges, hundreds of anti-personnel mines detonated. Gaps were formed in the minefield, through which the Red Army soldiers stormed to the German trenches. Then tanks drove through the same passages.

At 10.40 a.m., units of the 2nd Strike Army rushed to attack with terrifying cheers. The main blow fell on the Germans' 9th and 10th Luftwaffe Field Divisions, which were not distinguished by high resilience and professionalism. By the end of the day, the soldiers of the 48th, 90th and 131st Infantry Divisions, supported by the 152nd Tank Brigade, had achieved success. By the end of the day, the Russians had advanced 4km, capturing the strongholds of Porozhki and Gostilitsy.

The Germans had to withdraw to their second defensive line. On the first day, the commander of the 3rd SS Panzer Corps (III. SS-Panzerkorps), Obergruppenführer Felix Steiner, was forced to throw his only reserve into battle – the 4th Volunteer Panzergrenadier brigade 'Netherlands' (4.SS-Freiwilligen-Panzergrenadier-Brigade 'Nederland'). It consisted of Dutch volunteers. And it was the only unit in Army Group North that had tanks. The regiments of this brigade were alerted and transported by trucks to the breakthrough site.

The Soviets learned that Dutch infantry was operating in front of them the very next day. A captured corporal from the 1st Battalion, Becker Erickson, spoke in detail about the history of the formation of the brigade, its fight against partisans in the Balkans and the way to the Eastern Front. This Dutchman willingly gave the Russians all the secrets: the list of military equipment, the location of Steiner's headquarters, the strength of all battalions, etc. The commander of the 2nd Strike Army, General Ivan Fedyuninsky, was very surprised to hear about the Dutch SS. At first, he didn't even believe this information. However, it was soon confirmed by radio interception data. At that time, the Russian radio interception service also reached perfection. Listening to the enemy's entire broadcast, experienced translators quickly compiled reports, which were processed by analysts within an hour. Then all the information received was sent to the army headquarters. Since the Germans, unlike the Russians, rarely used ciphers, the Soviets knew about all their requests, reports and orders transmitted near the front line. It was from the radio interception that Fedyuninsky learned that in the first two days of the offensive, many German infantry companies had lost a third of their personnel, and soldiers from auxiliary units (sappers, builders, etc.) had been thrown into the front line.

Russian air operations were limited due to heavy cloud and fog. The planes mainly struck ground targets but, due to the poor visibility, they had to fly low, flying directly over the heads of the attacking soldiers and shooting at German trenches and pillboxes with cannon and machine guns at point-blank range. The Russians also deployed a large number of Il-2s as spotter aircraft for howitzer artillery.

Meanwhile, on 15 January, troops of the Soviets' 42nd Army launched an offensive from the Pulkovo area, that is, from the outskirts of Leningrad. Despite long and careful preparation, in the early days the Red Army achieved only minor successes, encountering the stubborn defence of the 50th Army Corps. Nevertheless, on 20 January, after fierce fighting, Ropsha, a city located 25km south-west of Leningrad, was captured.

Simultaneously with the Leningrad Front, the Volkhov Front under the command of General Kirill Meretskov went on the offensive. The Russians took into account their extensive experience of fighting in the past two and a half years and had begun to prepare carefully for the attack in September 1943. In the rear of the 54th and 59th Armies, in the middle of the swamps, a huge mock-up of German defensive lines several kilometres long was built. It included wire fences, ditches, minefields and rivers. Rifle divisions and assault groups were brought to this training site every week. At the same time, some of them imitated the defending Germans, the others the advancing Red Army. Soldiers were trained not only to sneak up to defensive lines and overcome them, but also to manoeuvre quickly in the depths of enemy defences, to pursue retreating units. Special attention was paid to the management of troops on the ground, the correction of artillery fire and the use of aviation. Large-scale exercises involving aircraft and tanks were conducted in December. At the same time, the Russians began to build camouflaged trenches that led to German positions, as well as advanced firing positions for artillery.

Another innovation used by the Red Army was false artillery firing. Before the start of the offensive, artillery opened fire on several sectors of the German defences at once. At the same time, only 30 per cent of shells and mortar shells were fired at the true area of attack, with the rest fired into sectors where no one was going to advance. This technique was supposed to confuse the Germans and wreak havoc on their defences. The task was facilitated by the fact that weak units of Army Group North operated in the Novgorod region. The 38th Army Corps defending there included the 1st Luftwaffe Field and 28th Jäger Divisions and the 2nd Latvian SS Brigade. At the same time, Latvians and Estonians were entrusted with defending the shore of Lake Ilmen. This area was considered the safest.

On the morning of 14 January, hundreds of guns opened fire on the western bank of the Volkhov River south of Novgorod. A little later, explosions began to be heard to the north of the city, as well as in the area of the Zakharya bridgehead (35km north of the city). It was there that the Soviets struck the main blow. But much more dramatic events took place on the western shore of Lake Ilmen. Early in the morning, while it was still dark, Latvian soldiers heard a strange sound coming from the east.

At first it reminded them of the noise of aircraft engines, and the SS thought that it was Russian U-2 night bombers flying. In fact, it was NKL-26 snowmobiles moving on the ice. These were self-propelled combat sleds on skis, 5.5m long and powered by an aircraft engine mounted in the rear. The two-man crew was in an armoured hull and was armed with a machine gun. The sled could carry up to six infantrymen holding on to the handrails. On the ice, these amazing vehicles could travel at 70kmh. Several dozen snowmobiles suddenly reached the shore, landing the first infantry. They were soon followed by the second and third waves. For the Latvian brigade, the appearance of Red Army soldiers on snowmobiles was a complete surprise. Chaos and panic ensued, which allowed the Russians to quickly seize a bridgehead, liberate fifteen villages and reach the Veryazha River. Throughout the day, the Russians used snowmobiles to deliver reinforcements and ammunition to the west bank, and evacuated the wounded on return trips. As a result of this brilliant operation, the Soviet 59th Separate Rifle Brigade managed to capture the village of Borki, 20km south-west of Novgorod, and cut the Novgorod–Shimsk highway.

When Küchler's headquarters learned that the Russians had crossed Lake Ilmen and the Latvian battalions had escaped, they found themselves in complete confusion. The first thing that came to the Germans' mind was to try to break the ice! On the morning of 15 January, Ju 87 Stukas appeared over the lake and dropped 80 high-explosive bombs on its surface. The thin ice cover cracked, but Russian snowmobiles easily avoided the affected areas and still darted between the shores. Two days later, the bridgehead was expanded to 6km wide and 7km deep. Moving through supposedly impassable swamps, the Russians desperately rushed forward and soon approached the muddy Novgorod–Luga highway. This was the last way the German units could escape in a westerly direction.

On 18 January, the commander of the 18th Army, General Georg Lindemann, ordered a retreat. However, he was too late. Abandoning all heavy weapons and self-propelled artillery, the Germans rushed to break through. But only half of this group was able to reach the huge Dolgovsky Moss swamp before the Russians arrived there. Almost the entire 1st Air Field Division and part of the 28th Jäger Division were cut off in this remote and wild area. The German soldiers desperately tried to make their way by detours through the swamp. Hundreds of soldiers died in this crazy campaign, many of them swallowed up by the Novgorod quagmire. Approximately 3,000 chose to surrender.

On 20 January, the Russians entered Novgorod. They saw the oldest city, from which Russian civilisation originated, and the largest historical monument, in a deplorable state. Of the 2,500 residential buildings, only forty survived. The Kremlin and the ancient Novgorod cathedrals were severely damaged. There were practically no residents on the streets. At that moment, Field Marshal von Küchler, commander of Army Group North, had to contact Hitler by phone. He informed him that the defences south of Leningrad and in the Novgorod region had collapsed, and the 26th Army Corps defending near the Mga station could be under threat of encirclement. The Führer was very disappointed by the fact that it was not possible to repel the attacks of the Soviets on the old defensive lines, which Nazi propaganda repeatedly declared to be 'impregnable'. But Hitler did not give any clear instructions on what to do next.

However, Küchler, who was always distinguished by determination and knew how to put a fait before the Führer, made this phone call more as a formality. He already understood that this time it would not be possible to contain the massive Soviet offensive. And his goal was to preserve his small forces and then withdraw them to a new defensive line.

All of Küchler's thoughts were already connected with Panther. This was the name of a powerful defensive line, which the Germans began to build through the sweat of the local population and German contractors in autumn 1943. It stretched from Narva through Chudskoye Lake–Pskov–Nevel–Vitebsk and further along the hills east of Orsha and Mogilev. In the band of Army Group North, the line included about 6,000 field fortifications (including 800 concrete bunkers), 180km of barbed wire and 30km of anti-tank ditches. Unlike the southern sector of the Eastern Front, where there was no time to start building Panther before the Soviet troops crossed the Dnieper, in the north everything was ready for a stubborn defence on new frontiers.

Without waiting for Hitler's sanction, Kuehler ordered the withdrawal of the 26th Army Corps from the Mga – an 'enchanted stronghold' that the Russians had not been able to capture during countless attacks that lasted for more than two years. Having gained a foothold on the new line along the Moscow–Leningrad highway, the Germans again stood on the defensive there.

It is worth noting that the winter of 1943–44 in Russia turned out to be very mild. Judging by the memoirs of German soldiers, on the Eastern Front they constantly froze and had to climb huge snowdrifts, while the air temperature was always -30 degrees. In fact, the Russian climate is very changeable. Even in the very harsh winter of 1941–42, frosts were often replaced by prolonged thaws, when rain fell instead of snow. The climate in Russia depends entirely on atmospheric cyclones and anticyclones. At the same time, the weather can change in a few hours. For example, in the evening the soldiers would go to bed in a severe frost, a heavy snowfall would began at night, but in the morning it would be raining and the temperature would rise above freezing.

In the winter of 1943–44, cyclones dominated Eastern Europe, which invariably brought warm air from the Mediterranean and the Atlantic. The snow cover was very thin, so it often melted, and it rained frequently in December and January. Such weather was more comfortable for soldiers who spent most of their lives in the trenches and moving to new positions, but it had a strong influence on the course of the fighting. The mud from the winter thaw hampered the movement of tanks, vehicles and horse-drawn wagons and slowed the transporting of infantry. It also greatly interfered with air force operations, with constant cloud cover hanging at an altitude of 50–100m, morning fogs and drizzle making navigation, searching for targets and conducting aerial reconnaissance difficult. And sodden and dirty airfields made it difficult for planes to take off and land. Bombers and ground-attack planes had to fly low over trees, although such flights in poor visibility were fraught with danger due to accidents and high losses from infantry fire.

In January most of the planes were still flying with summer black and green camouflage, covered with a thick layer of dirt. With high and medium altitudes usually occupied by impenetrable cloud, the air war moved to low level for a long time and air battles took place at a maximum of 500m, and most often at 300m and even 50m above forests, fields and villages. That winter, the Soviets began to use Polikarpov U-2 biplanes as their main bombers. Due to their slow speed and good view from the cockpit, these aircraft, resembling something from the First World War, were more suitable for flying in such weather. Flying directly above the ground, they dropped bombs with delayed-action fuses on suitable targets through the fog and haze. These unpretentious planes could take off even from muddy and unpaved airfields. The Luftwaffe adopted a similar approach to the Russian air force. In January 1944, they often used their lighter He 46 and Go 145 aircraft, the latter also a biplane, to adjust artillery fire and observe the enemy. Near Leningrad, they were sometimes seen in groups of four or five.

## Meeting with a Panther

By 26 January, the troops of the Leningrad Front liberated Krasnogvardeysk, and four days later they reached the Luga River, seizing a bridgehead on the west bank in the Ivanovsky area. Four days later, units of the Soviet 67th Army reached Siversky, where a large Luftwaffe air base had been located since the autumn of 1941. From now on, there was no continuous front; the main group of German troops (about fourteen divisions) retreated from the east, north-east and north to Luga, and the second one, consisting of five to six divisions, split into separate small combat groups, retreated west to Narva. Hitler was afraid that this would turn into an uncontrolled retreat and began a search for the culprits. On 31 January, Küchler was summoned to a meeting at the Wolf's Lair headquarters. There, the Führer accused the field marshal of not following orders, having insufficient fortitude and losing command of his troops. Küchler was dismissed, and Generaloberst Walter Model was appointed in his place. This commander had already gained fame as the 'fireman of the Führer'; a kind of 'superman' who, even in the most critical situation, was able to inspire troops and cope with any crisis. Hitler ordered the 'fireman' to urgently create a new line of defence along the Luga and Mshaga rivers to Lake Ilmen. Since the first attempts of the 2nd Baltic Front under the command of General Markian Popov to break through the defences of the 16th German Army south of Lake Ilmen had failed, Hitler still hoped to retain this desolate swampy and wooded area, which had proved so difficult to hold in 1942–43.

However, Model, who had never argued with the Führer but understood the real state of affairs perfectly well, realised that it would no longer be possible to stay at the specified line. However, he wanted to withdraw the divisions of Army Group North to the Panther line as soon as possible in order to take up defence there and exhaust the Russians, who would inevitably face problems due to stretched communications and lack of supplies.

At the end of January, Soviet reconnaissance aircraft were photographing the western bank of the Narva River, having discovered there a powerful line of defence consisting of many barriers, trenches and bunkers. All settlements were adapted to circular defence. This was the northernmost part of the Panther line, or 'Eastern Shaft', which the Germans began to build in the autumn of 1943.

On 3 February, the advance units of the 2nd Strike Army reached the Narva River and the city of Narva. The 43rd Rifle Corps immediately crossed the river north of the city, capturing two bridgeheads on the opposite bank. At the same time, the 122nd Rifle Corps captured two bridgeheads to the south. Narva was the most important stronghold in the Panther line and the 'gateway' to the Baltic region. Hitler stated that the retention of the city was of paramount political importance, including from the point of view of relations with Finland. Therefore, he gave the usual order – to defend it to the last soldier and rifle cartridge.

The defence of Narva, now declared a 'Festung' (fortress), was carried out by the 54th Army Corps of General Otto Sponheimer. At this time of crisis, he received small reinforcements in the form of the Panzergrenadier Division Feldherrnhalle and one regiment of the 58th Infantry Division. 'Glory to the soldiers who made the withdrawal. There can be no question of retreat now! Narva must be held to the last drop of blood. We will die for Narva, but we will not let the Russians into Germany!' said the pathetic appeal read to the soldiers.

In the following days, the war zone was again covered by heavy snowfalls and fog, which chained the aircraft of both sides to the ground. But the weather did not stop the advancing land forces of the Red Army. Taking advantage of the absence of a solid front line and the inability of the defender to quickly organise defence in conditions of mud and sparsely populated wooded areas, advanced units quickly bypassed strongpoints, again and again creating a threat of flanking and encirclement for the enemy. They forced the Germans to retreat further south and west.

However, the Soviet troops also experienced great difficulties. 'The troops encountered destroyed bridges, roads, and rubble on their way. This is the work of our partisans operating in the German rear. Progress was hampered by bad roads. Traffic jams up to 2 kilometres long formed on the roads. The rear wagons and artillery lagged behind. The queen of our battlefields, mother infantry overcame the difficulties of off-road, refusing to rest, moved forward, catching up with the enemy,' it was reported in the journal of combat operations of the 108th Infantry Corps, advancing to Gdov on Chudskoye Lake, also called Lake Peipsi.

The advance was often hindered by the Luftwaffe. On 5 February, the 108th Rifle Corps was subjected to air attacks by German aircraft that flew over the Gubin-Perevoz–Gdov highway and bombed infantry from a low level, with about thirty troops killed and injured. The next day, He 111s twice bombed detachments and convoys of the 90th and 126th Infantry Divisions. Eight Red Army soldiers were killed and forty-three were injured, with forty-two horses killed and injured. However, these separate raids could not stop the advance of the Red Army. On 12 February, they captured Luga, and units of the 42nd Army, which crossed the Plyussa River in several places, occupied Gdov with a rapid advance and reached Lake Peipsi. After that, General Model was forced to authorise the evacuation of the 16th Army from its positions along the Lovat River, as well as a general withdrawal to the Panther line. However, the Russians had already reached it in the Narva area.

On 11 February, the 2nd Strike Army launched an attack in order to expand the bridgeheads on the west bank of the Narva River. The Russians sought to reach the Baltic Sea to the west of the 'fortress' and completely surround it. After several days of fierce fighting, Soviet troops managed to achieve minor successes. Units of the 43rd Rifle Corps, advancing north-west of Narva, advanced 2km in a narrow area. South-west of the city, units of the 109th and 122nd Rifle Corps advanced 12km, but were also stopped by fanatical German defenders. The greatest success was achieved by the 30th Guards Rifle Corps, which reached the Narva–Yyhvi railway and highway on 17 February and captured Auvere. However, stubborn resistance and constant German counter-attacks in the Blue Mountains, the last natural obstacle separating the Red Army from the coast, forced the offensive to be suspended in this sector as well.

Near Narva, the Soviets again clashed with the Dutch from the 3rd SS Panzer Corps. Interestingly, after being captured, these soldiers from the Netherlands told the same story. They said they were tricked into joining some kind of 'security battalion' and promised that they would only protect the rear areas and fight saboteurs. However, then the unsuspecting 'Dutch sheep' were tricked into going to the front and forced to fight against the Russians on pain of death. For example, a captured soldier of the Nederland brigade, 25-year-old Willem van Deyk, who was captured on the banks of the Narva River, said that he worked as a concrete worker. 'In October 1943, I voluntarily joined the Dutch security battalion, but the Germans deceived me, sent me, like many others, to Alsace to an SS training camp. There I completed seven weeks of infantry training. In total, 2,000 recruits were trained there, mostly foreigners. At the end of November 1943, a hundred Dutch were sent to the 11th SS Reserve Tank Grenadier Battalion in Graz. I was enlisted in the 5th company of this battalion.' When the company arrived at the positions near Narva, it consisted of eighty soldiers, and the main armament of the Dutch infantry consisted of 10 MG42 machine guns. Van Deyk also said that the Dutch were 'apathetic' and did not believe in a German victory.

Using numerous units manned by citizens of different European countries on the Eastern Front, Hitler tried to give the war an international status. It was as if not just Germany, but 'the whole of civilised Europe' was fighting Bolshevism on a single impulse. In this, the Führer copied Napoleon, who in 1812 sent to Russia a huge 'Grande Armée', half consisting of Germans, Austrians, Poles and Italians. The fate of this army turned out to be tragic, with few of these soldiers returning to their homeland. Now history was repeating itself. The Dutch, Danes, French, Slovaks, Croats, Hungarians, Romanians and Italians fought in the Russian open spaces for incomprehensible purposes and died by the thousands allegedly to 'save Europe'. This made it easier for Stalin to produce propaganda. He inspired his troops with analogies to Napoleon's army: 'You see: then and now we are at war with the whole of Europe!'

Meanwhile, the chance of a rapid capture of Narva was missed. On 13 February, the Germans with heavy Tiger tanks launched a counter-attack north of Auvere with heavy Tiger tanks. On the night of 15 February and in the afternoon, they again attacked the bridgeheads south-west and north-west of the city. On 23 February, after receiving reinforcements, units of the newly formed task force Narva again launched counter-attacks along the entire front, supported by air strikes. The Luftwaffe bombed Soviet pontoon river crossings to make it difficult to supply bridgeheads. The next day, the Germans launched a powerful attack against the bridgehead in the area of Tyrvala (north-west of Narva), while one of the strike groups even tried to force the river under the cover of a smokescreen and cross to the north bank. Periodically, the Germans raised observation balloons, from which they corrected artillery fire. These were usually covered by a pair or four Bf 109s continuously circling a little higher.

However, the main role in ensuring that the Wehrmacht, in a situation that seemed catastrophic, still managed to first hold the front, and then clear the Narva–Tallinn railway line of Soviet troops, was played not by aviation, but by artillery. By concentrating many stationary and mobile artillery batteries on a narrow section of the front, skilfully combining the firing of long-range howitzers with field guns and rocket-propelled mortars, corrected from dozens of observation posts, the gunners completely took control of terrain that was convenient for defence. For example, on 20 February, more than 5,000 shells and mines of all calibres, including rockets, were fired at Soviet positions; on 27 February, 4,500, and on 5 March, 4,000. On some days, the Germans literally bombarded the crossings and starting positions of the 2nd Strike Army with a hail of ammunition, preventing any movement near their line of defence. And it was from artillery that the Russians suffered the greatest losses.

Despite the setbacks and the general strengthening of the enemy's defences, on 22 February Stalin ordered the Leningrad Front to cross the Velikaya River as quickly as possible, capture Pskov and Ostrov Island, and then develop an offensive against Riga. By the end of the month, the leading units of the 42nd and 67th Armies reached the main defensive strip of the Pskov–Ostrovsky fortified area, which was part of the Panther line. There, the offensive that started in Leningrad and Novgorod finally ran out of steam and for the next five months the fighting in this sector took on a positional character. The Germans also managed to hold a bridgehead on the eastern bank of the Narva River near Ivangorod. Despite the fact that the ambitious plans of the Soviet command to encircle and completely defeat Army Group North were not implemented, the Wehrmacht had suffered another heavy defeat, and the front line had shifted 100–250km to the west – to the borders of the Baltic region.

Chapter 2

# THE UKRAINIAN COLLAPSE

## Operation Waltraut is Manstein's Last Blitzkrieg

Army Group South of Field Marshal Erich von Manstein repelled the endless attacks of the Red Army in Ukraine during the winter. Hitler demanded the holding of the line of defence along the Dnieper, even when Soviet troops from the numerous bridgeheads they had captured were deeply wedged into the German defences.

At the end of December 1943, the Red Army launched an offensive south of Kiev in the direction of Vinnytsia, where Manstein's headquarters were located. The stretched defence of the 4th Panzer Army could not withstand the onslaught and crumbled on the first day. After that, the Russians moved in divergent directions and introduced a thousand tanks into the breakthrough. On 30 December, the Russians liberated Zhytomyr, on 4 January the Belaya Tserkov, and the next day Berdichev. The German 4th Panzer Army had to retreat to the south-west, while the 8th Army was still on the Dnieper in the Cherkassy area. As a result, a large gap was formed between the two German armies, into which General Nikolai Vatutin (commander of the 1st Ukrainian Front) immediately sent his tanks. On 8 January, the Russian 1st Tank Army reached Vinnytsia, and the 40th Army advancing from the left reached the approaches to Uman. The only obstacle to the Russian tanks rolling across the plain were attacks by the Luftwaffe. The combat log of the 8th Guards Mechanised Corps reported: 'The enemy's ground-attack planes Me 109 and Fw 190 were particularly active, attacking and firing machine guns and cannon at columns of troops approaching the Ilyintsy area. They literally chased individual vehicles, tanks and even small groups of people.'

The biggest nightmare for the Wehrmacht was Colonel Vladimir Gorelov's 1st Guards Tank Brigade. Due to the absence of German

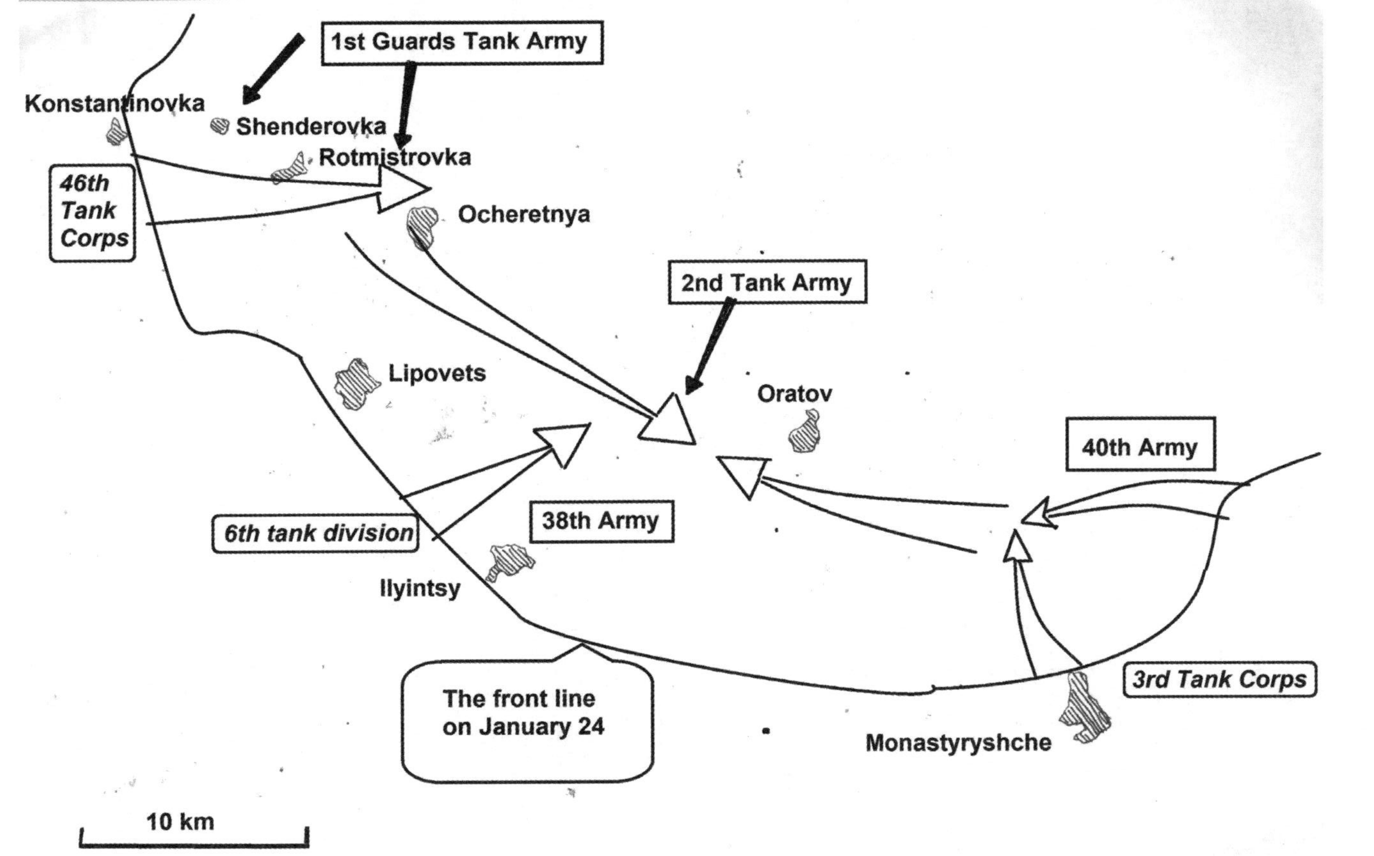
1st Guards Tank Army
Konstantinovka
Shenderovka
Rotmistrovka
46th Tank Corps
Ocheretnya
2nd Tank Army
Lipovets
Oratov
40th Army
6th tank division
38th Army
Ilyintsy
The front line on January 24
3rd Tank Corps
Monastyryshche
10 km

forces and cloudy weather, a group of twenty tanks and self-propelled guns made a 60km raid into the German rear. On the evening of 9 January, the first T-34s suddenly appeared in Zhmerinka, the most important railway station on the Lviv–Odessa railway line. At that moment, German reserves arriving by train were concentrated in the city and these were urgently transferred to the breakthrough area. Tiger tanks were still unloading on the railway platforms, where soldiers getting out of the wagons had been certain that the Russians were still north of Vinnytsia. Hospitals were filled with the wounded, while trucks and columns of soldiers were moving everywhere. Suddenly, explosions were heard in one of the trains arriving in Zhmerinka. The StuG self-propelled guns standing on the platforms began to explode, then the locomotive burst into flames. The German soldiers, engulfed in fire, jumped from the wagons to the ground on the move and fell into the snow to extinguish themselves. Then explosions rang out on the streets of Zhmerinka, from somewhere came the terrifying screams of 'Russische Panzer! Russische Panzer!'

Several T-34 tanks drove through the entire city, crushing vehicles, carts and guns and shooting fleeing German soldiers. Some of them reached the western outskirts of Zhmerinka, causing incredible chaos. This episode showed how well the Russians had mastered the tactics of blitzkrieg. At the beginning of the war, German tanks carried out multi-kilometre raids, and then suddenly appeared on the streets of cities, causing terror and panic. And now the Germans themselves were running away in horror from the T-34 tanks that had crawled out of nowhere, which were covered with mud from top to bottom and looked even more frightening.

Manstein was also in shock. After all, now the Red Army was already on the southern bank of the Southern Bug River (it was considered the 'new border' of Romania), in the deep rear of Army Group South. However, this moment was the high point of Gorelov's tank raid. In the evening of that day, the reserves gathered by Manstein, combined into the 1st Panzer Army, launched a counteroffensive. On 14 January, the 1st Guards Tank Brigade and the 20th and 21st Mechanised Brigades were caught in a pocket. With great difficulty, these units managed to break through to the north-east, abandoning almost all their tanks.

After a ten-day pause, Manstein completed the concentration of two strike groups and ordered the launch of an offensive on 24 January, dubbed Operation Waltraut. General Hans Gollnick's 46th Panzer Corps (two tank, two infantry, one Jäger and one mountain division) was advancing from the Vinnytsia region, and General Hermann Bright's 3rd Panzer Corps (three tank divisions) was advancing from Uman. In total, the Germans managed to concentrate 290 tanks (including forty-one Tigers and eighty-two Panthers) and eighty self-propelled artillery pieces on a narrow sector of the front. By this time, 328 tanks and fifty-four self-propelled artillery pieces remained in the opposing 1st Tank Army of General Mikhail Katukov. The Russian tank brigades, which had moved 150km away from their rear bases, were becoming exhausted and suffered from a shortage of fuel and ammunition. The unfolding battle was somewhat reminiscent of Operation Citadel near Kursk in July 1943. The Soviet troops occupied a square ledge about 100km wide, and the German panzer corps with a large number of tanks were forging the flanks of this arc. Shock fists from heavy Tiger tanks were moving ahead, crushing the defences and shooting at T-34 tanks from a long distance. They were followed by Panthers and Pz.III and IV medium tanks with armoured personnel carriers. They consolidated the success and provided infantry attacks. Both groups were supported by He 111s and ground-attack Fw 190s.

The Germans were successful, and they quickly crushed the Soviet defences on both sides of the salient. This is how this offensive was described in the combat operations journal of the Russian 38th Army: 'The enemy led the attack with tanks in echeloned groups of 50–60 pieces, together with self-propelled artillery pieces and assault troops on tanks and armoured personnel carriers. Interacting with the infantry, tanks and self-propelled guns opened volley fire from a distance of 2,000 metres at the positions of our anti-tank artillery. This tactic has almost paid off. Our inexperienced and poorly trained gunners prematurely opened fire on tanks from a long distance, giving away their location. The enemy actively used heavy Tiger tanks to fight our artillery, they exchanged fire with our artillery batteries.'

While the 3rd Panzer Corps was advancing on Oratov, the 6th Panzer Division attacked from the south in the direction of Rossosh, cutting the encircled Soviet grouping into pieces. At the same time, the Germans continued their attacks at night to prevent the Russians from gaining a foothold and entrenching themselves in new positions. Vatutin decided to delay Manstein's tank wedges by striking at the left flank of the 46th Panzer Corps in the Shenderovka area. The attack of the 7th Guards Tank Corps of General Sergei Ivanov began on the morning of 25 January. However, from the very beginning it faced great difficulty. At first, the T-34 tanks found themselves in a vast muddy swamp. Many of them got stuck, while others with great difficulty, sinking a metre into the mud, moved through the slush. When the first tanks approached Shenderovka, the Tigers, standing motionless on the hills, appeared ahead. The Germans fired at the barely crawling T-34s, while the Russians could not get close to firing range. Then Fw 190s appeared, which first dropped bombs, then turned around, descended to the level of 50–100m and fired cannon at the engine compartments of Russian tanks. Nevertheless, the Russians managed to break into Shenderovka and this village changed hands several times.

The next day, the battle continued, but the 7th Guards Tank Corps failed to advance beyond Shenderovka. The 54th and 56th Tank Brigades were almost destroyed, losing eighty T-34s, and several dozen more tanks were stuck in the mud. This allowed the Germans to continue their offensive. On 28 January, the strike wedges joined up, and the Russian 17th Guards and 21st and 40th Rifle Corps were trapped in the resulting pocket. Vatutin took this defeat hard, which overshadowed recent high-profile victories. But he had an important advantage over Manstein. Vatutin did not need to ask for Stalin's highest permission to break through, and he did not even have to call his general staff. Therefore, the surrounded troops immediately received the order to break through to the north. By dawn on 29 January, having broken through the German barriers in the Sinarni area with a desperate attack, the Russians had broken out of the pocket.

The 1st Tank and 38th Armies suffered the most in this battle. The former lost 10,000 men, including 3,333 killed, and the second lost 20,000 men, including 1,778 dead and 12,000 missing. After the Russians counted their losses, several groups of infantry managed to escape from German territory.

However, for the Germans it was also a Pyrrhic victory. The strike groups lost 140 tanks and self-propelled artillery pieces, that is half of their equipment. The striking power of Manstein's panzer divisions was greatly reduced, and already around the corner new fierce battles awaited them.

## 'Very strong, stubborn and stable army'

As it turned out, Operation Waltraut was Manstein's last successful offensive in his illustrious career. But he didn't have time to celebrate this tactical victory. Russian forces completed the encirclement of the German 11th and 42nd Army Corps of the 8th Army on the southern bank of the Dnieper River on the exact same day when the Germans surrounded the Russians between Vinnytsia and Uman. It happened in the Korsun region, just 100km to the east. Another pocket appeared, which included nine infantry divisions, one security division, three sapper battalions, four construction battalions, the Belgian SS brigade Wallonia, the SS division Viking, the Estonian battalion, the 810th Armenian battalion, the Russian Kuban cavalry regiment and other units. General of Artillery Wilhelm Stemmermann assumed overall command over the group. At first, the pocket's perimeter was quite large, but then it quickly shrank to 35km in diameter. Then events began to develop according to the standard Hitler scheme: a deblocking blow from the outside and an air bridge. But in this case, Hitler immediately allowed Manstein to act according to circumstances, including breaking through in a south-westerly direction. Responsibility for the supply of the blockaded group was assigned to Fliegerkorps VIII, while inside the perimeter the reception of transport aircraft was organised at the Korsun air base. Flights to the pocket began on the morning of 29 January, when the first fourteen Ju 52s took off from Uman with 30 tons of ammunition on board. As usual, He 111 bombers had to be involved in the supply mission. This practice had developed during the defence of the encircled Demyansk in February–March 1942. Then there was Stalingrad, and later twin-engine bombers regularly had to engage in the 'potato war', as the staff doctor of Kampfgeschwader KG27 'Boelcke' called such missions. This bomber unit, more than others, had to supply countless Hitler 'fortresses' with food.

The Red Army also had extensive experience in encircling German troops, and it was no secret to Russian commanders that the Germans would immediately organise an air bridge. In the very first days, anti-aircraft batteries were placed on the blockade ring, and fighters regularly patrolled in the sky above the pocket. The vulnerable Ju 52s were saved only by cloudy weather, as well as the pilots' ability to fly at just 50m.

On 2 February, a large group of prisoners fell into the hands of the Red Army. They said that the officers had demanded that the soldiers put up fierce resistance and not lose heart. The encircled had been promised that in three or four days an offensive of three panzer divisions would begin from the south, which would break through the blockade ring and free the units of the 8th Army. However, the commanders of the 2nd Ukrainian Front were optimistic about resisting the breakout attempt. By that time, ten rifle divisions and three tank corps were located on the outer ring of the blockade, and eight rifle divisions, three cavalry divisions, four tank regiments and one tank brigade were located on the inner ring. The Soviets had 243 tanks in this area. 'Thus, the superiority of forces is on our side, which makes it possible, combining offensive with defence, to repel any enemy tank attacks from the south and south-west and defeat the encircled enemy divisions,' the journal of combat operations of the 2nd Ukrainian Front reported.

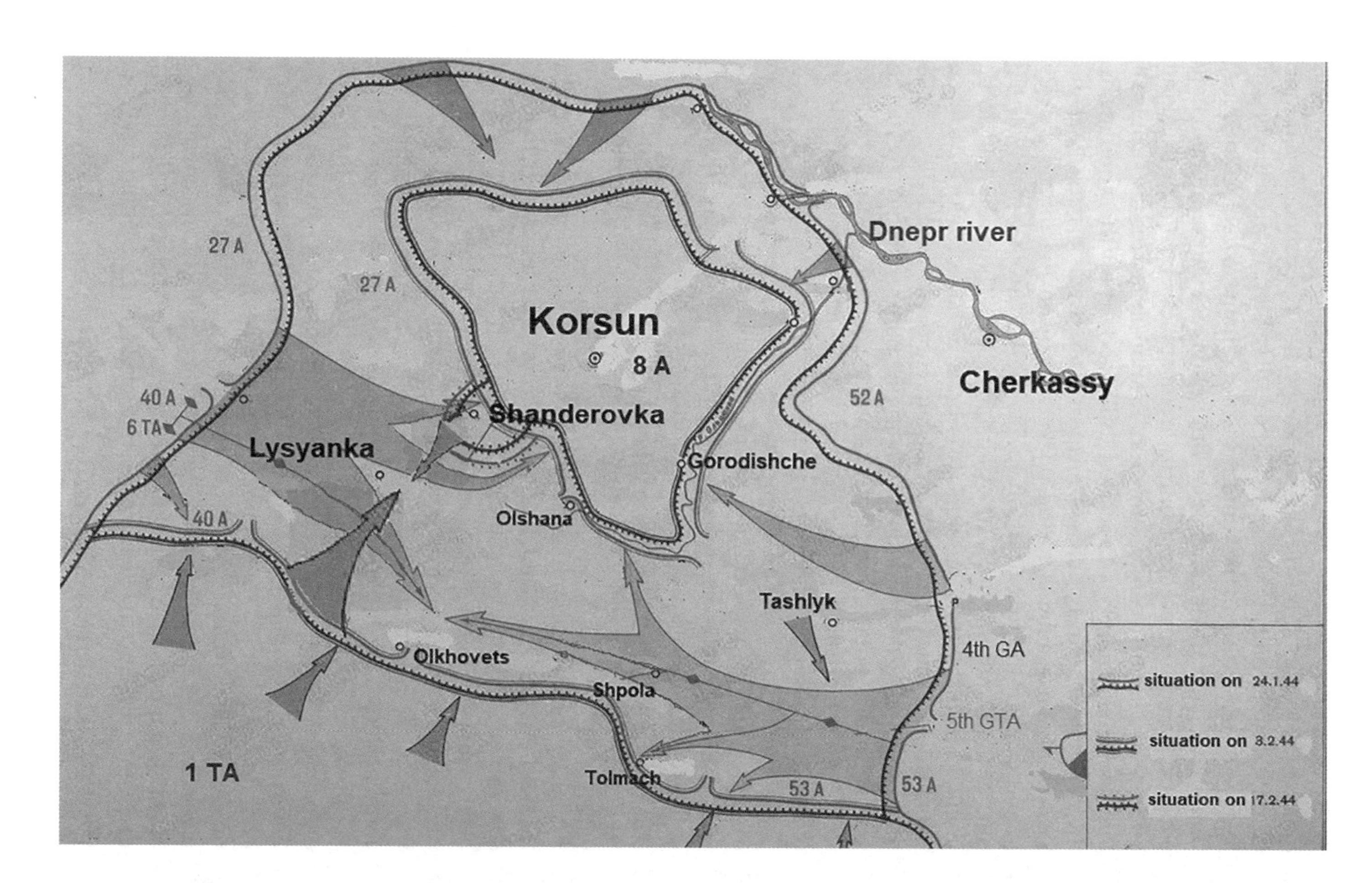

Dnepr river
Korsun
8 A
Cherkassy
27 A
27 A
52 A
40 A
6 TA
Shanderovka
Lysyanka
Gorodishche
Olshana
40 A
Tashlyk
Olkhovets
4th GA
Shpola
5th GTA
1 TA
Tolmach
53 A
53 A
situation on 24.1.44
situation on 3.2.44
situation on 17.2.44

The unblocking operation began on 1 February. From the south (from the Antonovka–Kaligorka area), a German strike group went on the offensive. The encircled troops attacked from the north. Tanks and infantry were moving to meet each other to connect in the Shpola area. By 5 February, the Germans had managed to make significant progress from both directions, narrowing the blockade ring. But at the same time, the Red Army attacked the defence perimeter from different directions and began to quickly compress it. During 4 February, the 52nd Army advanced 14km to the west. The next day, the cavalrymen of the 4th Guards Army surrounded and captured the important German stronghold of Olshana, south of Korsun. In addition, significant reserves were transferred to the Shpola area, which made it possible to repel further attacks. The Journal of Combat Operations of the 2nd Ukrainian Front reported: 'Despite the fact that the German group has been completely surrounded for several days now, and the offensive of our troops is steadily compressing the encirclement ring, despite the complete failure of unblocking the encircled troops from the south and the inability to get out of this ring of fire, despite the fact that the encircled suffer huge losses in manpower and equipment, there are no facts of demoralization and disorganisation in the surrounded divisions, only individual soldiers surrender, resistance is stubborn, counter-attacks do not stop. This phenomenon shows once again that we are fighting a very strong, stubborn and stable army.'

After repelling the first German attacks, the Soviet command issued an ultimatum to the encircled troops on behalf of Marshal Zhukov and Generals Konev and Vatutin. The text was typical and actually copied a similar ultimatum put forward thirteen months ago to the 6th Army in Stalingrad. The Germans were offered to surrender in full force and give up all military equipment intact. In exchange, they were guaranteed to keep their military uniforms, insignia, medals and officers' edged weapons (daggers), be provided food, medical care, and after the war departure to any country in the world. Later, Russian planes dropped messages from Field Marshal Friedrich Paulus and other generals who were captured in Stalingrad. They were intended for the command of the surrounded German group. Paulus wrote that Hitler had betrayed the interests of Germany, was sending his soldiers to certain death and asked those in the pocket to capitulate in order to avoid bloodshed. However, there was no response from the pocket to these messages. Most German generals, officers and soldiers still believed in Nazi propaganda and were ready to sacrifice themselves further for the sake of a senseless struggle.

Having failed to break through the blockade ring from the south in the Shpola area, Bright's 3rd Panzer Corps launched an offensive from the south-western direction along the Tikhonovka–Lysyanka–Shanderovka axis. The four panzer divisions that were part of it were able to quickly break through the front. On 7 February, the Germans captured the village of Vinograd, and the next day occupied Tatyanovka, Kosyakovka and Repki. At the headquarters of the 2nd Ukrainian Front, the optimistic mood changed to an anxious one. It became obvious that the Germans were breaking through to the Lysyanka–Shanderovka area in order to connect with the encircled troops.

However, the onset of another thaw made the roads almost impassable. The strike group had 126 tanks and self-propelled artillery pieces, which, due to mud, consumed three times more fuel than usual. But the Germans wouldn't be Germans if they hadn't come up with something! The crews had no choice but to resort to delivering fuel from stuck tanker trucks in buckets. It was easier to do this barefoot, since the human carriers got their boots stuck in the mud every ten minutes. Then it was decided to supply the advancing tank divisions by air.

It turned out to be a very dramatic situation. The unblocking group slowly moved in a narrow wedge in the direction of the pocket, being subjected to counter-attacks from both flanks. At the same time, mud-splattered Ju 52 planes periodically appeared out of the fog, dropping containers with ammunition, fuel and food rations on parachutes or without them. Mud and snow so softened the impact of the container on the ground that even 75mm and 88mm shells packed in heavy boxes did not receive any damage. It was harder with fuel, and one in five of the dropped fuel barrels exploded on impact. To escape anti-aircraft fire, the desperate pilots of German transport planes descended almost to the ground, literally hiding behind forests or low hills!

Meanwhile, the Russian 4th Guards Army captured the stronghold of Gorodishche, south-east of Korsun. All the streets of the destroyed city were clogged with abandoned and burnt-out vehicles, while boxes, various cargoes and weapons were scattered everywhere. The Germans could no longer hold the entire perimeter of the defence, concentrating all their troops in large strongholds. The air bridge worked smoothly, and the scale of the supply operation reached the level of Stalingrad. So, on 9 February, 199 Ju 52s and He 111s flew to the pocket, delivering 140 tons of ammunition and 34m$^3$ of fuel, with another 396 containers dropped from the air. Some 668 wounded soldiers were taken out on return flights. On 10 February, planes delivered 370 tons of cargo to Korsun, and 760 wounded were flown out.

The climax of the battle came on 12 February. German tanks reached the Gniloy Tikich River and reached the outskirts of Lysyanka. At the same time, the encircled troops began to break out of the Steblev–Tarascha area in a south-westerly direction. The Soviet command desperately took measures to keep the advancing Germans out of the pocket, but the concentration of troops was hampered by the same terrible mud caused by rains and melting snow. T-34 tanks got stuck and sank, while fuel trucks could not deliver fuel to them. Also, artillery could not get to the concentration areas because even horses could not get through the swamps that had been formed. 'The troops are operating in extremely difficult conditions with complete impassability of roads, with a shortage of fuel for tanks and vehicles. The soldiers are fed at the expense of local resources,' stated the headquarters of the 2nd Ukrainian Front.

The Russian Air Force was also experiencing serious problems. Due to the muddy conditions, airfields were unsuitable for intensive take-offs and landings, so most of the aircraft were idle. Many pilots could not find their air base after completing the mission and landed anywhere. The command of the ground forces demanded that that air force obtain accurate information about the enemy and its movements, but the pilots could not do this due to bad weather and a shortage of reconnaissance aircraft. On 12 February, the commander of the 1st Guards Assault Aviation Corps (1st SCHAK), General Aleksey Ryazanov, even had to form a special reconnaissance squadron consisting of six Il-2s. Experienced ground-attack crews, well-versed in the terrain, had to fly over German territory at low level and control the movement of tanks.

Soviet aviation also had to spend a lot of effort on supplying its troops in the pocket area. For example, from 8 to 16 February, the 326th Night Bomber Aviation Division (NBAD), equipped with U-2 biplanes, carried out 822 transport flights. Some of the cargo was dropped from the air, while some was unloaded during landings. In total, 49 tons of fuel, 65 tons of ammunition, and 620 rockets for Katyusha rocket-propelled mortars were delivered to the troops during this period. On 14 February, it was snowing heavily in the pocket area. Stalin's Falcons were inactive, so the command had no idea what was going on inside the blockade ring. When soldiers of the 52nd Army reached the city of Korsun in the evening in fog, they found only empty streets and fifteen damaged Ju 52s. The Germans had already headed to the south-west, moving all their remaining units to the Shanderovka area.

On 15 February, Russian intelligence found out that the Germans were burning and blowing up tanks and vehicles that could not be taken with them, and were preparing for a decisive breakthrough from the pocket. However, the Soviets failed to prepare for it because of the mud. By this time, Soviet tanks were without fuel and shells. For example, the 27th Tank Brigade had fifty T-34s, but there was only a third the required diesel fuel left, and half the ammunition. Two Guards airborne divisions were urgently deployed to the blockade ring. The paratroopers were ordered to dig in in an open area and repel attacks by German tanks with anti-tank rifles and grenades.

On 16 February, the Germans completely captured Lysyanka and expanded the bridgehead on the north bank of the Gniloy Tikich River. By 7 p.m., the village of Oktyabrsky was captured. As a result of fierce fighting, the strike group managed to break through a 20km-long corridor towards the pocket. Now the units of the 3rd Panzer Corps and those in the pocket were separated by about 7km. On the night of 17 February, a breakthrough began on a 4.5km-wide front. At 03.00, a huge force, led by tanks and self-propelled guns, entered the positions of the 180th Infantry Division and the 5th Guards Airborne Division, defending in the area of the villages of Komarovka and Khilki. The Russian infantrymen and paratroopers, who had almost no artillery and shells, were quickly crushed. After that, the Germans rushed in a continuous stream in a south-westerly direction. When dawn broke, the Red Army soldiers saw several columns of infantry, tanks and wagons with wounded moving from Shanderovka to Khilki. The headquarters of the 2nd Ukrainian Front ordered the commanders of aviation units to assemble all serviceable aircraft and strike at the Germans breaking through. However, due to a severe snowstorm, which reduced visibility to 1km, not a single Soviet aircraft took to the sky.

In the morning, most of the Germans, overcoming incredible difficulties, managed to connect with units of the 3rd Panzer Corps through the mud and streams. After that, the German troops began to withdraw to the south-west. Although the breakthrough was successful, and the 'second Stalingrad' did not take place, the damage to the Wehrmacht was still enormous. Of the 56,000 soldiers trapped in the pocket, 37,000 eventually managed to break through. But at the same time, they had to abandon all their artillery and heavy equipment. Moreover, most of them were no longer combat-ready troops, but a demoralised and exhausted rabble. Some 11,000 German and Belgian soldiers and collaborators were captured.

Fifty-five-year-old General Wilhelm Stemmermann, who personally led his troops into the attack at dawn, was not among those who escaped from the pocket. On 18 February, near the village of Petrovsky (halfway between Shanderovka and Lysyanka), Red Army soldiers found a corpse in a general's uniform in the snow. He was carrying a soldier's book No. 2, a driver's licence issued on 28 August 1930, a hunting ticket issued on 1 April 1941, and other documents with photographs. They had a first and last name on them – Wilhelm Stemmermann. In addition, the corpse was identified by prisoners who were personally acquainted with the general. By order of General Ivan Konev, Stemmerman (Hitler awarded him posthumously with Oak Leaves for the Knight's Cross) was buried with military honours in a separate grave in the cemetery of the village of Zhurzhintsy. So the future marshal showed respect for the Nazi commander, who did not abandon his soldiers but personally led them to salvation. This grave has been preserved to the present time. In parallel, Konev wrote a report to Stalin, in which he significantly embellished his successes. 'Our troops – infantry, tanks, cavalry and artillery – fell on the enemy, with fire, bayonet, tracks and sabres during the day they mercilessly destroyed the enemy,' he wrote. The Soviet Information Bureau also announced the complete defeat of the Wehrmacht and even its degradation: 'The captured Germans said that over the past 3–4 days, soldiers and officers of the surrounded troops committed mass suicides. Wounded German soldiers and officers were killed and burned on the orders of the High Command.' Stalin was satisfied and on 20 February he awarded Konev, commander of the 2nd Ukrainian Front, the rank of marshal.

## The Russian Cavalry is Attacking

Meanwhile, a crisis had arisen on the eastern flank of Army Group South. There, General Karl Hollidt's 6th Army was still defending a large salient in the Nikopol area and holding a bridgehead on the south-eastern bank of the Dnieper. Hitler claimed that this area was of paramount importance because of the manganese deposits, without which, allegedly, it was 'impossible to wage war'. The Führer often justified the retention of unfavourable positions for economic reasons, and he reproached his generals for 'ignorance of economics'. In addition, Hitler told Manstein that Nikopol was important because of its proximity to the Crimea, where Erwin Jaenecke's 17th Army, cut off from all sides, was still defending itself. Finally, the Führer's main 'trump card' in his endless discussions and disputes with military leaders was the 'political significance' of the Crimea and southern Ukraine. He claimed that if the Wehrmacht retreated from the region, Turkey would side with the Allies, and this would have 'fatal consequences'. As a result, the Soviets had another opportunity to surround an entire army.

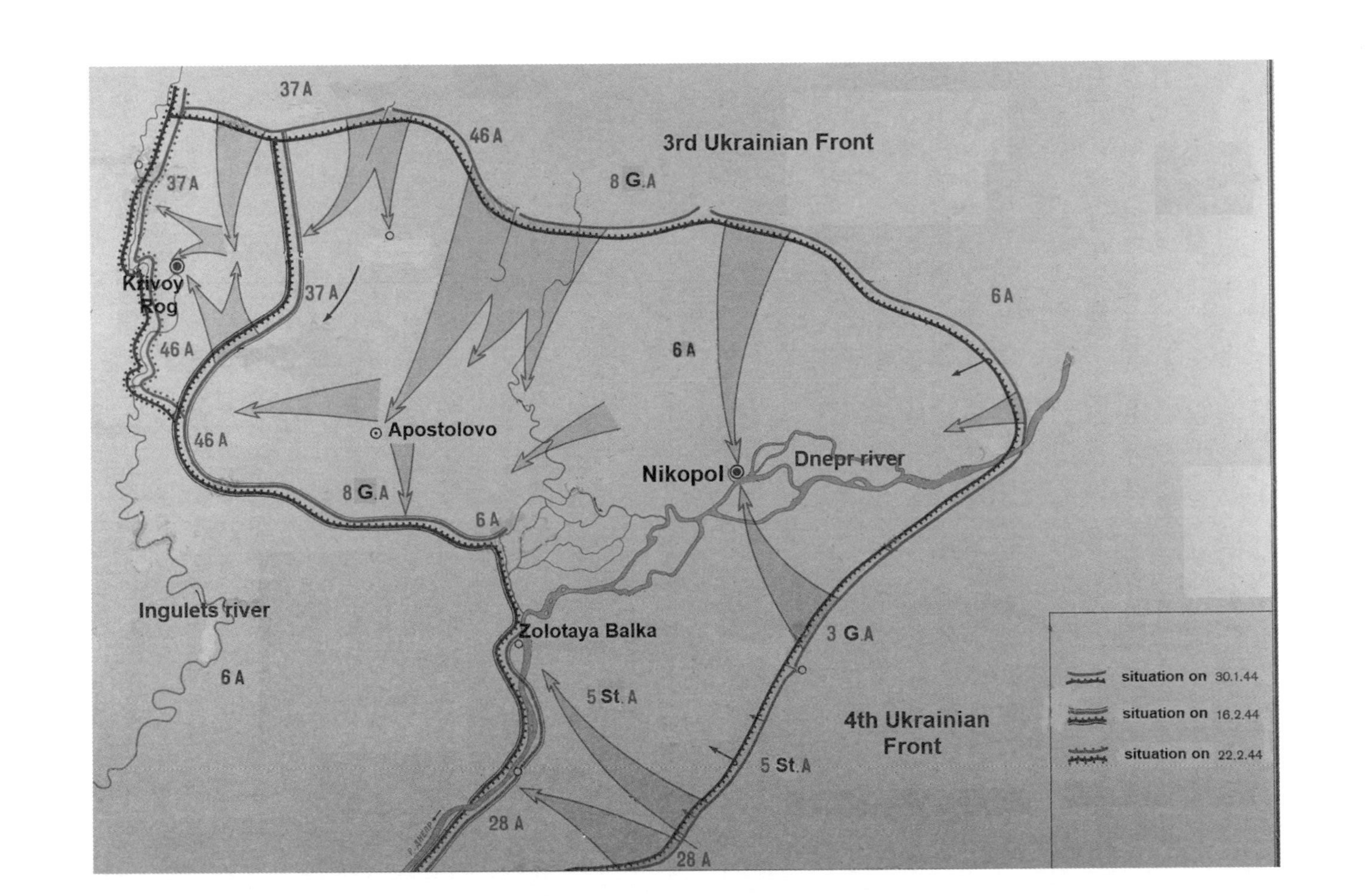
3rd Ukrainian Front
37 A
46 A
8 G.A
37 A
Krivoy Rog
37 A
46 A
6 A
6 A
Apostolovo
46 A
Nikopol
Dnepr river
8 G.A
6 A
Ingulets river
Zolotaya Balka
3 G.A
6 A
5 St. A
4th Ukrainian Front
5 St. A
28 A
28 A
situation on 30.1.44
situation on 16.2.44
situation on 22.2.44

On 30 January, the armies of the 3rd Ukrainian Front under the command of General Rodion Malinovsky launched an offensive to the north-west and north of Nikopol. They immediately managed to break through the German defences in several places and, despite desperate counter-attacks, the Russians began to advance to the Apostolovo railway station, the main rear base of the German 6th Army. On 1 February, Manstein gave the order to begin the gradual evacuation of the 29th Army Corps from the Nikopol bridgehead. In order to start a full evacuation, Hitler's permission was required, and it was very difficult to get it!

On 3 February, the 30th Army Corps retreated across the Kamenka River, which Apostolovo was only 11km from. And on the left flank, the Germans had to retreat to Avdotevka and Zlatoustovka, beyond which the road to the city of Krivoy Rog opened. Now the Red Army was already 60km north-west of Nikopol, which made further defence of this city with its manganese mines pointless. Two days later, the Russians were already in Apostolovo, which forced Manstein, effectively presenting the Führer with a fait accompli, to order a retreat. On 8 February, the Germans left Nikopol, avoiding being caught in another pocket at the last moment. In the destroyed city, the Red Army captured only small trophies: 200 trucks (mostly defective) and two railway trains. However, in order to escape, these soldiers still had to negotiate a narrow corridor along the Dnieper, which the 8th Guards Army was already ready to cut from the north. At the crucial moment, Hollidt managed to concentrate a strike force of 150 tanks south of Apostolovo, which attacked the sprawling Russian flank. Fierce fighting raged in the area for several days, which eventually allowed the 6th Army to be saved and taken across the Ingulets River. On 22 February, the Red Army liberated the city of Krivoy Rog. The manganese mines that Hitler was so worried about were lost.

It was from this battle that the ascent of the star of Hitler's new 'favourite' general of the mountain troops, Ferdinand Schörner, began. It was he who commanded the defence of the Nikopol bridgehead in autumn 1943 and, with weak forces, managed to repel all the attacks of General Fyodor Tolbukhin's 4th Ukrainian Front. In February, Schörner miraculously managed to get his troops across the Dnieper and take them beyond Ingulets. Hitler knew this fanatical general well from his actions in Lapland, the northernmost sector of the Eastern Front. Although Schörner did not achieve any impressive successes there, the Führer liked his adherence to Nazi ideology and his love of brutal discipline of the troops. The worse things turned out on the fronts, the more Hitler needed loyal military leaders who were ready to carry out any, even insane, orders from their boss without discussion. The Führer believed that it was precisely such violent fanatics who could save the Third Reich from collapse. Immediately after the end of the battle in the Nikopol area, Schörner was appointed chief of Staff of the Nazi Party at the Wehrmacht High Command. He was supposed to fulfil Hitler's long-held dream of instilling Nazi ideology in the army. However, the 'gendarme general' (as the soldiers called Schörner) did not hold this post for very long. After another collapse in southern Ukraine, he was needed again at the front.

As already mentioned, the winter in the south of Russia turned out to be very warm. And the so-called 'rasputiza' – the severe wetting of the surface layer of the soil – began in February. By the end of the month, the situation had only worsened. The terrain was becoming increasingly unsuitable for tanks. The commander of Army Group A, Field Marshal Ewald von Kleist, hoped very much that the mud would force the Russians to suspend major offensive operations, as had already happened in 1942 and 1943. However, these hopes turned out to be illusory. In 1944, the Red Army learned to advance through the mud!

Preparing for a new offensive, the commander of the 3rd Ukrainian Front, General Rodion Malinovsky, decided to place his main bet on cavalry. He summoned the commander of the cavalry-mechanised group, General Issa Pliev, and entrusted him with the risky task of crossing the Ingulets River near the city of Krivoy Rog, breaking deep into the German rear, sowing chaos there and cutting off the enemy's escape routes to Nikolaev. Experienced cavalryman Pliev had had to carry out similar missions more than once. The first time Soviet cavalrymen launched raids deep into German territory was during the Battle of Moscow. Since then, cavalry, as in the wars of the nineteenth century, hard remained a powerful weapon. This may seem ridiculous to the current generation of people, who say, 'What could horsemen do against tanks, artillery and machine guns?' In fact, horses in cavalry divisions were only a means of transportation. Unlike vehicles, armoured personnel carriers and motorcycles, these animals could move through almost any terrain and at high speed. The horses did not need petrol, and food for them could be found everywhere. Cavalrymen very rarely engaged in battle on horseback; they usually dismounted and fought like ordinary infantry. The supply of cavalry during deep raids was often carried out by air. In addition to cavalry, mounted mechanised groups usually included tank brigades (in light tanks) and motorised rifle brigades in American armoured personnel carriers. Suddenly appearing behind enemy lines, Stalin's cavalrymen terrified the Germans.

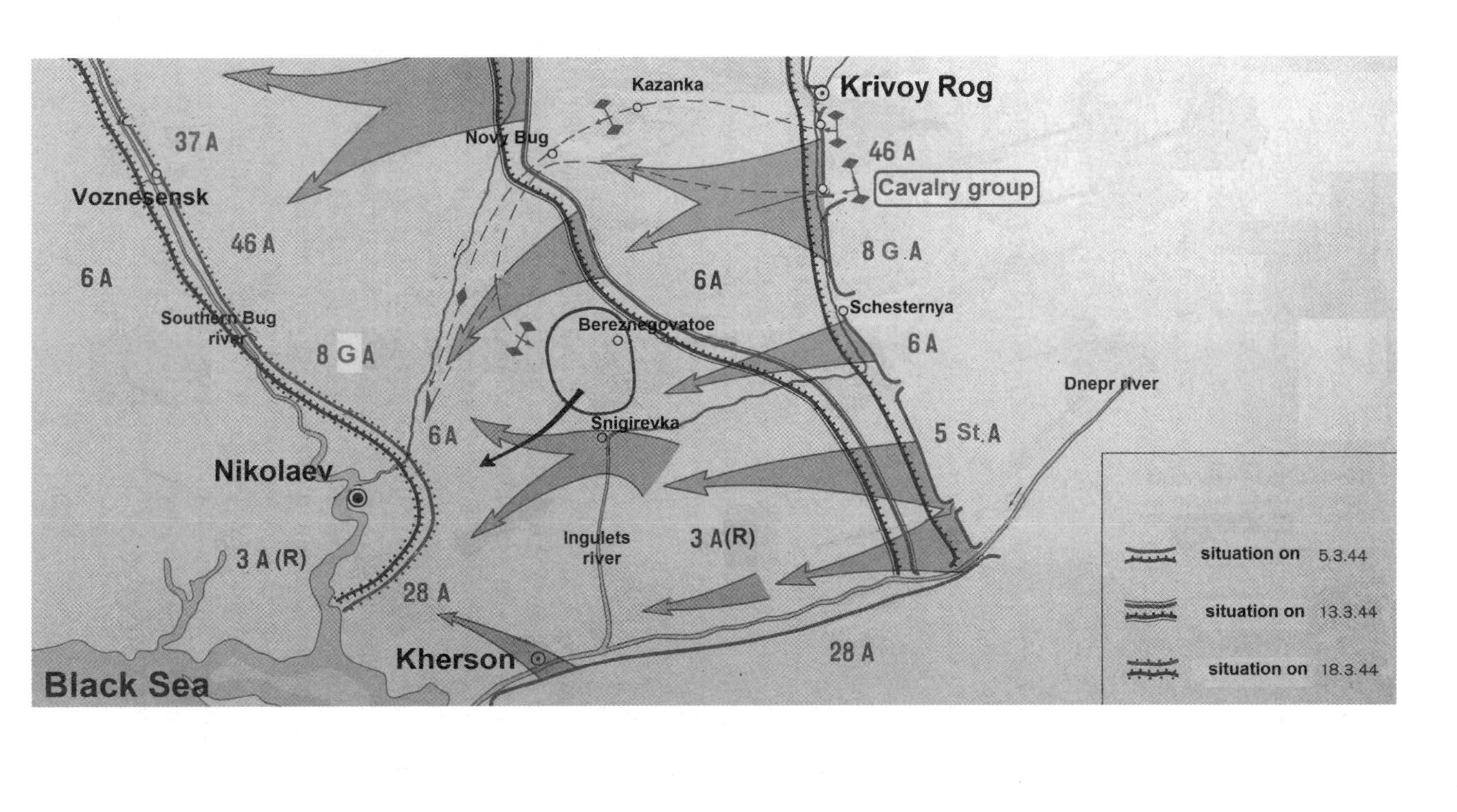
Kazanka
Krivoy Rog
Novy Bug
37 A
46 A
Cavalry group
Voznesensk
46 A
8 G.A
6 A
6A
Schesternya
Southern Bug
river
8 G A
Bereznegovatoe
6 A
Dnepr river
Snigirevka
6A
5 St.A
Nikolaev
Ingulets
river
3 A(R)
3 A (R)
28 A
28 A
Kherson
Black Sea
situation on 5.3.44
situation on 13.3.44
situation on 18.3.44

At 22.00 on 6 March, concentrating on a small bridgehead on the west bank of the Ingulets Pliev's cavalrymen rode forward rapidly. Despite the terrible mud, in just seventeen hours the group reached the village of Drendelevo, having covered 35km. And in the morning of the next day, the cavalry broke into the town of Novy Bug. The small German garrison fled in panic to the surrounding area, without offering any resistance. As a result, the Russians seized an elevator filled with grain, several hundred railway wagons, and at the nearby railway station the Germans abandoned four trains with ammunition and food. After feeding the tired horses and sleeping, Pliev's cavalrymen rushed south at night.

In the morning, they appeared near the Bashtanka, and it was only there, after a 90km raid, that they first encountered resistance from German troops. Sniper fire turned out to be especially dangerous. Within an hour, these managed to seriously injure two cavalry regimental commanders at once and wound two more senior officers. Then German fighters appeared in the sky, which fired at the cavalrymen for a long time. They managed to kill and injure many horses, as Pliev had no air defences. It was the air attacks that stopped the Russian cavalry at the moment when it was about to gallop towards Nikolaev. An even bigger surprise for the Russians was the appearance of … enemy cavalry! It suddenly appeared from behind a railway embankment and, with drawn sabres, rushed to attack one of the regiments of the 10th Guards Cavalry Division. A battle in the spirit of the Napoleonic Wars began, lasting about an hour. Later it turned out that the Russians had been attacked by a squadron of Kalmyks, which miraculously turned out to be at the disposal of the 6th Army. Later, the Germans brought an armoured train by rail, which immediately opened fire on the cavalrymen.

Having suffered serious losses, the cavalry-mechanised group nevertheless continued the raid and on 12 March reached the town of Snigirevka. Two cavalry divisions reached the village of Barmashovo, just 30km east of Nikolaev. The next day, the 4th and 5th Mechanised Brigades, which crossed the Dnieper, broke into Kherson. As a result, the 6th Army was again under threat of complete encirclement. General Hollidt gave the order to urgently flee to the Southern Bug River. One part of the German troops was moving towards Nikolaev along the Snigirevka–Nikolaev railway line, breaking through the barriers of the Russian cavalry and suffering from its sudden flank attacks. The second unit (79th, 304th and 370th Infantry Divisions and Romanian units) moved along the Kherson–Nikolaev railway line, being attacked by the Russian 2nd Guards Mechanised Corps. Due to the impassable mud, the Germans had to abandon almost all their self-propelled artillery and howitzers along the way, while hundreds of trucks also got stuck and drowned in puddles. It was only because the Red Army was experiencing similar difficulties that more of the 6th Army managed to escape again. The Russians reached the outskirts of Nikolaev by the evening of 17 March. However, the battles for this city, which was a large harbour with numerous shipyards, dragged on for ten days.

## Katukov's Trap

The forces of Army Group South did not have time to recover from the battles for Korsun, Nikopol and Nikolaev, as in early March, Soviet troops launched an even larger-scale offensive over a vast area from the Pripyat marshes to the mouth of the Southern Bug. Having concentrated two tank armies (680 tanks and self-propelled artillery pieces) to the south of Rivne, the 1st Ukrainian Front (on 2 March, it was personally led by Marshal Georgy Zhukov) launched them into an offensive in a southerly direction – towards Romania. At the same time, Marshal Konev's 2nd Ukrainian Front went on the offensive from the Korsun area to meet them.

Manstein foresaw this turn of events and guessed the intentions of the Russians. He managed to concentrate nine panzer divisions (1st, 6th, 7th, 8th, 11th, 16th, 17th, 19th and 1st SS Panzer Division Leibstandarte Adolf Hitler) in a narrow area between Tarnopol and Proskurov. Until 7 March, Zhukov's troops advanced without serious interference. On this day, the 4th Tank Army of General Vasily Badanov, moving in the vanguard, reached the Volochisk railway station, located on the Lviv–Odessa railway line. There, the Red Army captured several trains and huge warehouses filled with ammunition, fuel, food and construction materials: 1,000 high-explosive SC500 bombs prepared for the Luftwaffe, 40km of rails, 20,000 railway sleepers, 200 tons of cement, 100 tons of sugar and much more. But before the Russians had time to count the trophies properly, German tanks appeared from the south and south-east. At the same time, the 3rd Guards Tank Army of General Pavel Rybalko, advancing on the left flank, was attacked. As a result, mobile tank battles unfolded along the railway line, which lasted several days. The Russians had not yet managed to bring up their anti-tank artillery, and Badanov had very few large-calibre self-propelled guns. In these conditions, the attacks of German heavy tanks had to be repelled by T-34 tanks, which were not very suitable for this. Tanks with 85mm guns had just begun to enter the army and have not yet become widespread, and the T-34, with conventional, short-barrelled 76mm guns, could not effectively fight the Tigers and Panthers in a direct fight.

Within four days, the Russian 4th Tank Army lost ninety-seven tanks and thirteen self-propelled artillery pieces; that is, a quarter of its military equipment. By bringing his main forces into the battle, Manstein managed to delay the Red Army for a while. However, he failed to repeat the success of the recent Waltraut operation. The Red Army command quickly learned lessons from that defeat. Instead of going on the defensive and counter-attacking, Zhukov decided to simply bypass Manstein's tank divisions and move on.

Having regrouped his forces, pulled up reserves and moved Katukov's 1st Tank Army to the railway embankment, Zhukov resumed his offensive on 21 March. This time the Soviets were completely successful. Two days later, their tanks reached the town of Chertkov, and on 24 March they reached the Dniester River west of Kamenets-Podolsk. Without stopping there, the Russian tankers immediately crossed the river and drove on. On the evening of 25 March, mud-stained T-34s appeared at the Moshi railway station, on the banks of the Prut River. At that time there was a train there with German tanks and shells. Several shots fired at the wagons and subsequent explosions caused incredible confusion and panic. Having covered 135km in five days through the German rear, Katukov demonstrated that the Russians had learned the lessons of blitzkrieg perfectly! And now they were happy to take revenge on the Germans for the fear and humiliation experienced by the Red Army in 1941–42.

The widespread mud, which practically did not disperse due to the warm winter, only aggravated the complete chaos in German-occupied areas. Instead of armies and a single front line, various combat groups operated that were formed from units that happened to be in the same region. Infantry and tank divisions intermingled with each other, as well as various volunteer formations and rear units. The German command lost control of the situation, communication was carried out mainly by radio, and all ground supply lines were cut. All this was complemented by chaos at the airfields.

On 21 March, Konev's advanced units also reached the Dniester in the Mogilev-Podolsky area, and soon joined up with Badanov's 4th Tank Army there. As a result, a huge German group with a total strength of about 200,000 men was surrounded in the Kamenets-Podolsk area. The pocket included ten infantry, nine tank and panzergrenadier divisions and many disparate combat groups. The general command over these disparate units was carried out by the headquarters of the 1st Panzer Army of General Hans Hube. At the same time, some of the troops of the German 4th Panzer Army also fell into the pocket in Tarnopol.

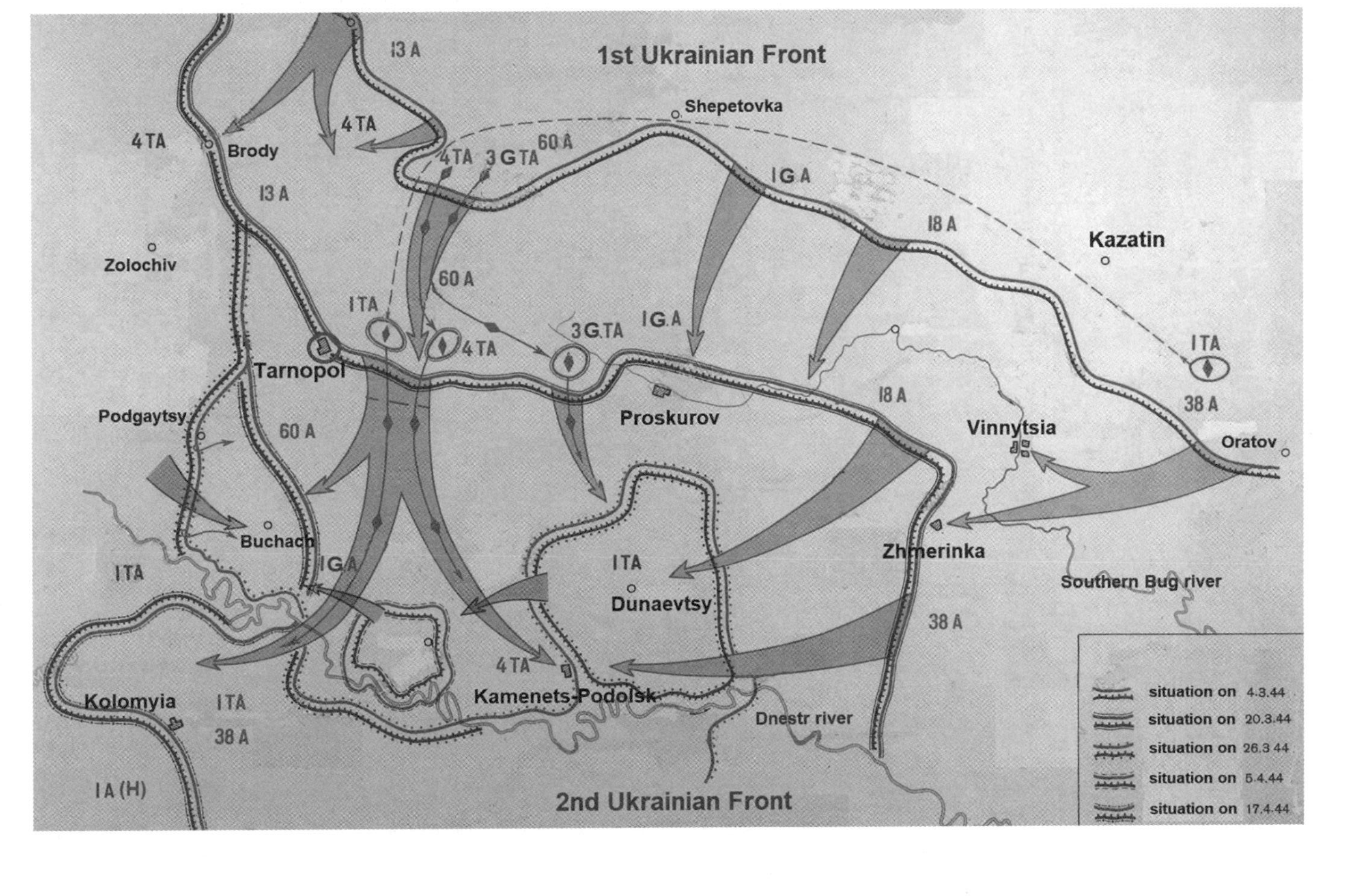
1st Ukrainian Front
2nd Ukrainian Front
Shepetovka
Kazatin
Brody
Zolochiv
Tarnopol
Podgaytsy
Buchach
Proskurov
Vinnytsia
Oratov
Zhmerinka
Southern Bug river
Dunaevtsy
Kamenets-Podolsk
Dnestr river
Kolomyia
13 A
4 TA
60 A
3 GTA
1 GA
18 A
1 TA
38 A
1 A (H)
situation on 4.3.44
situation on 20.3.44
situation on 26.3 44
situation on 5.4.44
situation on 17.4.44

It was another crisis that threatened a catastrophic collapse of Army Group South and the loss of an entire army. Manstein and Hube immediately realised that the only chance for salvation was an immediate breakthrough to the west. Hitler had not trusted Manstein for a long time and had already decided on his resignation. But he trusted Hube implicitly, who was part of the Führer's cohort of favourites and protégés. Together, Manstein and Hube were able to intimidate the dictator, put pressure on him and convince him of the correctness of such a decision. Depressed by the protracted series of defeats in Ukraine, Hitler quickly allowed a breakthrough out of the pocket.

This time, the Ukrainian mud benefited the Germans. The Soviet troops concentrated very slowly, their artillery got stuck in puddles, and fuel trucks with diesel fuel could not get to their tanks. The rifle divisions were also moving slowly because of the trucks stuck in traffic jams. As a result, the Russians had not yet managed to create a tight blockade ring, and their lines were immobilised. In addition, Hube first intended to break through in a south-westerly direction, towards Romania. This information was intercepted by Soviet intelligence, and Zhukov ordered to strengthen the south-western part of the pocket. However, Hube changed the plan and ordered all his troops to move west.

On 27 March, the vanguard of the 1st Panzer Army moved west to the Zbruch River, while the rearguard began to withdraw with fighting, and the remaining 220,000 men were between them. The advanced guard attack went well for the German forces. The northern column quickly captured three bridges over the Zbruch river, while the southern column was battered by a 4th Tank Army counter-attack that penetrated deep into the pocket, capturing Kamenets-Podolsk. The loss of this major road and rail hub meant that the escaping Germans had to detour around the city, slowing the movement to a crawl. A counter-attack soon cut off the Russians in the city, and the breakout recommenced. Moving by day and night, the forces kept moving. Soon bridgeheads were formed over the Seret river.

General Otto Dessloch's Luftflotte 4 received the usual order to organise an air bridge. Despite the bad weather, the supply operation began the very next day. Landing inside the blockade ring was carried out on a variety of sites. At night, these were indicated with the help of radio beacons and light signals, while special code signals in the form of crosses, circles and triangles were developed. For example, the KG27 bomber Geschwader used thirty different landing sites and designated container drop sites between 22 March and 11 April (shown in the German designation): Kurylowce-Murowane, Sauca, Wierzbowiez, Nefedowcze, Dunajewce, Sinkoff, Bolschaja Lewada, Berezanka, Bricani Targ, Wonkowzy, Lipcani, Gruzka, Rozca, Nowa Sulita, Kamenez Podolsk, Hotin, Surzence, Marianowka, Borszczow, Ulaskowce, Jezierzany, Nowosiolka, Kostiakowa, Mielnica, an der Straße Jagielnica-Czortkow, Fluste Miaste, Glebozcek, Worwolince, Berestek, Gleboka and Jagielnica.

At the same time, the breakthrough out of the pocket was facilitated by weak opposition from Soviet aircraft. By the end of March, the 2nd Air Army operating in the Kamenets-Podolsk area consisted of four aviation corps and five separate aviation divisions, which numbered 709 aircraft (279 fighters, 159 ground-attack planes, 57 bombers, 199 night bombers and 15 reconnaissance aircraft). However, due to the impassable mud at the air bases, only a small number of aircraft took off. Planes had to be towed from their parking areas to the end of the runaway by tractors because there was not enough fuel and engine oil (fuel trucks got stuck in the mud, and supplies were carried out mainly by air). Because of these problems, the Russians had to use U-2 night bombers for day air attacks. It was easier for these biplanes to take off from wet airfields, and the low speed and low altitude made it easier to find targets in foggy conditions and poor visibility.

Up until 3 April, both the commander of the Russian 4th Tank Army, Badanov, and the commander of the 1st Ukrainian Front, Zhukov, were confident that the Germans were breaking through to the south-west. Even when the infantry of the 38th Army arrived in Kamenets-Podolsk, Badanov decided to send his tanks to the west – to the northern bank of the Dniester, but in order to 'prevent the enemy from breaking through to the south'. For several days, Russian tank brigades fought with small groups of Germans moving from the east, but Badanov did not suspect that this was only a flank guard of the southern column of the 1st Panzer Army. In these battles, the Russians managed to capture 1,000 prisoners. However, the bulk of the Germans managed to escape from the pocket.

On 8 April, after stubborn fighting and a 300km dash to the west, the advanced units of the 1st Panzer Army joined the 2nd SS Panzer Corps in the Buchach area. According to Soviet information, the withdrawal of individual groups through the front line continued until 18 April. The last sorties of transport aircraft for supplies were carried out on 10 April. In total, the Luftwaffe carried out about 8,000 flights to the pocket, delivering 4,000 tons of cargo (an average of 200–250 tons per day), almost as much as the 6th Army in Stalingrad requested in December 1942.

Despite the success of the breakthrough, it was another defeat for the Wehrmacht, which led to the loss of huge territories, material reserves, a large amount of equipment and the withdrawal of troops into Romania. The material losses were extremely high, with most of the armoured vehicles, motor vehicles, artillery and anti-tank guns, as well as various equipment of the rear services, being lost, mainly through abandonment in the spring mud. After the breakout, the formations of the army retained only a small number of their vehicles, weaponry and equipment. As trophies, the Russians got 500 tanks and self-propelled artillery pieces, 600 armoured personnel carriers, 15,000 motor vehicles, 4,400 motorcycles, 400-ton heavy trucks, 200 buses, 338 car trailers, about 1,000 artillery pieces and much more. Most of this equipment was not destroyed in a hurry and was given to the Russians in complete safety. It took a month just to compile an inventory of all the trophies! A significant number of the captured vehicles, armoured personnel carriers, motorcycles and heavy trucks were later used by the Red Army.

## 'We ride our horses to where the enemy is visible'

Meanwhile, the Red Army launched a new offensive against Army Group A. The 37th Army managed to capture a bridgehead on the western bank of the Southern Bug River in the area of Konstantinovka and Voznesensk. It was from this point that the commander of the 3rd Ukrainian Front, General Malinovsky, decided to strike. On 28 March, the crossing to the bridgehead of the cavalry-mechanised group of General Pliev began. Due to heavy rain and the poor quality of wooden bridges built by sappers, this process was very slow, and several self-propelled guns even sank in the river. On the evening of 29 March, Malinovsky personally arrived at bridge crossing to speed up his subordinates.

The next day, the cavalry concentrated completely in the bridgehead, after which they rushed deep into German territory. The first target of the raid was the town of Berezovka, 45km south-west of Voznesensk. The route to it was not easy. For example, the 10th Cavalry Division was subjected to Fw 190 air attacks three times, as a result of which fourteen riders and ninety-five horses were killed. Nevertheless, at midnight on 31 March, the cavalrymen reached Berezovka, finding themselves in the deep rear of the enemy. The German command's hopes that mud would delay the Russian advance were again not realised. Where tanks and trucks could not pass quickly, horses could gallop! The Germans had previously mined the bridges over the Tiligul River and retreated to the south-western bank. However, this small water barrier with a width of only 20m and a depth of 1½m, of course could not detain the Soviet cavalry for long. On the night of 31 March–1 April, cavalry began crossing the river over quickly built wooden bridges. The Romanians defending on the opposite bank had simply fled by that time.

Pliev's next target was the Razdelnaya railway station. Advancing by day and night, the cavalrymen reached Novonikolaevka by dawn on 2 April. At 8 a.m., with terrifying cries and under the roar of hundreds of hooves, they burst into this settlement, forcing the Romanian garrison there to flee, abandoning all vehicles and artillery pieces. There was complete chaos and confusion in the enemy's rear. Bypassing small villages and strongpoints, the cavalrymen rode without stopping and by the next night they had reached the Kuyalnik River. Bridges across the river were blown up, but despite this, in the morning this water barrier was overcome. 'The movements were carried out in difficult meteorological conditions, a severe blizzard raged, the roads were slippery from the onset of ice, steep descents and ascents, deep ravines greatly hampered movement,' the journal of the 4th Cavalry Corps said.

On the morning of 4 April, the Russians reached the village of Poniatovka. There they got unusual trophies: seven 210mm Mrs 18 mortars, attached to tractors. The captured gunners said that they were taking these powerful siege guns to the railway station and were sure that the Red Army was still very far away. It is worth adding that during such raids, Russian cavalrymen rarely took prisoners, simply because there was no one to escort them to the rear.

At noon, the cavalry reached Razdelnaya station. The scouts saw through binoculars that there were several trains under loading, around which soldiers were fussing. Soon they noticed the horsemen and opened fire indiscriminately. The locomotives immediately began to raise steam in preparation for departure but it was too late. Soon General Issa Pliev himself arrived at the scene. Drawing his sabre and forming the cavalry into three large ranks, he personally led them into the attack. Seeing this terrifying sight – avalanches of horsemen galloping from three sides at once, the Germans and Romanians panicked, abandoning all heavy weapons and rushing off in different directions. The most dramatic thing happened on the railway and was a sight reminiscent of a Western movie. Two steam locomotives managed to start before the Russians reached the station. While the longer of the two trains train was accelerating, soldiers, distraught with fear, were running towards it from all sides. They clung to the running boards and grabbed on to the carriages, some even climbing on the roof.

Soon, the first cavalrymen appeared around the corner, brandishing glittering sabres in an intimidating manner. They mercilessly chopped down all those who came to hand with them and trampled them with horses. This further aggravated the unimaginable panic. While some soldiers were shooting at the Russians from the roofs of the wagons, others continued to grab at them. Some of the fugitives broke and fell, upon which others immediately rushed to take their place. The last carriages and railway platforms were plastered with bodies like flies. Meanwhile, the driver of the locomotive was desperately throwing coal into the furnace to increase speed. Both trains managed to escape but the Russians still seized a lot of booty: about 1,000 railway wagons and several warehouses with food and ammunition. Having covered about 150km in four days, the Russians found themselves north-west of Odessa. And behind the cavalry, tanks and motorised infantry were already pulling up. Everything happened as in the famous popular song about the Soviet cavalry: 'We ride horses to where the enemy is visible!'

Now General Hollidt's 6th Army was divided into two parts. Two army corps (nine divisions) retreated to Tiraspol. The remaining units (ten German and two Romanian divisions) were blocked in the Odessa area. On 7 April, Pliev's cavalrymen reached the shore of the Black Sea. Some German troops managed to break through the Soviet lines to the west. The rest had to be evacuated from the port city by planes and ships. Some episodes of this escape resembled scenes from Hollywood blockbusters. For example, Helmut Wolf, who served at the headquarters of Fliegerkorps I, ended up in Odessa after the German troops abandoned the city of Nikolaev. There, Wolf was detained due to numerous problems, and he remained until 10 April, when most of the port was already occupied by Soviet troops. While the last rearguard of the sappers left Odessa on amphibious ferries after destroying the port facilities, Wolf had only one intact He 111 bomber at his disposal, standing in a hangar on the edge of the airfield. Moreover, the Red Army soldiers were already on the opposite side of the air base. They were in no hurry, because they believed that all the Nazis had already escaped. The Germans started the engines, warmed them up a little and only then opened the hangar doors. To the surprise of the Russian infantrymen, a bomber packed with twenty people left from inside and then taxied at speed through puddles, breaking thin ice, to take off. 'Before reaching the edge of the airfield, he climbed only a few metres. In a low-level flight, we saw Russian soldiers looking at our plane in fright, and we were being fired at by all their guns. We were outside the Russian positions before there was any opposition,'

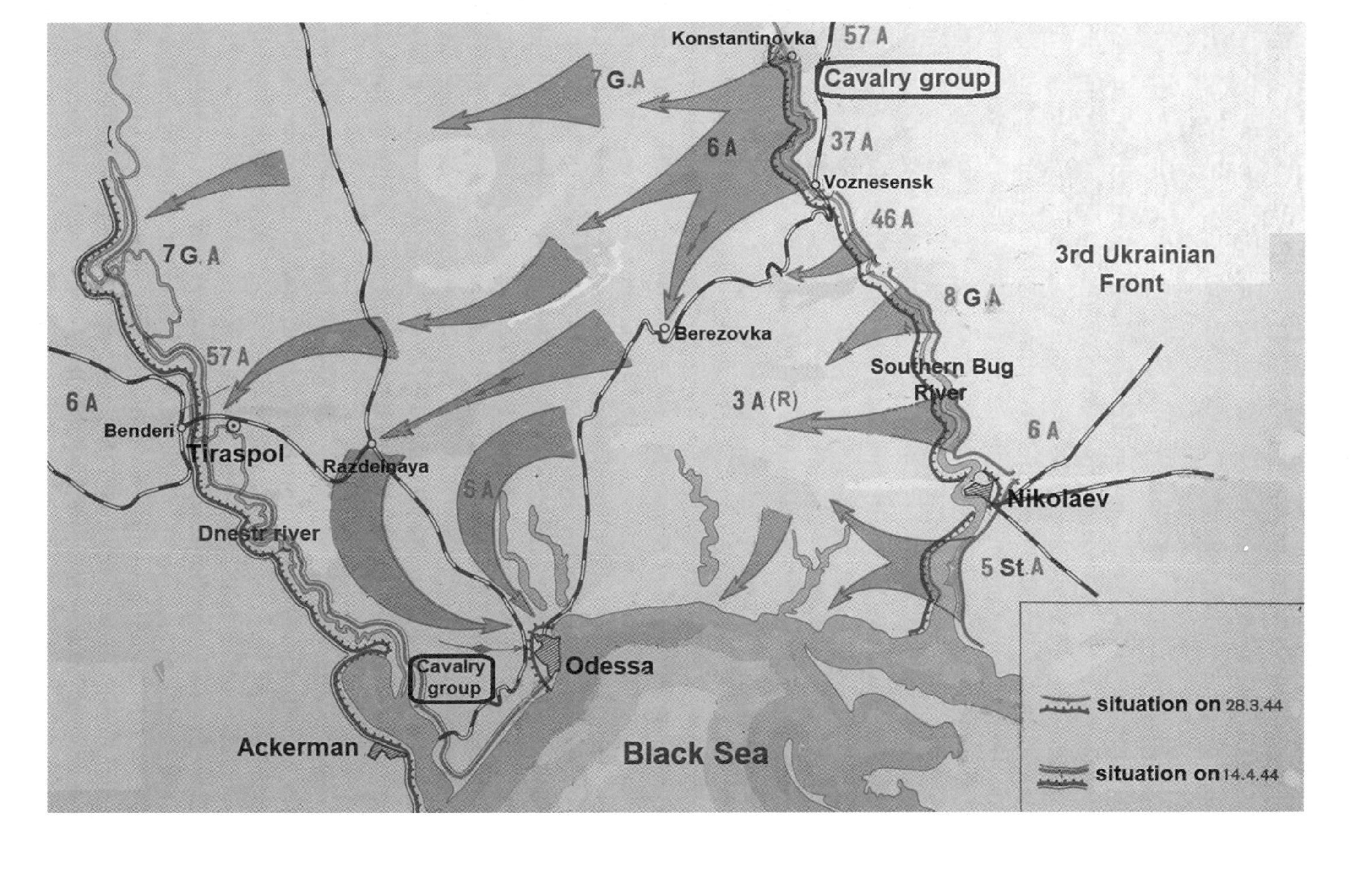

Konstantinovka
57 A
Cavalry group
7 G.A
6 A
37 A
Voznesensk
46 A
3rd Ukrainian
Front
7 G.A
8 G.A
Berezovka
57 A
Southern Bug
River
6 A
3 A (R)
Benderi
Tiraspol
Razdelnaya
6 A
Nikolaev
Dnestr river
5 St.A
Cavalry
group
Odessa
Ackerman
Black Sea
situation on 28.3.44
situation on 14.4.44

Wolf recalled. So, the 6th Army fled in disarray, forgetting all Hitler's exhortations about stubborn defence. And on 8 April, Army Group 'A', renamed South Ukraine, was headed by Ferdinand Schörner. Soon he would have to repel another Soviet offensive.

## Deadly City

In addition to the 'wandering pocket' in the Kamenets-Podolsk area, the Germans had to rescue two more blockaded garrisons during the same period. In mid-March, the troops of the 2nd Belorussian Front (under the command of General Pavel Kurochkin), advancing through the forests along the Pripyat marshes, reached the city of Kovel. Since it was the last German stronghold on the way to Brest-Litovsk – in the deep rear of Army Group Centre, which was still defending on the banks of the Dnieper, the German command ordered the defence of Kovel 'at any cost'. Then Hitler joined the case, declaring Kovel another 'Festung'. As a result, the Red Army surrounded the city, but could not advance further. The defence of the city was personally led by the commander of the 5th SS Panzer Division 'Viking', Obergruppenführer Herbert Gille.

Despite the shortage of transport aircraft involved in supplying other pockets, the Germans still managed to create another air bridge. DFS 230 cargo gliders from Schlepp.Gr.1, as well as He 111 bombers from I./KG27, were mainly sent to Kovel. They dropped containers by parachute. The supplies delivered allowed the garrison of the city to repel the Russian attacks and hold out. Meanwhile, a strike group was quickly formed consisting of the 8th Company of the 5th SS Panzer Regiment (sixteen Panthers), the 190th Assault Gun Detachment (seventeen StuG self-propelled guns) and two incomplete grenadier battalions. These were very weak forces, but the mission was facilitated by the short distance to the pocket (about 20km) and the lack of Russian forces, who had not yet managed to create a strong external encirclement front.

The SS attack began at noon on 29 March. Taking advantage of the snowfall that had begun, they reached the Russian positions unnoticed and quickly captured the village of Cherkassy. The breakthrough of several Panther tanks through the swamp played a decisive role. They bypassed the right flank of the defenders and shot up the anti-tank guns that had not had time to turn around. On the morning of 30 March, moving along the railway embankment, the Panthers reached the outskirts of Kovel. This unexpected success was due to the commander of the tank company, SS Obersturmführer Karl Nicolussi-Lek, who at the crucial moment simply ignored the command's order to 'stop and wait for reinforcements'. On 5 April, the blockade of Kovel was finally ended, and the city remained in the hands of the Wehrmacht for several more months.

The 'military fate' of a small garrison in Tarnopol, 180km south of Kovel, became much more dramatic.

This western Ukrainian city was captured by the Wehrmacht on 2 July 1941. At the same time, most of its population, unaware of the state of affairs at the front, did not even think about evacuating before it was too late. The fate of most of these people turned out to be tragic for several reasons. Firstly, about 40 per cent of the inhabitants of Tarnopol were Jews. Secondly, from 1929 to 1939, this city was part of Poland, and a lot of Poles lived Tarnopol and the surrounding area. Meanwhile, on 30 June 1941, in Lviv, Ukrainian nationalists proclaimed the restoration of Independent Ukraine under German patronage, while they considered western Ukraine their patrimony, and fiercely hated Poles and Polish Jews. It is not surprising that on the second day of the occupation, a pogrom began in the city, during which the SS and Ukrainians literally competed among themselves as to who could burn down more Jewish houses and kill more civilians. The Germans took the lead: their victims numbered about 1,000, while the Ukrainian 'militias' massacred only 600. Most were simply shot, while others were beaten to death with sledgehammers and beheaded.

In September, the German occupation authorities, led by Gerhard Hager, announced the creation of the Tarnopol ghetto in the area of the Old Square and the Small Market Square, where 12,000–13,000 remaining Jews were resettled. The death penalty was imposed for illegal exit from the territory, and food was imported according to rationing. The order was maintained by the Ukrainian auxiliary police. As a result of malnutrition, several hundred ghetto residents died of starvation the following winter.

The fate of the survivors was also predictable, and their lives were actually limited by the capacity of the Nazi death camps. In the summer of 1942, the new Belzec death camp, north-west of Lviv, was put into operation. Its 'death district' included the whole of western Ukraine. On 31 August, the first batch of prisoners were escorted by Ukrainian police to the railway station and put on a train. So that the victims, including women and children, would not be bored and languid during the transition, the guards organised musical accompaniment. All the way to the station, the Ukrainian orchestra played cheerful marches and melodies. The train stood at the station for two days waiting for another train with Jews. The passengers were not given any water or food and hundreds of them died before arriving in

Belzec. On 10 November, Ukrainians conducted the second convoy of 2,500 people from the ghetto to the station in the same way, with an orchestra. A small number of Jews remained for some time in a labour camp set up on the site of the liquidated ghetto, but by the end of 1943 they were also killed. By that time Tarnopol was almost empty.

In March 1944, a completely different 'music' began to play in the air, the clang of tracks and the roar of shots from approaching Soviet tanks became a kind of funeral march for the OUN (Organisation of Ukrainian Nationalists) and the UPA (Ukrainian Insurgent Army).

On 26 March, the Germans took up a circular defence in Tarnopol, hoping for a quick relief. The supply of the fortress was mainly carried out by He 111 bombers from KG27 and He 111 cargo bombers from TGr.30, as well as with the help of DFS 230 cargo gliders from Schlepp. Gr.1. The operation took place in conditions of strong opposition from Soviet air defences, especially anti-aircraft artillery. Therefore, all missions took place only in the early morning and evening with limited visibility. If you add to these conditions to blizzards with strong winds, it becomes clear that the pilots of the German gliders face a desperate mission. Having detached themselves from the He 111 tow planes, they had to overcome the anti-aircraft barrage, find a small runway on the outskirts of the city, and then land on it on the first approach. However, the Germans also found a way out in this situation. After uncoupling from the towing He 111, the gliders circled in the air for a while, while the bombers descended and began bombing the positions of anti-aircraft batteries, dropping one or two fragmentation bombs each. Thus, the bombers forced the Russian gunners to flatten themselves to the ground and diverted their fire. At the same time, the DFS 230s were speeding towards the city and landing.

There was not much activity from the Soviet air force due to bad weather. It was only on 31 March, when the sky became clear, that it gathered its strength. Twenty-six Pe-2 dive bombers and eighty-three Il-2 ground-attack planes accompanied by forty-one fighters staged a massive raid on Tarnopol. Then, close to the evening, a second air strike was carried out on the city with the participation of twenty-seven Il-2s escorted by thirty-four fighters. In total, 45 tons of bombs were dropped, causing numerous fires.

While the landing site remained in the hands of the defenders, the volume of supplies was kept at the level of 12–15 tons per day, but when it was captured it was only possible to drop cargo by parachute. The volume of deliveries immediately decreased to 8 tons per day. However, even these cargoes most often did not reach the troops on the ground. On 1 April, the commander of the garrison, Generalmajor Egon von Neindorff, radioed that the previous night, out of ninety dumped containers, only five ended up in the hands of German soldiers. The rest ended up on Soviet territory, in lakes and swamps, or were simply lost among the ruins.

The assault on the city was entrusted to Soviet stormtroopers. The first assault engineering sapper brigades were formed in the Red Army in the spring of 1943 on the basis of engineering sapper units. They were designed specifically for breaking through powerful fortified positions, storming cities and sabotage operations in the enemy's immediate rear. This was done on the basis of the rich experience gained during the first two years of the war. During the counteroffensive near Moscow and the parallel operations in other sectors of the front, the Russians had to liberate many cities in fierce battles. Large settlements were well suited for defence, especially in winter. Stone houses, factory buildings and other structures in themselves were convenient for defence; in addition, it was easier to keep warm and hide from shelling in them than in field trenches and dugouts. These tactics were often used by the Germans, and the defence of many cities stretched over many months and even years.

The assault units were elite. They enrolled only athletic, hardy soldiers under the age of 40. Preference was given to experienced soldiers who had previously distinguished themselves during the storming of German strongholds during reconnaissance raids behind enemy lines, who knew sapper and demolition work well. The armament of stormtroopers usually consisted of PPSh submachine guns (later Sudaev submachine guns), flamethrowers, knives, grenades, 'Molotov cocktails', explosive charges, and various devices for mine clearance and cutting barbed wire, etc. Unlike most Red Army soldiers, stormtroopers often used camouflage suits and steel breastplates. They were usually worn before battles in the city on a padded jacket with the sleeves torn off. Together with the gasket on the inside, this device served as an additional shock absorber when bullets and shrapnel hit the breastplate. The stormtroopers underwent long-term training for assault operations in special training models of cities. The full-time strength of the brigade numbered about 2,200 men, and organisationally it consisted of a headquarters, a company of engineering intelligence and management, five assault engineer battalions, a company of mine-detecting dogs and a light ferry fleet.

During the storming of Tarnopol, Soviet stormtroopers actively used high-explosive FOG (powder) flamethrowers. This was a type of jet flamethrower that used very high pressure due to the detonation of a special propellant charge. This design made it possible to throw flames at a distance of 130–150m. In addition, Russian assault groups actively used thermite balls, which were fired from special Ampulomet cannon. Approaching the building occupied by German infantry, the Russians first put up a dense smokescreen that completely blocked visibility in the surrounding streets. Under the cover of heavy smoke, soldiers dragged Ampulomet cannon and high-explosive flamethrowers mounted on special frames to the building. As soon as the smoke cleared, the Russians flooded the building with jets of flame and pelted it with thermite balls. As a result, in a few seconds the stone house turned into a bonfire. All that remained of the German soldiers were charred skeletons. Then the assault group moved to the next house that had been turned into a strongpoint and did the same thing. To support their assault groups, the Russians actively used 152mm self-propelled artillery guns. They usually fired at the corners of the house, which allowed them to quickly destroy the supporting structures of the building and cause its collapse.

The successful use of such tactics, which the Red Army later used in the siege of Budapest and other European cities, made it impossible to defend it for a long time.

However, the Germans had their advantages. In the old part of Tarnopol there were a huge number of deep cellars and tunnels, many of which remained from the Middle Ages. These dungeons were used to store ammunition, set up infirmaries and shelter infantry from artillery fire and air attacks. The Germans did not even have time to explore many basements. In one of them, Russian stormtroopers found … a Jew and an NKVD officer. It turned out that these two had hidden in the basement of an abandoned building back in the summer of 1941, and they lived there for almost three years. These brave souls survived not only the German occupation, the Ukrainian raids, but also the brutal assault on Tarnopol!

The first unblocking strike was launched on 25–26 March. However, it did not bring success. The new commander of Army Group South, Walter Model, who arrived in Lviv (appointed instead of Manstein), ordered the preparation of a new strike. The main hope was pinned on the recently arrived 9th SS Panzer Division 'Hohenstaufen' from France under the command of Gruppenführer Wilhelm Bittrich. However, the concentration was extremely slow due to the incredible mud at the intended starting point of the attack (17km west of Tarnopol). As a result, the offensive, the course of which was personally controlled by Model from the forward command post, only started on 11 April. However, by that time it was too late to save the pocket.

By 4 April, the Russians had captured most of the city, and on 13 April they launched a final assault. The next day, the German defences collapsed. On the night of 14–15 April, approximately 1,500 soldiers, including Ukrainians from the Galicia division, broke through the remnants of the levee of the Lviv highway through Tarnopol Lake, ending up on the other side of the Seret River in the village of Zagrebelye. General von Neindorff, who had previously tortured Model with his telegrams demanding that the offensive be accelerated, also decided to break through to the west. He drove to Zagrebelye in the last surviving tank, and then went on foot. However, by that time, the unblocking group was able to get only 12km closer to Tarnopol. Only thirty to forty men people were able to reach the German positions. Neindorff was not among them, he died on the way. Two and a half thousand German soldiers joined the long list of prisoners of war.

## The Russians are Entering Romania

The result of the Red Army's winter offensive in Ukraine was the almost complete liberation of the territory of this republic (with the exception of the westernmost regions), as well as access to the Carpathians and the invasion of Romania. Against the background of these successes, in early April, Joseph Stalin ordered the commanders of the 2nd and 3rd Ukrainian Fronts, Konev and Malinovsky, to immediately, without any pause, launch an offensive deep into Romania. In Moscow, it seemed that the German–Romanian defence had collapsed and it was important not to allow the enemy to gain a foothold on new defensive lines. The new operation pursued primarily political and military-economic goals: to knock Romania and Bulgaria out of the war and deprive the Third Reich of access to the oil fields in Ploieşti. Hitler understood all this too. The closer the Red Army approached Romania, the more he demanded loyalty from his ally and the mobilisation of all human and material resources. On 25 October 1943, the Führer wrote in a letter to Antonescu: 'The decisive moment has come when we must do our best to provide our soldiers with everything to fight the enemy standing at the gates of Romania.'

In November, when the Russians liberated Kiev, the Führer demanded that Antonescu immediately send new divisions to the front. In response, the Romanian dictator complained about the heavy losses and difficulties. On 15 November, he wrote to Hitler: 'In 1942, we gave 26 divisions with the best weapons and sent almost all the heavy artillery. We lost 18 divisions on the Don and at Stalingrad, and the remaining eight divisions were exhausted in the Kuban. In addition, seven of our divisions are currently cut off in Crimea.' Antonescu also complained about difficulties of a military-economic nature. He noted the frankly low combat qualities of his troops. Meanwhile, in January 1944, Hitler ordered the development of a plan for the occupation of Romania in case of its withdrawal from the war. Under the guise of strengthening the air defence of Ploieşti, additional units were sent there. At the end of February, Hitler met with Antonescu, at which the Führer tried to convince his Axis partner of the inaccessibility of the Atlantic Wall and promised to hold the Crimea at all costs.

On 23–24 March, new negotiations between the two dictators took place at the Wolf's Lair headquarters. Hitler again tried to inspire the marshal with optimism, promising to launch a major counteroffensive in order to block the Russian way to Romania. In addition, he painted a rosy picture of 'decisive changes' in favour of Germany, which were soon to take place on the Eastern Front. The Führer firmly promised that Army Group South would in no case allow the Red Army to approach the Romanian borders. Moreover, he was referring to the old borders, forgetting that Romania's 'possessions' at that moment formally extended to the southern Bug River!

After returning to Bucharest, the Romanian dictator became convinced that the news he was receiving from the front did not correspond to what Hitler had said. He sent the Führer a letter, not without reproaches, in which he wrote: 'When I returned to my country today, I found that the situation looks completely different than it seemed to me when I was in the Main Apartment ... The situation from Tarnopol to the Bug estuary is very serious. The enemy group that crossed the Dniester is already in the area of Iasi. The enemy is conducting a powerful offensive between the Dniester and the Bug. It turns out that the German front in this area is pushed much further south than it was imagined at the time of my departure from the Main Headquarters.'

In response, the Führer called on Antonescu 'to accelerate the mobilisation and deployment of Romanian divisions and withdraw every combat-ready unit northward to the Prut.' He called on the marshal again and again to fight to the end. Meanwhile, on 8 April, the Russian 27th, 40th and 2nd Tank Armies launched an offensive against Targu Frumos and Pashkani. At the same time, the 52nd and 6th Tank Armies launched an auxiliary strike north of Iasi. In Romania itself, panic reigned these days, cases of mass desertion began in the army, and the military leadership constantly appealed to dictator Ion Antonescu in the spirit of, 'boss, it's over!'

It was at this moment that Ferdinand Schörner took command of the new Army Group South Ukraine. First of all, he launched a counter-attack in the area of Targu Frumos. On 10 April, the motorised infantry division 'Grossdeutschland' (Division Großdeutschland) launched an attack from the west, while the Romanian 1st Guards and 7th Infantry Divisions attacked from the south, which managed to push the Soviet troops north. As a result, units of the Soviets' 3rd Guards Airborne, 93rd Guards Rifle and 206th Rifle Divisions were surrounded, and the weakened 2nd Tank Army suffered heavy losses.

However, the Soviet command, despite the fatigue of the troops, the lack of ammunition and fuel, was not going to abandon its plans. At the end of April, the commander of the 2nd Ukrainian Front, General Konev, received an order to break through the enemy's defences in the area of Targu Frumos, then enter the communications of the Iasi–Kishinev group of Germans and advance south. For the operation, the 7th Guards Army and 5th Guards Tank Army were concentrated in this sector. The first of them consisted of 53,500 men (11,500 'active bayonets') and 938 guns. The density of artillery in the offensive zone was 124 guns per kilometre of the front. The 5th Guards Tank Army of General Pavel Rotmistrov, consisting of the 3rd Guards Tank Corps and the 18th and 29th Tank Corps, was concentrated in the initial area a week before the attack. At the same time, its units were severely exhausted, and its armoured vehicles were badly worn out after 300–400km marches through mud and soaked roads. Nevertheless, Romistrov's army was an impressive force. The 3rd Guards Tank Corps alone consisted of 130 T-34s, thirty-three Valentines and forty-two Sherman tanks, and twenty-one Su-85, twenty-one Su-76 and eighteen ISU-152 self-propelled guns. In total, the army had 330 tanks and self-propelled artillery units and 25,000 soldiers.

The Soviet generals pinned their main hopes on the weak 'political and moral condition' of the enemy troops, especially the Romanian ones. 'The difficult living conditions at the front (Romanian soldiers receive 700 grams of bread and half a litre of soup per day), the lack of goals and prospects for struggle and hatred against the Germans are the main factors determining the political and moral state of Romanian soldiers. Most of them do not want to fight,' the corresponding summary of the headquarters of the 7th Guards Army said.

However, the condition of some of the Soviet troops was also a problem. For example, on the eve of the operation, the 6th Guards Rifle Division received a replenishment of 200 men. Of these, 82 per cent had no uniforms at all, and the remaining 18 per cent were 'not fully equipped' (there were no shoes). The recruits had no weapons at all. These Guards were apparently hastily mobilised from the recently liberated territories of Ukraine.

By this time, the Germans and Romanians had managed to create a fairly powerful line of defence in the Prut and Seret interfluve (defile). Its forward positions with field fortifications ran along a chain of commanding heights, while in the rear there were long-term fortifications with many bunkers, an anti-tank ditch and four lines of barbed wire. The relief in the form of a hilly ridge with ravines, covered with dense stunted forest, was well suited for defence and hindered the actions of tanks. Starting on 25 April, German reconnaissance aircraft, taking advantage of the good weather, photographed the positions of the Soviet troops. As a result, the Germans managed to determine in advance the directions of attacks and the places of the greatest concentration of tanks. On the morning of 1 May, the Luftwaffe and FARR (La Forțele Aeriene Regale ale României, Romanian Royal Aviation) unexpectedly launched a preemptive air strike on Soviet howitzer artillery positions in the area of Vaskania and Beiceni. Then, at 18.00, Stukas and Hs 129s attacked the concentration areas of Soviet troops around Dumbravica. 'Enemy aircraft in groups of 30 to 70 aircraft of the type Ju 87, Ju 88, Caproni continuously bombed our troops on the front line, areas of concentration of troops and roads during the day,' the combat operations journal of the 5th Guards Tank Army reported.

Soviet aviation in this sector of the front was significantly weakened by the beginning of May. The 4th Fighter Aviation Corps of General Alexander Utin included five fighter aviation regiments (6th, 183rd, 193rd, 240th and 427th IAP), but by the beginning of the offensive they had only forty-seven serviceable aircraft. At the same time, there were almost no fuel reserves at the air bases of Putenesti, Bivolari, Tabera, Annopol and others.

At dawn on 2 May, after an hour of artillery preparation, the 7th Guards and 5th Tank Armies launched an offensive towards the city of Roman. As soon as the message about this arrived at the headquarters of the German and Romanian air forces, everything that could fly began to be scrambled, according to a pre-prepared plan. Old aircraft from the FARR 2nd Air Corps also flew out to bombard the Soviet troops. These included the PZL.37 'Moose', IAR JRS-79B and even old IAR-39 biplanes used as light bombers.

According to Soviet information, groups of four to six Fw 190 fighters appeared first over the battlefield, then twin-engine bombers appeared, followed by a large group of Ju 87s, which flew in a circle and then began to dive alternately at various targets. The attacks of the dive bombers were repeated every three hours.

The Soviet troops managed to break through the enemy's first line of defence in places and advance in a southerly direction for 10–12km, occupying Dumbravitsy, Vaskaniy, Buzhkha and Jurazheechy. This success cost the Russians great sacrifices. For example, the 3rd Guards Tank Corps lost fifty T-34 and Valentine tanks and 300 men killed and wounded.

The next day of the operation was marked by fierce fighting. The 29th Tank Corps launched its first attack at 11.00 a.m., but it was repelled by artillery fire and attacks by German Ju 87s. At 6 p.m., the second attack began, but it soon choked for the same reason. During the day, the corps lost seven tanks and self-propelled guns. But the biggest damage was again suffered by General Ivan Vovchenko's 3rd Guards Tank Corps, which lost fifty tanks and 600 personnel.

On 4 May, the Soviet strike force tried to resume attacks along the entire front, but they again ran into stubborn German–Romanian defences. 'The advancing troops were met with heavy fire and counter-attacks by infantry under the cover of enemy bomber aircraft, they did not advance and conducted a fire battle on the occupied lines,' the headquarters of the 24th Guards Rifle Corps reported. Only the neighbouring 25th Guards Rifle Corps managed to advance 1½km, reaching the enemy's advanced trenches.

By 6 May, the Soviet offensive had finally run out of steam, largely due to the local advantage of the Germans and Romanians in the air. In total, the Luftwaffe and FARR carried out about 4,000 sorties during 2–6 May, to which the 5th Air Army responded with only 1,970 sorties, and most of them fell to U-2 light night bombers. The Soviet troops suffered heavy losses. During the first three days of fighting, the 5th Guards Tank Army lost 155 tanks, almost half of those available at the beginning of the offensive. The losses of the 7th Guards Army amounted to 3,140 men killed and wounded, i.e. almost a third of its active soldiers. The next morning, after a long two-hour artillery preparation and several massive air attacks, the Germans launched a counteroffensive on the left flank of the 7th Guards Army, with forty to forty-five heavy tanks and self-propelled guns attacking there. As a result of the death of the commanders of the 223rd and 475th Rifle Regiments, the units of the Russian 53rd Guards Rifle Division were disorganised and retreated, leaving the villages of Sekereshti and Kukuteniy. Thus, the Germans managed not only to hold their positions, but also to regain part of the lost territory.

All these events allowed both the German command and, first of all, Antonescu and his entourage to exhale. The immediate threat of the Red Army's entry into the Balkans was averted, and a new powerful line of defence was created. These successes of Ferdinand Schörner were primarily due to the fatigue of the Soviet troops after the protracted winter offensive, as well as the transfer of a large number of German reserves to Romania. Such a German strategy of sending the best troops to be concentrated in crisis areas, however, ultimately only played into the hands of the Red Army. Having forced Hitler to plug the gaps in one place, Stalin later struck in another.

Chapter 3

# HITLER THROWS STRATEGIC BOMBERS INTO BATTLE

In March, Hitler's entourage was in a very anxious mood. The Red Army's offensive in Ukraine seemed endless, and it was unclear how to stop it. At that moment, the Führer suddenly found an ace in his pocket – strategic bombers. Even after the Stalingrad disaster, Germany for the first time thought about massive raids on Soviet military-industrial centres and the creation of strategic aviation. The main lobbyist for this decision was Reich Minister Albert Speer. On 30 May 1943, he proposed to Hitler the formation of a committee of civilian industrial experts who would advise the Luftwaffe General Staff on priority military and economic goals. It was headed by Dr Karl Krauch, Director of Electric Power Planning at the Reich Ministry of Armaments, a member of the board of IG Farben. Later, the structure was informally named 'Karl's Committee' after his name.

From 4 to 25 June 1943, the Luftwaffe carried out the first strategic operation against the industrial centres of the Volga region. A total of 993 sorties were carried out and 1,538 tons of bombs were dropped on three main targets (Gorky, Yaroslavl and Saratov). As a result, four large, about twenty medium-sized and many small enterprises were completely destroyed, the restoration of which took from four to six months. The Russians had to significantly reduce the production of tanks, vehicles, aircraft, artillery pieces and other military equipment.

In July, Karl's Committee concluded that a large-scale air attack against Soviet military industry was practically impossible, firstly, due to the limited number of bombers and their maximum range of 800–900km, and secondly, due to the huge spread of potential targets in the area from Moscow to Omsk and Central Asia. Industrialists quickly came to the conclusion that the only way to deal a painful blow to the 'Soviets' was to 'focus on one vital point' (Schwerpunktbildung). As such, twenty-three hydroelectric and thermal power plants were identified, as well as twenty main transformer stations located in the region with the symbol 'Moscow – Upper Volga' (MOW). Five generating plants were located in Moscow, the rest supplied electricity to the capital and the industrial districts of Yaroslavl–Ivanovo, Gorky and Tula–Stalinogorsk.

In August, after the suicide of the Chief of the Luftwaffe General Staff, General Hans Jeschonnek, the former commander of Luftflotte 1, General Gunther Korten, became his successor. He was on good terms with Speer. In September, General Karl Koller became the head of the operations department of the Luftwaffe General Staff. Both of them were supporters of strategic air attacks and engaged in the creation of a fleet of strategic bombers. They decided to combine most of the aviation groups available on the Eastern Front, equipped with twin-engine He 111 and Ju 88 aircraft, as part of General Rudolf Meister's Fliegerkorps IV. On 26 November 1943, the Luftwaffe High Command issued an order stating: 'We intend to use the bulk of heavy bomber units reinforced by specialised units that will be combined under the leadership of the Fliegerkorps IV headquarters in the planned fight against the Russians. The task of these units will be to inflict devastating blows on the Russian military industry in order to reduce the endless growth in the production of tanks, guns and aircraft. And this should have a greater effect than destroying them on the battlefield.'

By December, it was possible to assemble the minimum required number of bombers. Eight aviation groups from KG3, KG4 and KG55 were combined as part of Fliegerkorps IV. There were only about 250 bombers in total. In parallel, intensive training of crews began. Major Reinhard Graubner's II./KG4 underwent the most thorough training, which was to perform the role of pathfinders (target markers) in the operation. It was expected that by the beginning of 1944, at least one air group equipped with He 177 Greif (Griffin) heavy bombers would arrive on the Eastern Front. Speer proposed using them to bomb power plants in the Urals, the total installed capacity of which was estimated by German intelligence at 2.2 million kilowatts.

By the end of January, preparations for an air attack against the power plants of the MOW region and other designated targets were generally complete. However, the order to start the operation had not been received. The reasons for the delay were anyone's guess. Firstly, the winter turned out to be very warm and cloudy with a minimum number of clear days. It is clear that it was possible to attack such point targets located deep behind enemy lines only at night and in clear weather. Secondly, Hitler did not give a direct order. At that time, the Führer was completely absorbed in another operation – Steinbock (Capricorn). It started on the night of 22 January and represented another series of massive raids on London. Time passed, but the order to attack still did not arrive. During the first months of 1944, Fliegerkorps IV was in constant readiness to strike at Soviet power plants, until at the end of March, the Führer's long-awaited order finally arrived. But, it was completely different ...

Strategic bombers were tasked with completely paralysing railway traffic along the Kiev–Korosten–Sarny–Kovel line, as well as the Shepetovka–Zdolbunov–Rivne–Kivertsy–Kovel railway line located south of it. Sarny and Shepetovka stations were identified as the main targets. This was supposed to make it difficult to supply Soviet troops, bring reserves to the front line, and simultaneously destroy the maximum number of new units and military equipment before it was sent to the front.

By the beginning of the operation, dubbed 'Zaunkönig' ('Royal Fence'), there were about 300 bombers in Fliegerkorps IV. They were mostly He 111H-20s. It was the last modification of the bomber, which differed by having more powerful engines and more capable defensive weapons.

On the night of 27–28 March, fifty aircraft carried out the first raid on the Sarna railway hub. It turned out to be completely unexpected by the Soviet air defences, and the target was completely destroyed. On the night of 31 March–1 April, a total of 138 aircraft took part, which dropped bombs on the railway stations of Sarny, Fastov, Bila Tserkva, as well as the railway bridge across the Dnieper in Kiev. On the night of 4–5 April, Sarny and Korosten stations became targets. The next night 185 He 111s and Ju 88s attacked the railway hubs of Rivne and Korosten.

The next target of the Fliegerkorps IV headquarters was the large Kiev-Darnitsa marshalling yard. At 23.30, Soviet radar stations detected two single targets that were moving south-east from Ovruch and Pripyat towards Kiev. At 00.11, an air surveillance post located in the Radchi area (Sarny–Olevsk railway section) reported that a large group of enemy bombers had appeared from the north-west, from the Pripyat marshes, flying in the direction of Korosten. Soon, it was reported from the Ovruch area that the planes were moving further to the south-east, probably towards Kiev. After a few minutes, the grouped targets were already clearly visible on radar. At 00.20, the anti-aircraft guns of the 317th ZENAP (anti aircraft artillery regiment), covering the capital of Ukraine, began a barrage, but the sky remained empty, and the searchlights went into the void. In fact, the German

Sarny
Korosten
Rivne
Zdolbunov
Zhytomyr
Kiev-Darnitsa
Fastov
Shepetovka
Berdichev
Kazatin
Bila Tserkva
Zhmerinka

planes bypassed the city from the north, after which they turned around and began to enter their targets in turn. The first pathfinders from II./KG4 appeared over Kiev, which dropped coloured marker bombs from a great height.

The Germans chose the target and the time of the strike extremely well. By the evening of the 7th, a huge number of trains had accumulated at the Darnitsa marshalling yard, and trains with fuel and ammunition, wagons with soldiers, cavalry horses, wounded soldiers and civilians stood on parallel and access rails. Train No. 15046 with the 1st Separate Detachment of Anti-Aircraft Artillery of the Polish Army (Wojsko Polskie) under the command of Lieutenant Colonel Wlodzimierz Sokolowski also happened to be there. He was heading to the Zhytomyr region.

At 00.30, the bombing began and it lasted almost two hours. Railway tanks with fuel and wagons containing shells and mines began to burn on the tracks and explode one after another. Therefore, the flames spread to neighbouring trains, and from them to other trains with ammunition. In the midst of this pitch-black hell, figures of soldiers, railway workers and civilians rushed around in panic. The shockwaves from the explosions was so strong that the wagon wheel axles flew several kilometres away, with some falling in the centre of Kiev! The station was completely destroyed, with about 5,000 military personnel and civilians killed, as well as almost 500 railway workers. Eight bombs hit a Polish train, as a result of which three guns were destroyed and fifty-two anti-aircraft gunners were killed (including the commander of the 1st Battery, Lieutenant Ivan Kononenko).

On the night of 7–8 April, 166 bombers attacked the Fastov station, and a day later the Korosten station. The next mission within the framework of Operation Zaunkönig, in which 148 He 111s and forty-two Ju 88s took part, was on the night of 15–16 April and its target was Sarny station. According to Soviet information, 400 high-explosive bombs were dropped. The next night, 183 bombers struck the railway hub of Shepetovka. On the night of 17–18 April, a repeat air attack was carried out against the Kiev-Darnitsa station. The journal of combat operations of the 317th anti-aircraft Artillery Regiment (317th ZenAP) reported: ‘The bombing was carried out from horizontal flight and diving using marker bombs. In total, about 400 high-explosive bombs of 250–500kg calibre were dropped at the Darnitsa station. As a result of the bombing at Darnitsa station, railway tracks were partially destroyed, the exit to Brovary station was destroyed, 4 wagons with ammunition, 3 railway tanks, up to 30 empty wagons burned, a train with coal and 20 wagons with various property were set on fire. 20 soldiers and 16 civilians were killed at Darnitsa station.'

Fourteen anti-aircraft batteries fired at the bombers, which dropped 4,600 shells. According to German information, two of the 167 bombers involved in the raid were lost.

After a short break, the operation continued on 27 April. Sarny station was again designated as the main target, and Rivne station was designated as a back-up. A total of 191 aircraft (145 He 111s and forty-six Ju 88s) took to the air, however, due to bad weather, most of the crews were unable to reach the target areas. On the night of 30 April–1 May, 144 He 111s, forty-three Ju 88s and one Do 217 carried out a massive raid on Zdolbunov station. The next target, a day later, was the railway hub at Shepetovka. The tactics were the same: around midnight, the first marker bombs were dropped over the target, and five minutes later the bombing began, which lasted intermittently for an hour. As a result, 175 rail links of tracks, twelve switch rails, a depot, a pumping station, a water intake lock and eighty spans of wires were destroyed, with seven steam locomotives and thirty-five wagons also wrecked.

The personnel of the 7th Battalion of the 7th Railway Brigade, responsible for this railway section, arrived at the site twenty minutes after the attack and immediately began restoration work. At 03.00, through traffic was resumed along one of the tracks, then during the next day workers gradually put the railway hub into operation. This example shows how quickly Russian railway workers restored traffic through large railway hubs, but this only concerned the rails themselves. The restoration of the rest of the railway infrastructure (pressure and distribution network, pumping stations, warehouses, etc.) required at least another ten to fifteen days of continuous work.

On the night of 5 May, Sarny station was again designated the main target of the raid, but due to bad weather, only fifty-six bombers out of 241 were able to find a back-up target, Rivne. The following night, Fliegerkorps IV carried out the third massive raid on the Kiev-Darnitsa marshalling yard. This time, all 217 aircraft reached the target, dropping 319 tons of high-explosive and fragmentation bombs. As a result, the tracks on the Poltava railway line were destroyed, along with twenty wagons. The Soviets learned quickly from previous raids. Taking into account the sad experience of the past five weeks, Russian rail workers did not allow trains to accumulate on spare tracks or a build-up of congestion, especially at night. Trains approaching Kiev were delayed at intermediate stations or on the track in between, waiting there for their turn to sort and pass the bridge over the Dnieper. These measures made it possible to avoid large losses, although they slowed down the movement.

From 27 March to 5 May, the Luftwaffe carried out 2,700 sorties and attacked seventeen targets, on which 3,500 tons of bombs were dropped. The losses averaged 1.4 per cent of the bombers involved. Although the losses in rolling stock (wagons and locomotives) were relatively small, and the Russians quickly repaired the damage, these air attacks undoubtedly had an indirect effect on slowing down the Soviet offensive.

Chapter 4

# THE END OF HITLER'S GOTENLAND

## Hunting for Worms

The battle for the Crimea continued intermittently for two and a half years. Both warring parties attached the utmost importance to the possession of this peninsula. Hitler considered the Crimea an 'unsinkable aircraft carrier' that allowed him to control the Black Sea and exert political pressure on the Balkan countries and Turkey, as well as 'native German land', 'Gotenland' (in ancient times Crimean Goths lived there), on which an exemplary European resort was to appear in the future. Stalin also attached the utmost importance to the retention and then reconquest of the Crimea, despite the fact that the peninsula was actually a 'dead end' through which it was impossible to break either into the enemy's rear or to advance anywhere at all. The Soviets stubbornly made naval landings there and threw large aviation and naval forces into battle, while the Führer tried to hold the Crimea with the same fanaticism and was not bothered by the huge expenditure of forces and resources, or even the danger of losing an entire army of 200,000 men.

In the autumn of 1943, in the course of a rapid offensive, the Russians approached the northern part of the Crimea. Even then, the Wehrmacht command insisted on the immediate evacuation of the peninsula. However, Hitler, in his characteristic spirit, categorically forbade any withdrawal. He believed that he got won the peninsula in a fierce struggle and was not going to give it up without a fight. As a result, the entire 17th Army was cut off from the rest of the troops. On 23 October, units of the Soviet 51st Army occupied Melitopol, after which the 4th Ukrainian Front, under the command of General Fyodor Tolbukhin,

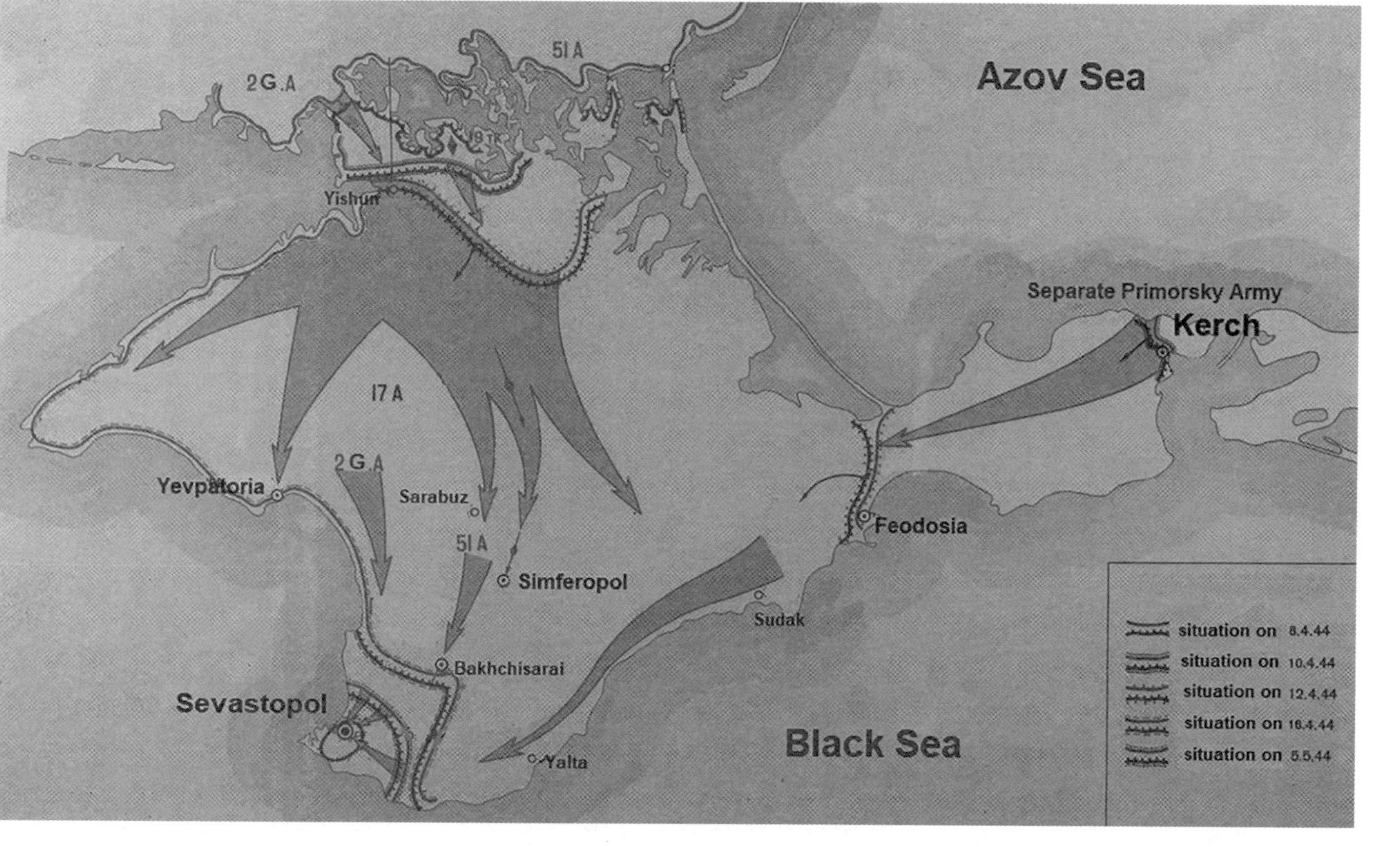

Azov Sea
2G.A
5I A
19 TK
Yishun
I7 A
2G.A
Yevpatoria
Sarabuz
5I A
Simferopol
Bakhchisarai
Sevastopol
Yalta
Sudak
Feodosia
Separate Primorsky Army
Kerch
Black Sea
situation on 8.4.44
situation on 10.4.44
situation on 12.4.44
situation on 16.4.44
situation on 5.5.44

continued its rapid offensive to the lower reaches of the Dnieper and the Crimea. On the evening of 31 October, the advanced units of the 19th Tank Corps reached the Turkish Rampart – an ancient earthen wall behind which the Crimean Khanate, a vassal of Turkey, hid from the Russians in the eighteenth century.

This Rampart was located in the north-western part of the Perekop Isthmus between the Black and Azov Seas. At the same time, on the night of 1 November, the North Caucasian Front under the command of General Ivan Petrov launched an operation to force the Kerch Strait. The landing took place on armoured boats, seiners, motorboats and even rowboats under enemy fire. As a result, the Soviets managed to capture two bridgeheads on the west bank; in the area of Eltigen and east of Kerch.

However, further battles turned out unfavourably for the Red Army. In the north of the peninsula, the Germans surrounded the advanced units that had broken into their rear and quickly restored their defences along the Turkish Rampart. In the east of the peninsula, Romanian units were able to eliminate the Eltigen bridgehead after fierce fighting, and in the Kerch area the Germans built an impregnable line of defence. The battles for the Crimea took on a positional character and continued throughout the winter and spring.

By April 1944, the Crimea had turned into an enclave that lived its own special life. Most of the peninsula was not affected by military operations, railway trains (including passenger trains) ran regularly between Kerch, Feodosia, Dzhankoy and Sevastopol, ships docked and sailed in harbours, and soldiers went on holiday and returned on smoothly flying transport planes. At the same time, Russian partisans were active in there, controlling entire areas, especially in the mountains. They even had their own airfields, where Soviet planes landed from time to time. During the two and a half years of occupation, both sides had already become accustomed to such a situation; they did not stop fighting, but only slightly interfered in each other's lives. Civilian life also flowed steadily: fishermen went out to sea to fish, many vehicles drove along the roads, performances were held in city theatres, and movie premieres were shown regularly in cinemas. But a storm was raging outside the peninsula. In mid-March, the defence of Army Group A almost collapsed. On 13 March, the 6th Army left Kherson, the largest stronghold closest to the Crimea. Then the Germans lost Nikolaev and Odessa. Despite this, Hitler rejected all proposals to evacuate the Crimea.

On the morning of 8 April, the troops of the 4th Ukrainian Front, after a record eight-hour artillery preparation, attacked the positions of the German 17th Army on the Perekop Isthmus and on the southern shore of the shallow Sivash Bay. According to the operational plan, personally approved by Stalin, only a week was allotted for the liberation of the Crimean Peninsula. For example, the 19th Tank Corps of General Ivan Vasilyev (the main striking force of the 4th Ukrainian Front) was supposed to capture Simferopol on the fourth day, which was considered the most important stronghold in the south of the Crimea and a key strategic point. The main task was to cut off the Germans' routes to the ports, to prevent them from moving away and boarding ships in an organised manner. This plan looked tempting and very optimistic, if not adventurous. Recall that the distance from the northern tip of the peninsula to Sevastopol is 160km in a straight line, and from Kerch 250km. Mostly it is a sparsely populated, waterless steppe with a poorly developed road network, rapidly turning into highlands in the south. By the beginning of the attack, the 19th Tank Corps had 233 tanks and self-propelled artillery pieces.

In the northern part of the peninsula, the Soviet troops were supported by the 8th Air Army of General Timofey Khryukin, which numbered 802 aircraft (196 bombers, 235 ground-attack planes, 351 fighters and 20 reconnaissance aircraft). General Vershinin's 4th Air Army operated in the east of the Crimea, which had 539 aircraft, including 239 fighters. And this is not counting the air force of the Black Sea Fleet. The opposing forces of German and Romanian aviation looked much more modest. By early April, only 134 aircraft were based the Crimea, including 33 Bf 109s, 38 Ju 87s and 20 Fw 190s.

However, the Luftwaffe proved again that even with the huge numerical superiority of the enemy, they were still capable of delivering effective strikes. On the third day of the battle, when the German defence was still holding out but there were already signs of a crisis, two squadrons specialising in the destruction of armoured vehicles arrived in the Crimea. The first of them – 10.(Pz)/SG9 – was equipped with twin-engined Hs 129B-2 aircraft. They were equipped with a pair of 20mm cannon and could additionally carry a container with a 30mm cannon or bombs and containers with SD2 fragmentation bombs under the fuselage. The second squadron – 10.(Pz)/SG3 – was equipped with Ju 87G-2 aircraft, which had two long-barrelled 37mm guns. On 10 April, Hs 129B-2s and Ju 87G-2s began combat sorties, which was just in time. In the evening, the headquarters of the 4th Ukrainian Front decided to introduce its main striking force, the 19th Tank Corps, into the breakthrough.

At about 17.00, a group of nine German aircraft 'bombarded' the initial positions of the tankers in the Armyansk area with a large number of SD2 fragmentation bombs. As a result, almost the entire command staff of the compound was put out of action, including General Vasilyev, who was seriously wounded. Vasilyev's deputy, Colonel Ivan Potseluyev, took command of the unit, as he received only a slight wound. As a result, the departure of the 19th Tank Corps to the line of attack was delayed for several hours. And it was only at 05.00 on 11 April that tanks and self-propelled guns began an offensive in the direction of Dzhankoy.

However, it was impossible to stop the Russians with the help of a dozen planes. By eight o'clock in the morning on 11 April, tanks and motorised infantry of the 19th Tank Corps were able to break through the German defences in the Tomashevka area. Having reached the operational area, they continued their offensive in the direction of Dzhankoy. The commander of the 8th Air Army, Timofey Khryukin, sent a telegram saying: 'The main defence of the enemy in Crimea has been torn, the enemy is fleeing in panic, pursued by our tanks and planes.'

It also became clear to the German command that the defence of the 17th Army in the north of the Crimea had collapsed. The troops were ordered to move at maximum speed to Sevastopol and the commander of Fliegerkorps I, Major General Paul Deichmann, ordered all aircraft to be relocated to the Chersonesos air base. This facility was destined to play a crucial role in the Crimean disaster. The airfield was located 10km south-west of Sevastopol, on a tiny peninsula between the Black Sea and Kazachya Bay. The runway was located on a plateau, which in the south dropped off into the sea from a height of about 30m. The coating was partially made of peat, the rest was covered with sand or stones.

Meanwhile, Russian tanks first reached Dzhankoy, and by evening Colonel Pyotr Arkhipov's 79th Tank Brigade had captured Karankut airfield. There were captured rich trophies – barrels of fuel and stacks of bombs, which the Germans did not have time to take out. The last German planes took off from Karankut half an hour before the arrival of the first Russian tanks. The rapid breakthrough of Tolbukhin's troops in the north of the Crimea put German and Romanian troops, still defending themselves in the eastern tip of the peninsula, in a dramatic position. In October 1943, after the evacuation of the Kuban bridgehead, the eastern part of the Gotenland seemed to be an impregnable forward bastion, providing the southern flank of the Eastern Front. Six months later, this position turned into a remote enclave, deep in the rear of the Red Army. While some of the Romanian soldiers could still look at the Caucasus Mountains through binoculars, their comrades were already fighting fierce battles on the territory of Romania itself – 800km west of Kerch! It is clear that there could be no question of any 'stubborn defence', only thoughts of evacuation reigned everywhere. The soldiers waited tensely for the signal to run away. And they would have to run very far – almost 250km! According to Soviet plans, after the breakthrough of the enemy defences in the northern Crimea, the troops in the east were to launch an offensive. However, the first days of the operation to liberate the Crimea at the Kerch bridgehead passed quietly.

On the evening of 10 April, pilots of Russian reconnaissance aircraft reported that a large number of explosions and fires had been observed in the front line, and heavy traffic in the south-westerly direction was on the roads. It became clear that the Germans and Romanians had begun to leave their positions on the coast en masse and retreat along the roads to the south-west. The next morning, Russian soldiers entered the empty central quarters of Kerch without a fight, not meeting a single German there. Although the commander of the Separate Primorsky Army, General Andrei Yeremenko, had clear instructions to 'not let the enemy' leave, he missed the moment of launching an attack and actually gave the Germans and Romanians a small head start.

The retreat to the west was carried out in various ways. Some of the troops and property were sent by rail, others moved by trucks and horse-drawn wagons. A significant number of soldiers had to walk. On the rocky roads of eastern Crimea, these numerous columns became an easy target for Russian aircraft. At the same time, there was no fighter protection as all German aircraft were at that moment in the western part of the huge peninsula.

The first target of Russian aircraft were railway trains, as well as the famous German rail destroyers. During the retreat, German troops always sought to disable the railway lines in order to make it difficult for the Russians to advance further and supply their troops. Two types of rail destroyers were used for these purposes. The first of them was a copy of the Russian 'Chervjak' (Worm) model back in 1915, named after the surname of its creator, Lieutenant Chervjak from the 4th Railway Battalion. It consisted of a loop bent from rails, wider than the railway track, which, with the help of loops riveted at its tapering ends, was attached to the coupling device of the locomotive. To start the work of the 'Worm', it was first necessary to disassemble one of the joints of the rails and detach the rails from the sleepers, after which the loop was fed under the rails. The locomotive began to pull the loop, which tore the rails from the sleepers along with the crutches, while bending the rails themselves. The result of the Worm's work was dislodged and damaged sleepers and deformed rails, which forced the enemy to actually rebuild the track.

However, the Germans made their original contribution to the destruction of railway tracks. At the end of 1942, the Krupp company developed and began serial production of the 'Hook' (Hagen) rail destroyer. It was a two-axle platform loaded with very heavy ballast, at one end of which a powerful hook made of an I-beam or welded from sheet metal was attached to a hinge. Before using the destroyer, a team made the necessary gap between the sleepers, into which the hook itself was lowered with the help of jacks. The locomotive pulled the platform at a speed of about 10km/h, and the hook literally opened the railway track. The sleepers broke in half and the rails bent. In 1943–44, such rail destroyers became a real headache for Russians. For the destruction of such equipment, a pilot was immediately awarded a medal.

At 14.30, a pair of Bell P-39 fighters from the 66th IAP departed for a 'free hunt' to destroy steam locomotives on the Tashlyar–Vladislavovka railway segment. Near the Seven Wells station at the semaphore, the pilots saw two steam locomotives with wagons and a platform to which a rail destroyer was attached. Second Lieutenant Shugaev and Second Lieutenant Petrov completed four passes, firing at the target with their 37mm guns. After that, the locomotives were enveloped in clouds of smoke and steam, and a large explosion occurred in one of the wagons. Later, a broken train and an abandoned Worm-type rail destroyer were discovered by the advancing troops of the Separate Primorsky Army.

Meanwhile, the columns of the German 5th Army Corps, retreating in the direction of Feodosia, were subjected to brutal Soviet air strikes all day. Major Elman Krause, who was captured the next day, said: 'At about 5–6 a.m., the first groups of Russian ground-attack planes appeared, which at a low level attacked automobile columns that came up behind the division's rearguards. As a result of this raid, several vehicles were set on fire and 5 drivers were killed. The air raids continued throughout the morning, and the Russian pilots, meeting no resistance from the air defence and fighters, became so emboldened that they literally flew over their heads.'

Krause was echoed by the commander of the Romanian 6th Cavalry Regiment, Captain Commander Theodore Paulian, who was captured on the same day: 'Already at dawn, my regiment, which was on its way to the intermediate line passing along the Tatarsky rampart, was raided by Russian aviation. The Russian planes were flying at low altitude in threes, and flying up to the column of the regiment, turned around, dropped to low-level flight and opened heavy fire from cannon and machine guns, simultaneously pelting the column with small fragmentation bombs. After the soldiers scattered and lay down in roadside ditches and on the field, the Russian ground-attack planes attacked artillery batteries following the regiment, pelting them with rockets.'

The Germans, as often happened, simply abandoned their allies to their fate, ordering them to leave on their own, hiding behind the rearguards.

By the evening of 11 April, advanced mechanised units of the Separate Primorsky Army reached the Ak-Monai (now Kamenskoye)–Dalniye Kamyshi (now Primorsky) line.

The next day, the mass exodus continued. Some of the railway trains managed to slip to Sevastopol through the Dzhankoy station in the north of the peninsula. Everything that did not have time to be taken out was either abandoned or hastily loaded on to ships in the port of Feodosia or in Sudak. The last train to leave Feodosia station was a steam locomotive with four wagons and a rail destroyer attached to it. As it was later established, it was a 'Hook', which in Soviet documents was called a 'Scorpion', probably because of the external similarity of its hook with the curved tail of this arthropod. In the morning, LaGG-3 fighter pilots from the 249th IAP, performing a reconnaissance flight, discovered this small train on the Vladislavovka–Islam-Terek section. At the same time, the pilots saw the Scorpion in operation, and the broken sleepers and twisted rails remaining behind it. Soon the locomotive was fired at by P-39 fighters, after which the Germans blew up the rail destroyer and fled on a trolley towards Islam Terek.

On 13 April, the troops of the 4th Ukrainian Front captured Sarabuz airfield, which for two and a half years had been the most important base of the Luftwaffe. At the same time, the troops of the Separate Primorsky Army, moving further west, reached Feodosia, the Islam-Terek railway station and Koktebel. Then they entered the town of Karasubazar (now Belogorsk), where they joined forces with Tolbukhin's troops.

The Germans continued to flee. The march of the 5th Army Corps retreating from the east was the most dramatic. A narrow coastal highway led from Feodosia to Sevastopol, sandwiched between high mountain gorges and the sea. This winding road, passing by small resort towns, was 250km long. Thousands of Romanian and German soldiers in vehicles, on horses, donkeys and on foot moved day and night, driven by Soviet units advancing from behind and panicked rumours of the approach of Soviet troops from the north.

On the left, the soldiers saw the endless Black Sea, and on the right, menacingly looming mountain ranges teeming with partisans. From above, these defenceless columns were attacked regularly by Russian planes. Usually fighters approached the target at an altitude of 1,200m, then dived at an angle of 50–60 degrees, firing cannon and machine guns. At an altitude of 50–100m, these terrifying planes flew over the heads of frightened soldiers, then went on a second lap, returned and everything started over again. Because of these air attacks, the soldiers constantly panicked. The men fired randomly into the air, hid behind rocks and trees, and lost their units. From time to time, there was congestion, exacerbating the chaos. Broken and damaged vehicles and horse-drawn carts were dumped into the abyss. There was no time to dig graves, usually bodies were just stacked on the side of the road and sprinkled with stones.

On the afternoon of 14 April, the troops of the 4th Ukrainian Front captured Simferopol, and, moving further to the south-west, reached Bakhchisarai. Then, by nightfall, they reached the villages of Mamashai, Duvankoy, Hajika, Biyuk, Karalez, Adym and Chokrak. So, the Russians found themselves 50km west of the columns of the German 5th Army Corps, which were still passing Alushta and Gurzuf. The troops of the Separate Primorsky Army moving behind occupied Sudak in the morning, and in the evening they were already fighting with German rearguards north-east of Alushta. Thus, the Red Army was already 15–20km north-east of Sevastopol. The units of the 17th Army, not particularly lingering on the intermediate lines, quickly retreated further to this city.

It should be noted that, unlike Demyansk, Kholm, Stalingrad and other cities previously declared by Hitler as 'fortresses', but which actually represented piles of urban ruins, Sevastopol was a real, full-fledged fortress. There were numerous bastions around it, preserved since the Crimean War of 1853, and field fortifications from the period of the First World War. In 1941–42, this sea stronghold was further fortified by the Russians during their defence of it. And although many defensive structures were destroyed during the assault, by 1944 the Germans had partially restored them, turning the city into a powerful fortress again. It was this fact that ultimately saved the 17th Army from total annihilation.

On 15 April, the advanced units of the 4th Ukrainian Front attempted to immediately break through to Sevastopol. Tankers of the 19th Tank Corps, together with several rifle divisions, managed to reach the Mekenzievy Gory railway station and the vicinity of the village of Bartenyevka (now the northern outskirts of Sevastopol). However, further on, the Russians came across minefields, ditches and heavy fire from 88mm anti-aircraft guns.

On this day, the troops of the Separate Primorsky Army, advancing along the Black Sea coast, reached Alushta, and in the evening reached the village of Biyuk Lambat, 9km north-east of Gurzuf. At that time, the bulk of the troops of the 5th Army Corps had already passed Yalta and were 80km from Sevastopol. Yeremenko counted his trophies over the five days of the chase: 6,000 horses, 450 artillery pieces, 25 tanks and self-propelled artillery pieces, 20 steam locomotives and 700 wagons. About 20,000 people, mostly Romanians, were taken prisoner. It was a great success, but the general, who at one time led the defence of Stalingrad, was not happy. The Germans had succeeded in almost the impossible. Having covered more than 250km in five days (approximately equal to the distance between London and Liverpool), most of the troops managed to avoid encirclement and captivity.

During 16–17 April, the great exodus of the 17th Army ended. To the east of Sevastopol, the Soviet offensive finally stopped, and in the south-east, the last German units reached Balaklava. On 18 April, the troops of the 4th Ukrainian Front reached the line Saharnaya Golovka Mountain–Sapun Mountain–Karan village. From there, Sevastopol harbour was only 8km away. As a result, Sevastopol was surrounded by the troops of General Fyodor Tolbukhin, and along the way they cut off the Separate Primorsky Army. So Yeremenko lost the race to Sevastopol and on the same day, on Stalin's orders, he was recalled from the Crimea. After that, there was a pause in the battle. The Germans and Romanians retreated to well-fortified positions, and the troops of the 4th Ukrainian Front ran out of steam, suffering serious losses on the way to Sevastopol. For example, only thirty serviceable tanks and eleven self-propelled artillery pieces remained in the 19th Tank Corps.

This allowed General Jaenecke to begin evacuating people and various cargoes from Sevastopol. By the end of April, older soldiers, construction battalions, gendarmerie and police units, as well as all Russian volunteers were taken to Romania. Ammunition, fuel and equipment were delivered back to the 'fortress', as well as replenishment for infantry units. One of the captured German non-commissioned officers then said that his marching company of 277 men was formed in Königsberg and transported by rail to Constanta. Arriving there on 28 April, he witnessed large-scale loading and unloading operations. Russian volunteers and wounded who arrived from the Crimea were loaded on to the vacated trains, which immediately left towards Bucharest, and the new arrivals, on the contrary, boarded high-speed landing barges, which were also loaded with ammunition.

In the period from 11 to 30 April, sixty-three naval convoys consisting of 503 vessels passed between the Crimea and Romania, while their losses were minimal. However, Hitler still did not want to part with his beloved 'Gotenland' and, contrary to common sense, was going to hold Sevastopol.

On 28 April, a proclamation was read to German soldiers by the commander of the 17th Army, Generaloberst Erwin Jaenecke, which ended with a pathetic and at the same time ambiguous phrase: 'Death is behind us, victory is ahead!' As it soon turned out, this address became a farewell for Jaenecke. On 29 April, he flew to the Führer's headquarters in Berchtesgaden, where he offered to immediately evacuate the remaining troops to Romania. The general described the situation and explained that the organised operation of the air bridge and loading on to ships was possible only as long as German troops controlled Sapun Mountain, and Cape Chersonesos was outside the range of Soviet long-range artillery fire. But if these positions were breached, and the harbours and airfield began to be shelled, then chaos would arise. Hitler was initially shocked by what he heard and did not react in any way to the general's words. But then, when Jaenecke was already on his way back to the Crimea, he became furious and ordered his arrest. As a result, the general was detained in Galac, and General Karl Almedinger took command of the 17th Army instead.

While there was a pause on the ground, major air battles unfolded in the air. During the day, Russian ground-attack planes and bombers carried out attacks against German defensive lines and communications and bombed Chersonesos airbase. At night, Russian Il-4 medium bombers dropped bombs from 2,000m on Sevastopol harbour and Chersonese. These raids were complemented by raids by U-2 light night bombers. These biplanes flew in large numbers at low level, pelting the Germans with small fragmentation bombs. The main mission of the Russian light bombers was to exhaust the enemy. Endless bombing did not allow the Germans to sleep peacefully, as swarms of mosquitoes, U-2s, continuously 'bit' the Wehrmacht along the entire front line.

The Luftwaffe were also active. In addition to Fw 190 and Bf 109 fighters based at Chersonesos, Fw 190s from Schlachtgeschwader SG10 flew in from Romania every day. After flying almost 400km over the sea, they first dropped their bombs on Soviet troops, and then engaged in battle with the first Russian fighters they came across. When the Fw 190s' fuel ran out, they landed in Chersonesos, refuelled and flew back to Romania. He 111 bombers were also active, which, as usual, had to combine bombing and transport missions. Taking off from Romanian air bases, the planes dropped bombs on various targets, then landed in Chersonesos. There, He 111s loaded wounded soldiers and flew to Romania.

German fighters, in the face of the huge numerical superiority of the Russians, had to use non-standard tactics. They did not conduct their famous 'free hunting' at high altitude with sudden attacks out of the sun, but, on the contrary, from low level. Having thoroughly studied all the features of the terrain, which consisted of valleys and gorges surrounded by hills, mostly facing the sea, the JG52 pilots developed typical fixed routes that passed through the lowlands, then over the water, and then again through the lowlands. Speeding at a low level through the gorges, the German pilots avoided unnecessary encounters with Soviet fighters, as their main targets were the Il-2 ground-attack planes.

The culmination of the Battle for the Crimea came on 5 May. By this time, the Russians had concentrated 253,000 soldiers, about 5,000 artillery pieces and mortars, and 106 tanks in the Sevastopol area. From the air, they were supported by about a thousand aircraft. After an hour and a half of shelling, the 2nd Guards Army launched an offensive in the northern sector of the front in the direction of the Mekenzievy Gory railway station. However, the German resistance turned out to be unexpectedly stubborn, and the Red Army soldiers were met everywhere by a barrage of artillery, machine-gun and mortar fire. At the first opportunity, the Germans tried to carry out counter-attacks and restore the situation. As a result, by the end of the day, the Russians managed to advance only 500–1,200m deeper into the German defences, mainly in the Belbek area. The next day, the situation repeated itself, and General Almedinger optimistically reported that 'the attacks of the Soviets were repelled'.

However, this was only an overture to the battle. At 09.00 on 7 May, after a powerful artillery bombardment from 2,000 guns, units of the 51st and Primorsky Armies went on the offensive. Fierce fighting went on all day, with the Germans periodically launching counter-attacks, sometimes ending in hand-to-hand fights. This day was the culmination of the air battle over the Crimea. Taking advantage of the clear weather, the 8th Air Army carried out 1,500 sorties. More than eighty aerial battles took place, some of them lasting twenty to thirty minutes at different altitudes, from 100 to 3,000m. The Il-2s approached the front line at an altitude of 1,000m, found their targets, and then bombed and shelled them, making several passes. The German anti-aircraft artillery snarled desperately, and the pilots of the few German fighters made four or five sorties.

By evening, the assault groups of the 51st and Separate Primorsky Armies had come close to Sapun Mountain, a key 200m-high hill that dominated the southern approaches to Sevastopol. At 18.00, after a short shelling, the infantry rushed into the attack with shouts of 'hurrah', and with a swift rush managed to break into the lower tier of trenches on the eastern slopes of the hill. The Germans retreated to the second tier and from there began to pour machine-gun fire on the Red Army. But then, one by one, three six Il-2s appeared from the east. Already on the way to the target, the group leaders received a radio signal: 'Hit the second and third tiers, our soldiers are on the bottom!' Despite frenzied small arms fire and anti-aircraft guns firing from the top of Sapun Mountain, the aircraft stubbornly attacked the target. They fired rockets at practically point-blank range and hit trenches and bunkers with their cannon and machine guns, then dropped bombs, and at the last moment, when the crest of a huge hill pitted with craters was right in front of their eyes, they turned away, roaring literally over the heads of the Germans. After that, the Il-2s turned around and went on a second run, again pouring cannon fire into the trenches and dugouts. The Soviet soldiers crouched below saw three planes at once, engulfed in flames, crash into the hillside, which by the end of the bombing was enveloped in huge clouds of smoke and dust. Several more planes trailing a plume of smoke were trying to turn around in an easterly direction. Inspired by this suicidal air attack, which caused complete confusion to the enemy, the infantrymen rose and rushed to the top of the mountain. At 6.30 p.m., the first groups rushed in and hoisted the red banner, although fierce hand-to-hand fighting was still going on all around. Fighter squadron JG52 set a record on this day. Its few pilots who fought in the Crimea claimed fifty-one aerial victories. The Soviet air force really made great sacrifices for the capture of Sapun Mountain. The losses of the 8th Air Army amounted to fifty-one aircraft, most of them Il-2s, but at least half of them were actually shot down by gunfire from the ground.

By the end of the day, the soldiers of the 51st and Separate Primorsky Armies had completely captured Sapun Mountain. This event was the turning point of the battle. German–Romanian units began to gradually retreat from the burning and destroyed environs of Sevastopol to Cape Chersonesos. It became clear that the complete collapse of the defence of the 'fortress' was only a few days away. What happened was what the now disgraced former commander of the 17th Army, Generaloberst Erwin Jaenecke, had warned Hitler about on 29

April. After the capture of Sapun Mountain, Soviet artillery was able to fire from there at the Chersonesos airfield and ships in Sevastopol harbour. This made it impossible to further supply the German troops, and therefore continue the defence of Sevastopol. Now this fact was repeated to the Führer by the commander of Army Group Southern Ukraine, Generaloberst Ferdinand Schörner. Only then did Hitler reluctantly allow the complete evacuation of all troops from the Crimea.

## 'Everything was the same as always, only a little worse'

On 9 May, the Germans had to withdraw from Sevastopol. They retreated to the 'Turkish Rampart', an ancient line of defence that ran along a ridge of hills south of Streletskaya Bay. There, Russian tanks from the 19th Tank Corps were stopped by fire from 88mm anti-aircraft guns, and the Soviet offensive temporarily stopped until the next morning, awaiting the arrival of reserves. At 8 p.m. that day, the headquarters of the 4th Ukrainian Front reported the complete liberation of Sevastopol. Nervousness and panic were increasingly felt at the headquarters of the German 17th Army and in its units. Many had concerns that there might not be enough 'tickets from Hell' for everyone. Up to this point, the Germans and Romanians were generally organised, despite the air attacks and shelling, while numerous ships and vessels plied between Sevastopol and Constanta. However, now the evacuation had entered a crisis phase, Romania did not have a clear idea of what was happening in the Crimea.

In the evening of that day, the last German fighters were forced to evacuate from Chersonesos air base and fly to Romania. The landing of transport planes had also become impossible. The German and Romanian soldiers had only one way to escape: by sea. At about 03.30 on 10 May, a convoy code-named Patria arrived at Cape Chersonesos, It included two R-bote type boats and two of the newest diesel-electric ships *Totila* and *Teja*. Interestingly, both ships were built at the Hungarian shipyard Ganz & Co. in 1940 by order of the Soviet government. They were supposed to be called *Simferopol* and *Sevastopol*, but the war altered these plans. In 1942, both ships were completed and became part of the Hungarian merchant fleet with the names *Magyar Tengeres* and *Magyar Vitez*. Then, they were bought by Germany and received the names of the Ostrogothic kings. Both transports were armed with two 37mm anti-aircraft guns and six 20mm anti-aircraft guns. At dawn, loading began on *Teja* and *Totila*, anchored 2km from the shore. At first, soldiers at the berths south-west of Chersonesos were loaded on to amphibious ferries of the Siebel type from the 770th Airborne Battalion, which then delivered them aboard transports.

At 06.00, Soviet air attacks began and soon *Totila* received the first three bomb hits. A fire started on the ship, and in addition she received a hole in the bow below the waterline and began to sink. Ferries that had previously loaded soldiers on to it now began to rescue them and transport them back to shore. At 08.20, *Totila* was attacked by thirteen more Il-2s and then ten A-20s, after which the diesel-electric ship, enveloped in clouds of smoke, rolled on to her side and sank. The Germans managed to get most of the crew and passengers ashore, where they had to wait for a new 'ticket' to Romania.

Meanwhile, after the first air raids the transport *Teja* paused the loading and hurriedly left for the open sea. For seven hours, the ship was subjected to air attacks, and at 15.30 she finally sank 37km from Cape Chersonesos. The nearby *Räumbootes* (minesweepers) *R35* and *R164* and a Siebel ferry rescued about 400 people from the water. The exact number of deaths on *Totila* and *Teja* is still unknown, but before the air attacks began no more than 3,000 people had managed to board them. While the huge ships were sinking, the main part of the headquarters of the 17th Army successfully escaped from Sevastopol on a torpedo boat. The commander of the 49th Mountain Corps, General Walter Hartmann, remained in charge of the troops remaining in the Crimea.

The evacuation drama continued on the night of 10–11 May. Among the ships that arrived that night at Chersonesos was the flagship of the Romanian Royal Navy, the destroyer *Regele Ferdinand* (King Ferdinand). Built in the late 1920s in Italy based on the British Shakespeare class design, it had a length of 102m, a total displacement of 1,880 tons and a speed of up to 37 knots. The main armament of the ship consisted of five 120mm guns. At dawn, the destroyer put to sea, packed with soldiers. It was accompanied by the *Romania* minelayer, the transport *KT-25* and the submarine hunter *Uj-110*, all headed for the shores of Romania as part of the Ovidiu convoy.

At 07.00, the convoy was subjected to the first air attack, which lasted for three and a half hours. One of the bombs hit the bridge of the destroyer and killed two officers. Other hits led to small fires, but the biggest problem was an unexploded bomb that pierced the fuel tank and caused a serious leak. At 10.50 a.m., when the Crimean coast was still clearly visible astern, the Romanian sailors saw another group of Soviet aircraft approaching from the north at low altitude. The destroyer's 120mm guns began a barrage and a wall of water appeared in front of the attackers. Then its anti-aircraft guns began to fire furiously. However, this time the Russians' target was the *Romania*, which was slightly behind. Soon the ship was enveloped in flames and smoke, after which she abruptly lost speed. There was no question of a rescue operation in this case, so the convoy continued without slowing down.

At 11.30 a.m., another group of Soviet aircraft appeared. They were a dozen Il-2s that were operating at the limit of their range. Despite fierce fire from all the guns, from which the sky was coloured with dozens of 'blotches' from the explosions, they stubbornly attacked their target. With horror, hundreds of soldiers and sailors watched this spectacle, desperately shooting at the approaching planes with rifles and even pistols. Soon they roared over the ships, after which at least two bombs, as well as many rockets, hit the destroyer, which was performing an evasive manoeuvre. Shells and bullets rattled on the sides and decks. As a result, the radio room was smashed and the starboard fuel lines were damaged. After that, the ship's speed began to drop sharply, and then it turned out that the engines did not have enough fuel. However, a team of sailors was hastily formed, which organised the delivery of fuel to the engine room in buckets, passed along the corridors from hand to hand. At 13.28, when the Crimean coast itself had already disappeared over the horizon, the last group of Soviet aircraft appeared over the *Regele Ferdinand*, in the form of five Pe-2 dive bombers. Despite the fact that the ship could not manoeuvre and was moving very slowly, all the dropped bombs fell far away. As a result, the destroyer managed to get to a safe distance from the Crimea before she ran out of fuel. By evening, the damaged *Regele Ferdinand* had been towed to Constanta harbour. Twelve crew were dead and twenty-six seriously wounded.

Fortunately for the Germans who were still in the war zone, there was a lull at Cape Chersonesos all day on 11 May. Tolbukhin did not dare to make a final attack, and the Soviet soldiers watched angrily as the landing barges packed with soldiers left the harbour. The next night, General Hartmann decided to undertake a final evacuation. The first convoys to load at dusk were Pioneer (tanker *Dresden*, three submarine hunters) and Astra (minesweepers *KT-24*, *KT-29* and *R-205*). They took on board about 3,000 to 4,000 men, after which they set off to the west under cover of darkness. Around midnight, Romanian ships anchored: the minelayer *Amiral Murgescu* and the auxiliary cruiser *Dacia*. By that time, the situation was becoming more and more alarming for the Germans. The entire coast was shrouded in clouds of acrid smoke, the sky was constantly illuminated by the reflections of fires and bombs periodically dropped from Soviet planes rumbling in the dark. Explosions were constantly booming in the water and on land. The sailors looked with tension at the dark silhouettes of ferries and landing boats darting between the shore and the ships, simultaneously looking with horror at the clock, then at the sky, where the silhouettes of U-2 biplanes periodically swept by, then at the southern part of the horizon, at any moment expecting to see a torpedo from a Russian submarine or boat.

When the loading was already over, at about 02.00 there was an explosion on the stern of *Dacia*. This immediately led to unimaginable panic and wild screams in the dark, but then it turned out that the ship had received only minor damage. Twenty-eight people died, including three members of the crew. Soon, having taken on board 2,200 people, *Amiral Murgescu* (General Hartmann evacuated on her) and *Dacia* weighed anchor and set off. The faces of the soldiers who escaped from this hell at the last moment were unusually spiritual and happy, despite the hardships they had endured. Finally, the Crimean coast, engulfed in fire, was left behind. No one knew exactly how many people remained on the beachhead at that time. Meanwhile, new ships were passing towards the ships in the darkness, just approaching Chersonesos.

At 01.00, in accordance with the plan of the final phase of evacuation, the last German units secretly left their positions on the Turkish Rampart and moved to the piers in an accelerated march. As it turned out, the decision to end the evacuation on that day, 12 May, although the 17th Army had every chance to hold the bridgehead for another twenty-four hours, was fatal for many soldiers. However, the Soviet command also made serious mistakes. After midnight, the scouts of the 32nd Guards Rifle Division captured a German prisoner who said that the troops had received an order to withdraw to Cape Chersonesos. At 03.00, the most powerful shelling began, which involved about 1,000 guns, although the shells fell on the already empty positions. Only an hour later, the Russians launched an attack and at 04.30 occupied the Turkish Rampart, from which there was still another 6km to Cape Chersonesos through rugged and cratered terrain.

Meanwhile, the evacuation continued. Loading on to the last vessels and ships, including the destroyer *Regele Maria* (Queen Maria), the gunboat *Dumitrescu*, the steamer *Geyserich*, tugs, minesweepers and several dozen Siebel ferries and high-speed landing barges, was carried out in panic, haste and chaos. Most of the ships set off overcrowded, with soldiers literally clinging to the decks and superstructures like flies. The last Do 24 flying boats also flew away packed to the brim. After 03.30, most of the ships stopped loading and went out to sea in order to get as far away from the shore as possible in the dark. Dawn in the Crimea began after 05.00.

However, teams of high-speed barges coming from Romania, despite an order to stop the operation, continued to approach the shore at their own risk, picking up up to 1,100 people each. As a result, the Germans and Romanians managed to accomplish the impossible on the last night, literally evacuating about 12,000 soldiers under the nose of the Red Army.

To this day, there is no complete and reliable data about what happened on the morning of 12 May in Chersonesos. It is believed that at about 08.00, the commander of the 73rd Division, Generalleutnant Hermann Bohme, who had taken command of the remaining soldiers, announced the surrender. Generalmajor Erich Gruner, commander of the 111th Infantry Division, was captured with him. The rescue operation at sea continued until 14 May. That day, the Do 24T-3 flying boat flew almost to the Crimean coast and returned to Romania, lifting seven people out of the water. They were passengers of several wrecked ships who had been in the water for several days. They miraculously survived and had waited for rescue. The crew of the Do 24 saw countless pieces of wreckage, empty dinghies, boats, life rafts and floating corpses at sea.

Of the approximately 200,000 men who made up the German–Romanian population of Gotenland in early April, 35,000 did not reach Sevastopol at all. About 30,000 more died in the battles for the city, drowned during the evacuation or were captured at Cape Chersonesos. Most of the 17th Army – about 135,000 men – managed to reach Romania after suffering severe hardships. However, it was no longer an army, but a collection of disparate units that had partially lost their combat capability and abandoned all their heavy weapons and equipment. Most of the returning soldiers went on leave, to hospitals and to replenish thinned-out divisions in other sectors of the front. And many Romanians, as soon as they set foot on their native shore, hastened to desert, voluntarily running home.

Ferdinand Schörner blamed the losses on the Kriegsmarine commanders on the Black Sea, claiming that they had conducted evacuation poorly. However, the Führer's devoted general kept silent about who was the true culprit of the next disaster and the resulting senseless death of his troops.

Chapter 5

# HITLER'S LAST SUMMER OFFENSIVE

After the Soviet offensive in Ukraine stopped in early May, the Wehrmacht command breathed a sigh of relief. It would seem that the time had come to put its battered and scattered units in order, and at the same time to equip a new line of defence on the outskirts of the Carpathians. However, Hitler was not going to rest and dig in. On the contrary, he decided that it was time to fulfil the promise he had made to Marshal Antonescu and undertake a 'major offensive against the Russians'.

The configuration of the front line seemed to favour this idea. In early April, the Germans launched a strong counter-attack on the left flank of the 1st Ukrainian Front in the area of Buchach and Kolomyia, pushing the Russians back 50–60km. And in early May (as already mentioned above), the Germans and Romanians managed to contain the offensive of the 2nd Ukrainian Front in the Iasi area. As a result, a huge protrusion in the front line was formed at Chernivtsi with a length of 200km and a width of 70km. It was here that the Führer decided to repeat what he had failed to do a year earlier at Kursk; that is, to strike the southern flank of the Chernivtsi salient from the Iasi area, create a threat of encirclement and force the Soviet troops to withdraw beyond the Prut River. And if it did not work, then at least his forces could throw them over the strategically important boundary, the Zizhiya River. This made it possible to eliminate the immediate threat to Iasi and Targu Frumos and to regain several hills that had been lost.

For this purpose, a strike force was formed consisting of five German divisions (14th, 23rd and 24th Panzer, 3rd and 79th Infantry) and two Romanian divisions (11th Infantry and 18th Mountain). According to the plan, the 14th and 23rd Panzer Divisions were to strike in the area

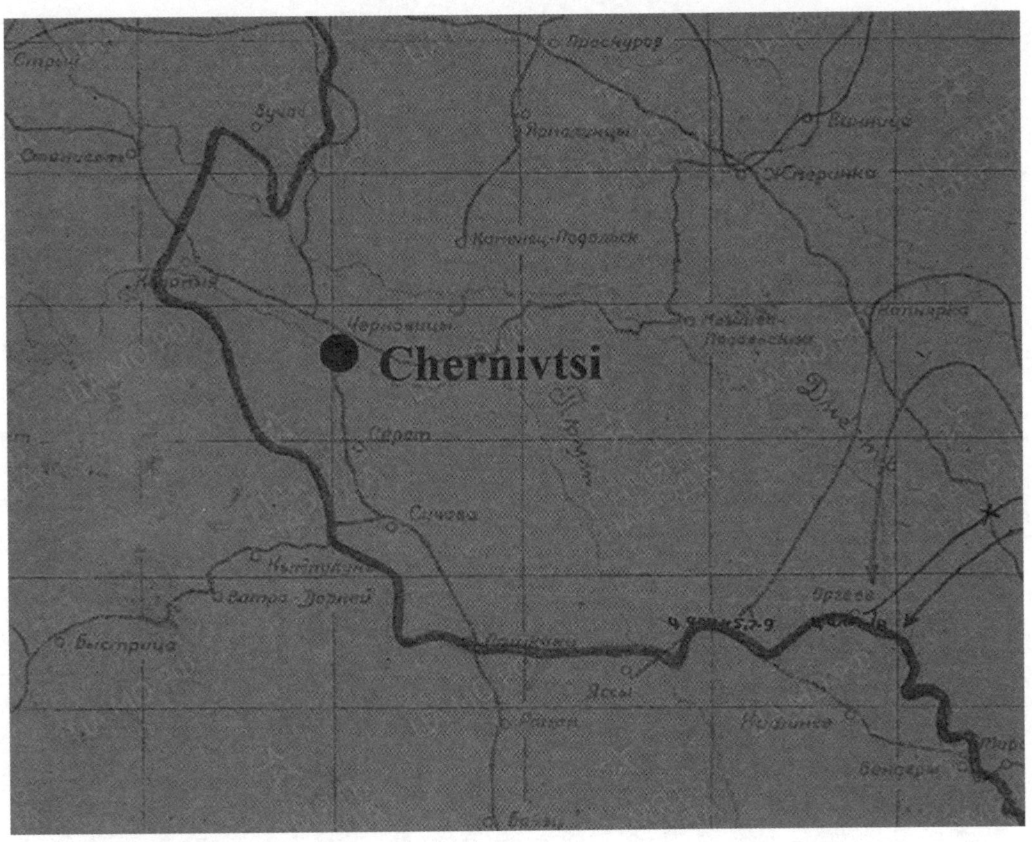

Chernivtsi and the surrounding area.

of the villages of Rediul Aldey and Stynka, and then advance to Rediu-Metropoliei. The 24th Panzer Division was to advance in the direction of hill 162, Budeul Impocita.

The operation was prepared in strict secrecy, and in a spirit unusual for the Germans (they were very fond of pretentious names!) it received the simple Russified name Sonya. Unlike Operation Citadel, preparations for this attack were carried out quickly and unnoticed, and the headquarters of the 2nd Ukrainian Front turned out to be unaware of the plans. Malinovsky simply did not believe that the enemy, battered and exhausted by protracted battles, would decide on a powerful offensive. From the position of common sense, it really didn't make sense. But Hitler was guided only by political and psychological motives. He hoped that a successful offensive would restore the Romanians' faith in victory and quell the pacifist sentiments in that country. In addition, he wanted to demonstrate to everyone that although wounded and tortured by endless battles in pockets, the Wehrmacht was still capable of advancing. The commander of Army Group Southern Ukraine, Ferdinand Schörner, did not object and took the task very seriously.

On 30 May, at 04.40 (Moscow time), shelling began, in which about 300 German and Romanian guns participated. Then the roar of aircraft engines was heard in the sky. First, twin-engine bombers struck the positions of the 48th and 73rd Rifle Corps and the bridge crossing over the Prut River, then Stukas and other ground-attack planes appeared, attacking field fortifications, artillery positions and various targets in the Russian rear. After that, throughout the day, the Soviet troops were subjected to continuous bombing from the air. 'Aviation, with massive raids by groups of 8–60 aircraft, continuously bombed the combat formations of troops of 73 and 48 Rifle Corps and bridge crossings over the Prut River during the day. A total of 663 aircraft overflights were noted during the day,' the 52nd Army Combat Operations magazine reported. In fact, the Luftwaffe carried out more than 2,000 sorties, and the 1st Romanian Air Corps 476.

'The operation came as a complete surprise to the enemy, as strict measures were taken to comply with the secrecy regime, and the disguise was carefully organised,' the journal of combat operations of the 4th Romanian Army reported. And it was true. Although several prisoners had been captured by the 27th and 52nd Soviet Armies the day before (the Russians called them 'tongues') and the headquarters of the 2nd Ukrainian Front knew the location of most German divisions, none of the prisoners knew anything about the upcoming offensive.

No other intelligence information indicating preparations for an attack was received.

The main blow fell at the junction between the 48th and 73rd Rifle Corps. By the end of the day, the Soviet defences had been breached on a fairly wide front, and the 294th Infantry Division was forced to retreat to Bakhna, the Lucheniy Sturzolei and partially to the northern bank of the Zizhiya River. The 254th and 373rd Rifle Divisions retreated to Stynka, and the 116th Rifle Division retreated to Budeu and the southern shore of Lake Nou.

Having learned about the German–Romanian offensive, Malinovsky began to hurriedly transfer reinforcements to the area of the breakthrough. At 10.00, the headquarters of the 5th Mechanised Corps of the 6th Tank Army, located on the eastern bank of the Prut (in the Nikoen–Gyrtopul Popiy area), received an order to immediately move to the Stynka area, after which, together with the 73rd Rifle Corps, it was to counter-attack the enemy that broke through. At that time, the corps consisted of the 9th Mechanised Brigade, the 233rd Tank Brigade, the 458th Mechanised Regiment and the 1494th Self-Propelled Artillery Regiment (six Su-85s). It is clear that it was very difficult to make a 20km a day march with the whole corps in a few hours under attack by enemy aircraft. Therefore, it was necessary to move to the designated area and engage in battle in parts.

The 233rd Tank Brigade, consisting of fifty-four tanks (mainly Sherman) and a battalion of machine gunners, was the first to move west along the Falesti–Skuleni highway at 11.00. When the tankers reached the bridge crossing over the Prut, they saw a sight that rather resembled May of two years ago. German and Romanian planes appeared group after group over the river and dropped bombs, huge water columns rose everywhere, and trucks and horse-drawn carts burned on the banks. Having barely moved to the west bank, the 233rd Brigade, being subjected to air attacks and stopping constantly, was able to reach a vineyard 2km north-west of Stynka. Then the self-propelled artillery guns of the 1494th SAP arrived there.

This concentration of equipment was quickly detected by German reconnaissance aircraft. The Germans pulled the tanks back, pushing forward anti-tank and anti-aircraft artillery, then the vineyard was bombed heavily. In response, Soviet bombers raided Stynka. Finally, at 20.30, tanks with an infantry assault group and assembled infantry of the 254th Infantry Division went on the attack. The group managed to reach the south-western outskirts of Stynka, but there it was subjected to heavy flanking fire and new air attacks. Having suffered heavy losses, the brigade retreated to its original positions under the cover of darkness. The 9th Mechanised Brigade at the bridge crossing over the Prut and along the road was also subjected to fierce aerial bombing and strafing, and only arrived in the combat area at night, so it did not have time to take part in the attack.

The Soviet 5th Air Army carried out 703 sorties during the day, losing about two and a half times the aircraft lost by the Luftwaffe. In the sky over Iasi, famous Soviet aces Grigory Rechkalov, Alexander Klubov, Nikolai Gulaev and Ivan Kozhedub and their German rivals Helmut Lipfert, Gerhad Barkhorn, Wilhelm Batz and Erich Hartmann came face to face. Russian pilots reported fifty-four aerial victories, while anti-aircraft artillery claimed another fifty-six.

Romanian and German aircraft did suffer serious losses on the first day of the operation: twenty-seven aircraft, including ten Ju 87s, five IAR-81s, five Bf 109s, five JRS-79s and two Fw 190s. Of these, at least eleven were shot down in aerial combat. German pilots claimed sixty-eight aerial victories, and Romanians claimed seven more. In fact, the irretrievable losses of Soviet aviation in this massacre amounted to thirty-six aircraft. The 9th Guards SHAD suffered the most damage. In 117 sorties, it lost ten Il-2s, of which six were shot down by German fighters.

On 31 May, the Luftwaffe and FARR flew 1,500 and 300 sorties respectively. Over the positions of the 233rd Tank Brigade, about 800 overflights of German and Romanian aircraft were noted. The tankers lost thirty-three tanks and fifty-eight men during the day. Nevertheless, they managed to repel eight tank attacks and generally hold their positions.

Soviet aviation responded with 888 sorties, a quarter of them flown by the 1st Guards SHAK of General Vasily Ryazanov. The main targets of the Il-2 ground-attack planes were the positions of tanks and artillery around Cuza-Voda. Every time the sixes and eights of the planes flew there they found themselves in a 'hornets' nest'. Anti-aircraft guns fired at them from below, and on the approach to the target area and on the way back they met groups of Fw 190s, which boldly made frontal and rear attacks at every opportunity. Large groups of fighters circled above, which attacked the Russian ground-attack planes in a dive. 'The Nazis this time used, although not new, but still a different tactic of air attack compared to previous battles. Acting in two powerful echelons – upper and lower, they solved two tasks simultaneously: they bombed our ground troops and tried to block ground-attack planes at all costs. And they suffered losses,' recalled Semyon Donchenko, at that time a colonel, deputy commander of the 9th Guards Assault Aviation Division (9th GSHAD).

As a result, the 1st Guards SHAK suffered even greater losses than the day before: eighteen Il-2s, of which at least seven were shot down by German fighters.

Following the results of the hardest day of combat, Stalin's Falcons reported forty air battles and sixty-four downed aircraft. And they slightly overestimated their own success. Romanian aviation lost twenty aircraft, a record for all the years of the war. The Luftwaffe lost seven aircraft, but among those shot down was the Bf 109G-6 of one of the best fliers: the commander of II./JG52, Major Gerhard Barkhorn. Returning in the evening from his sixth combat flight of the day, his fighter was hit at point-blank range by a Russian P-39 Airacobra. Wounded in the right leg and arm, the pilot parachuted over Barkhorn territory and was out of action for four months. In turn, the German pilots were credited with seventy-six aerial victories (including forty-two over P-39s!). In fact, the Soviet air force lost about forty aircraft, while thirty fighter pilots were killed or missing.

By the evening of 31 May, German and Romanian troops reached the area of the Budeul Impucit line–hillside 162–hill 156–Vulturul. According to Romanian data, the losses of Soviet troops in two days amounted to sixty tanks, seventy aircraft and 110 prisoners. These figures were close to the actual ones. The losses of the 52nd Army amounted to about 5,000 men killed, missing and wounded, with 122 artillery pieces and guns destroyed as a result of air attacks and artillery shelling. The attackers also suffered serious losses. The 11th Romanian Infantry Division alone lost 920 men killed, missing and wounded.

Despite some successes, the Germans and Romanians failed to completely eliminate the Soviet bridgehead on the southern bank of the Zizhiya River. In this regard, a new operation was quickly developed under the code name Katya. The reinforced strike group was to strike at the right flank of the Soviet 27th Army and advance towards the railway line in the area of Leccani to the intersection of the railway with the highway 5km south-west of Epureni. Next, it was necessary to capture Ridiu-Mitropoley and connect with the Miet group advancing from the Stynka area.

The new offensive started at dawn on 2 June. The Luftwaffe and FARR again bombed and strafed in large groups on the positions and rear of the Soviet troops and the crossings of the Prut River. Soviet observers recorded 1,347 overflights of enemy aircraft in the Iasi area. With the support of aviation, the Germans attacked with tanks in the area of hills 156, 158 and 197. The journal of combat operations of the 5th Mechanised Corps reported: 'Having pulled up additional forces, the enemy at 4.00 after a massive artillery bombardment threw 500 men into the attack with the support of 5 tanks. As a result of a two-hour battle, the enemy managed to break through the defences of the 111th Infantry Division in the direction of the village of Gospodsky Dvor and advance into the forest on Mount Kirpitiy. The enemy began to threaten the inner flanks of the 2nd and 4th Motorised Rifle Battalions of the 45th MDBR and forced these battalions to retreat to the southern bank of the Zizhiya River with a blow to the flanks. The situation has become extremely threatening.' At the same time, the commander of the 2nd Motorised Rifle Battalion, Major Mikhailov, was seriously wounded and the commander of the 156th Tank Regiment, Major Vorotilov, was missing.

In addition, at 05.30, the Germans from the area of Silishta, Tautoschi went on the offensive against the right flank of the 27th Army. As a result of fierce fighting, the Germans and Romanians managed to break through the front and wedge into the defence of the 223rd and 337th Infantry Divisions to a depth of 2½km. By evening, the Germans captured the Gospodsky Dvor and Zahorna, generally fulfilling the plan of the first day of the operation. The Soviet troops lost about 2,000 dead and wounded. However, the losses of the attackers were also considerable, mainly from artillery fire. Thus, the Grossdeutschland division lost nine tanks and forty-one more were damaged.

On 3 June, the Germans and Romanians captured hill 162 and pushed the right flank of the 52nd Army. In addition, they tried to break through to the Rediu-Metropoliei. The headquarters of the 5th Mechanised Corps ordered the 233rd Tank Brigade to urgently move into the area and attack the Germans in the area of hill 181. In the evening, a fierce tank battle took place there, during which the brigade lost six tanks. It could not occupy the height, but prevented the Germans from breaking through to Rediu-Metropoliei.

On 4 June, the Germans, supported by tanks and StuG self-propelled guns, again attacked the 50th and 254th Rifle Divisions of the 73rd Rifle Corps and by evening captured hills 152 and 154, as well as the village of Molniesti.

On the night of 5 June, Soviet long-range bomber aircraft entered the battle. The 3rd Guards Long-range Aviation Division (3rd AD DD) was ordered to raid Chisinau railway station. At that time, the 10th Guards Long-range Aviation Regiment (10th Guards AP DD), which was part of it, had thirty-three serviceable Il-4s, and the 20th Guards AP DD thirty-four of the type. At 21.00, a weather reconnaissance aircraft took off from the Belaya Tserkov airfield, whose crew reported on the radio at 22.50 that there was cloud cover above the target at an altitude of 3km. At 23.40, the air division commander gave the order to take off, and soon fifty-four bombers were airborne. At 01.31 marker bombs were dropped over Chisinau, after which 63.5 tons of high-explosive and incendiary bombs were dropped within twenty minutes.

Meanwhile, on 5 June, the battle reached its climax. At dawn, after heavy shelling and an air attack, the 11th and 3rd Romanian Infantry Divisions, 79th German Infantry Division, and the 14th and 23rd Panzer Divisions again launched an offensive against the Russian 73rd Rifle Corps in the area of hills south of the Zizhiya River. By mid-afternoon, one group of German tanks had broken into a grove north-east of Molniesti, and the other had reached hill 159 and a grove north of it. However, the Germans failed to build on their success, and by evening their armoured vehicles were forced to retreat. In the sector of the 27th Army, the Germans reached the south-eastern outskirts of Rediu-Metropoliei.

On the night of 5–6 June, 500 Soviet bombers carried out a massive raid on Iasi. Fifty-one Il-4s from the 3rd Guards AD DD participated in the operation. Since the front line passed close to the target, in such cases Soviet infantrymen lit bonfires shortly before the air attack to mark their positions. Immediately at the moment of the approach of the bombers, white flares were also fired and two searchlights were turned on, indicating the direction to Iasi. 'When approaching the target, the crews observed: excellent illumination of the target with marker bombs, a strong ground artillery firefight on the front line, intense bombing and a large number of fires at the railway hub and the southern outskirts of the city of Iasi,' said the 3rd Guards AD DD' combat log.

The next night, Russian bombers made a second raid on Iasi. Some 56.5 tons of high-explosive bombs were dropped on the railway station and the north-western quarters of the city. Interestingly, for some reason the Romanians thought that these air attacks were carried out by American aircraft. As a result of the two raids, headquarters buildings, barracks, telephone and telegraph communications were destroyed. The headquarters of the 4th Romanian Army lost contact with its units.

As a result of the offensive, the German and Romanian troops managed to move the front line away from Iasi, capture and hold a number of commanding heights and inflict serious losses on the Red Army. However, even the minimum goal – to throw the Russians back over the Zizhiya River – was not achieved. 'Operation Katya was an excellent lesson in tank offensive combat in conditions of strong and organised defence. The moral condition and behaviour of the Romanian troops was excellent. There was full cooperation with the

German troops,' wrote the commander of the 4th Romanian Army, General Ion Rakovice.

However, the commander of the 2nd Ukrainian Front, General Rodion Malinovsky, despite the very modest successes of the enemy, was very unhappy and gave a dressing-down to his subordinates. 'However, instead of perseverance in defence, commanders still live by the skills of mobile forms of combat characteristic of an offensive operation. As a result, there were cases when units left their lines without orders, criminally giving advantageous lines of defence to the enemy,' his order said. Malinovsky forbade any withdrawal from positions without an order and even decided to revive the forgotten blocking detachments. The losses of the Red Army in this battle amounted to more than 19,000 people killed and wounded. Just the 5th Mechanised Corps lost 2,636 men and 91 tanks between 30 May and 8 June.

This battle was Hitler's last summer offensive. It showed that the Germans could still attack, but they could no longer achieve serious successes. The advance of 5–10km looked ridiculous against the background of the grandiose successes of the Red Army.

Russian artillery firing in the Leningrad area.

A German dugout destroyed by artillery fire near Leningrad.

NKL-26 snowmobiles before the attack near Lake Ilmen.

A T-34 tank from the 1st Tank Army on the attack. Ukraine, January 1944.

German military equipment in the Korsun pocket area.

This STZ-5 NATI tractor is towing a 122mm M-30 howitzer in the Nikopol area.

Cavalrymen from General Pliev's cavalry-mechanised group in Ukraine.

German troops retreating along the roads of western Ukraine. (Boelcke Archiv)

German vehicles buried in the mud in the area of Proskurov. (Boelcke Archiv)

Russian armoured vehicles cross the Dniester River.

‘Hook’ rail destroyer (‘Hagen’).

Tanks of the 19th Tank Corps enter Sevastopol.

Cape Chersonesos in Sevastopol after the Germans fled.

Il-2 ground attack aircraft.

Soviet Tu-2 bomber.

Soviet sappers in Vitebsk.

Night attack by Soviet tanks.

Destroyed German armoured vehicles in the Bobruisk area.

Destroyed German armoured vehicles in the Bobruisk area.

The Polikarpov U-2 (Po-2) light bombers played a very important role in the battles.

Pliev's cavalrymen on the attack. Belarus, July 1944.

Belarusian women partisans in liberated Minsk.

He-177 bomber over Russian forests.

Soviet sappers building a bridge crossing.

A tank from the 4th Tank Army moving through the forest.

A StuG III Ausf G self-propelled gun captured by Russian gunners.

Russian tanks on the streets of Lviv.

Soviet tankers preparing to cross the Vistula.

German tankers from the 19th Panzer Division preparing for a counter-attack on the Magnushev bridgehead.

German 600mm heavy mortar Karl-Gerät 'Ziu' fires on Warsaw, September 1944.

A 600mm shell hits a high-rise building in Warsaw.

Ukrainian 'Cossacks' and SS officers in Warsaw.

Chapter 6

# 'H' HOUR

## 5,000 Russian Planes in the Sky!

In June 1944, there was a lull on the Eastern Front. Active hostilities took place only on the Karelian Isthmus, where on 9 June the Leningrad Front under the command of General Leonid Govorov launched an offensive against Finnish troops. The Finns had been preparing their defences for a very long time, building many trenches, bunkers and minefields. The best units of the Finnish army were concentrated to the north-west of Leningrad (on the old Russian–Finnish border). Despite this, the troops of the Soviet 21st Army managed to break through the enemy's defensive lines unexpectedly easily. By the evening of the first day of the offensive, the Finns had retreated 10–12km. The Russians skilfully manoeuvred their infantry and tanks, consistently introducing them into the gaps that had formed and quickly expanding the breakthrough. In the evening of 14 June, the situation became critical as the the vanguards of the Red Army broke through to Kuuterselka. The Finnish command had to bring its main reserves into the battle: a single tank division and a Jäger infantry brigade. These units fought selflessly, suffered heavy losses, but were unable to stop the enemy. Pursuing the Finns, the Russians quickly reached Vyborg and on 20 June liberated this city almost without a fight. After that, the Finnish government rejected another ultimatum from Stalin, considering it 'too humiliating'.

Meanwhile, the Red Army struck again, this time in the area of Lake Onega. In this taiga forest region, the Finnish army also could not withstand the blow and began to slowly retreat to the north-west. However, Finland's withdrawal from the war was postponed again.

In mid-June, when the battle broke out in Normandy, an unusual lull reigned on the Eastern Front, stretching 2,000km from Narva to the mouth of the Dniester. The weather was warm, and millions of soldiers in the trenches rejoiced at the respite and tried not to think about the upcoming battles. Almost nowhere was there any gunfire, artillery cannonade, or the hum of aircraft in the sky. It is no coincidence that in some places rumours even spread among the troops that after the Allied landings in France some kind of truce would be concluded. This information was circulated both in the Wehrmacht and in the Red Army. Russian prisoners told the Germans about the upcoming 'truce', and German prisoners ('tongues') told the Russians. In fact, that mysterious June silence was deceptive and became the harbinger of a real storm.

The only sector of the Eastern Front where the Wehrmacht managed to hold its positions in the spring of 1944 was Army Group Centre, commanded by Field Marshal Ernst Busch. Earlier, he had commanded the 16th Army for a long time, and from January 1942 to mid-1943 it conducted heavy defensive battles on the Lovat River. Then Busch managed to hold his position, despite the brutal and endless attacks of the Red Army. And the defence of the small towns of Demyansk, Staraya Russa, Holm and Velikiye Luki became a model of such tactics for Hitler. As the greatest specialist in 'fortresses', Busch became commander of Army Group Centre at the end of 1943. The Führer believed that he would cope with his mission again and repel any Russian onslaught by standing on the defensive. By June, Busch's forces consisted of four armies, which numbered 486,000 soldiers, 570 tanks and self-propelled artillery pieces, and 3,236 artillery pieces. With these forces, it was necessary to defend a huge 800km front.

The operational plan of the Belarusian offensive, Operation Bagration, began to be developed by the Soviet General Staff in April 1944. The general idea was to deliver powerful blows to the flanks of the front, which resembled a balcony extended to the Soviet side, and surround the main forces of Army Group Centre east of Minsk. It was an extremely ambitious plan, the main authors of which were General Konstantin Rokossovsky, and Marshals Alexander Vasilevsky and Georgy Zhukov. The idea was to indicate in every possible way an upcoming offensive in the northern sector (in the area of Polotsk and Vitebsk) and, conversely, carefully conceal the second direction of the main attack – on Bobruisk. To do this, a large-scale disinformation campaign was launched, which included a variety of activities. The most interesting of them was the false basing of aircraft.

By the summer of 1944, it was obvious that one of the signs of an imminent offensive was a large concentration of aircraft (especially

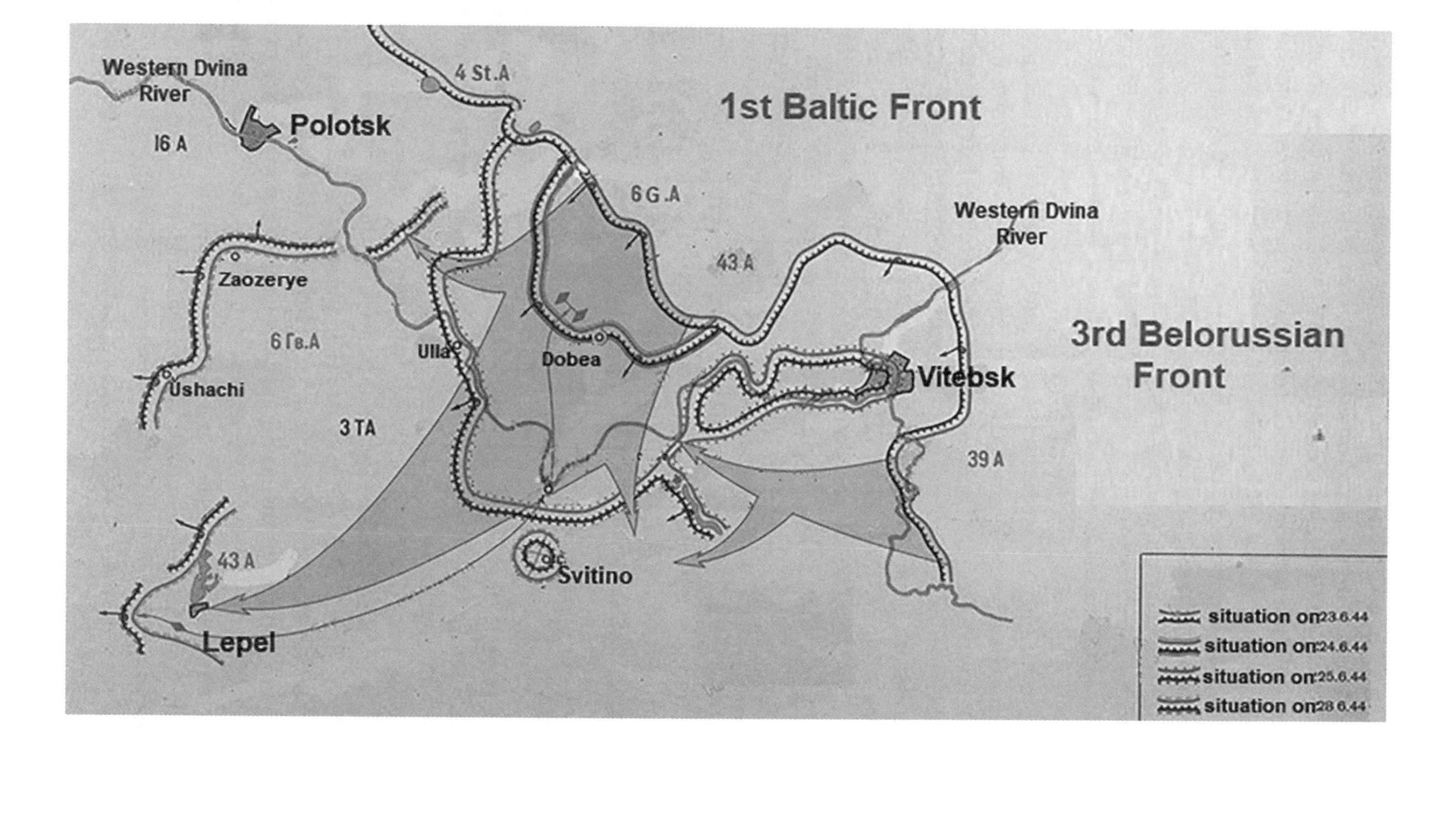
Western Dvina River
Polotsk
16 A
4 St.A
1st Baltic Front
6 G.A
Western Dvina River
43 A
Zaozerye
6 Гв.А
Ulla
Dobea
Ushachi
3 TA
3rd Belorussian Front
Vitebsk
39 A
43 A
Svitino
Lepel
situation on 23.6.44
situation on 24.6.44
situation on 25.6.44
situation on 28.6.44

Il-2s) at front-line air bases. The absence of such, on the contrary, indicated to the enemy a continuation of the lull. Therefore, in the Vitebsk region, a few days before the start of the offensive, intensified sorties by reconnaissance groups and massive air attacks by ground-attack planes of the 3rd Air Army on German strongholds and rear areas began. In the zone of the 1st Belorussian Front, the Russians, on the contrary, did not give themselves away in any way, displaying a 'peaceful' life. They defiantly built defensive structures, deepened their trenches, and swam in rivers and lakes. But the main thing was that only a small number of the aircraft of the powerful 16th Air Army were at the front-line air bases, while the main forces of several air corps were located at distant rear bases and were well camouflaged. All advanced air bases were distributed prior to the attack among the units that were to be relocated to them immediately before it began.

The Soviets placed a special emphasis on aviation and air power. As part of the four air armies attached to the 1st Baltic, 3rd, 2nd and 1st Belorussian Fronts, there were 5,228 aircraft, including 2,488 fighters and 1,746 Il-2 ground-attack planes. The opposing Luftwaffe forces were significantly weaker. There were forty-seven fighters, forty-two ground-attack planes and about twenty Ju 87Gs with 37mm guns at Belarus's air bases. To this can be added about 200 He 111 bombers from Fliegerkorps IV, about seventy heavy bombers from KG1, two staffel of night fighters and several air groups of reconnaissance aircraft. In total, Luftflotte 6 had about 450 aircraft, but at any moment it could be strengthened by transferring air groups from other sectors of the front.

At midnight on 22 June, the headquarters of the Russian air armies received the so-called 'H' time: the beginning of the artillery shelling at 07.00, with the offensive at 09.00. Three hours later, the order was sent in cipher to the headquarters of the air divisions and aviation regiments. At 04.00, all the pilots were assembled, after which the setting of combat tasks for the units began in accordance with pre-developed plans. The first air strike on German defence lines was carried out by Russian long-range bombers. At the same time, many targets were located directly in front of the positions of the Soviet troops and therefore it was necessary to develop a complex guidance system. For example, in the positions of the 3rd Army in the Rogachev area, lines of flares that were supposed to indicate the direction of the target to the crews were placed in a forest clearing near the observation post of its commander, General Alexander Gorbatov. To prevent the fire from being visible from enemy positions, a duralumin shield was installed in front of each flare, which reflected the light in an easterly direction.

The bombing strike in this sector was a particularly responsible mission, because before the offensive, Deputy Supreme Commander Marshal Georgy Zhukov, member of the Military Council of the 1st Belorussian Front Nikolai Bulganin, Commander of the Red Army Air Force Marshal Alexander Novikov and Deputy Commander of Long-range Aviation General Nikolai Skripko were at the command post of the 3rd Army. Having received a message from his headquarters that at 22.00–22.30 the bombers took off from their bases and were moving towards the target, Skripko, together with Novikov, climbed to an observation post in a pine tree. 'Let's see how ADD [Long-Range Aviation] hits his own,' the aviation commander jokingly said, settling into his seat.

Most of all, both were worried about the fog, which began to form over German territory closer to midnight. When Skripko was informed that the bombers were on the way, he ordered at his own risk that they should continue the mission according to plan. Skripko remembered: 'And now you can already hear the growing sound of engines. Single planes are passing right above us. These are pathfinders. Blinding burning marker bombs flash up and slowly descend on parachutes. It seems that they are illuminating us. Then we see the explosions of incendiary bombs. A powerful and menacing rumble is growing. Bombers are flying in the night sky in a continuous stream, with a density of 8–10 planes per minute. In the distance, the bright flashes of the first dropped bombs are already flashing, heavy explosions are heard. But immediately the crews of the aircraft report that the target is not visible from the raised clouds of dust and smoke. The situation soon became even more complicated. Pockets of fog have formed. The commanders of the air groups anxiously report that the flares cannot be distinguished – everything is covered with fog.' As a result, the frustrated Skripko had to instruct most of the planes to bomb a back-up target – the Parichi area (in the offensive zone of the 65th Army).

The largets Soviet air strike of the entire war was eventually partially thwarted by the suddenly deteriorating weather. From 06.00 to 11.00, a downpour passed over eastern Belarus, which at once rendered 60–70 per cent of Soviet air bases unusable. And in some places, due to zero visibility, combat operations became impossible for several hours. Many of the bombers and ground attack-planes that took off were unable to find or accurately identify the designated targets. Nevertheless, despite the fact that most of the planned attacks were carried out with great delay, the actions of the air force were still effective. Time also contributed to this, it was the day with the longest daylight of the year.

In total, on the first day of Operation Bagration, Soviet aviation carried out 3,639 sorties and lost fifty-nine aircraft, including thirty-three Il-2s. The German command noted the powerful Soviet air strikes in the Vitebsk sector. 'During today, a critical situation has been created on the front of the 3rd Panzer Army, as a result of the fighting south-east and north-west of Vitebsk. Continuing its offensive, supported by significant tank and aviation forces, the enemy prevented the creation of a new closed line of defence,' the morning report from the headquarters of the 3rd Panzer Army to the headquarters of Army Group Centre said. By the morning of 24 June, the German command still did not realise the full extent of the crisis and was trying to patch holes in the already crumbling front. Thus, the 53rd and 9th Army Corps were ordered to urgently withdraw to the Western Dvina River in the Ulla and Beshenko-vichy (the Tiger line) area and occupy a new line of defence there. Vitebsk itself, despite the obvious threat of encirclement, was ordered to be held.

The headquarters of the German 3rd Panzer Army complained throughout the day about the dominance of Soviet aviation in the air and the lack of its own. 'In addition to the strongest enemy artillery fire, large concentrations of infantry and tank forces in all directions, our command and troops are under the unheard-of influence of enemy fighter and assault aircraft, which greatly hampered all movements and almost completely destroyed telegraphic communications,' the report said. As it turned out, the Luftwaffe's fighters could not provide serious support to their troops in the Vitebsk area due to the loss of the advanced Ulla airbase, and all ground-attack planes were thrown into the 4th Army sector. The headquarters of Army Group Centre replied that due to the lack of forces, the Luftwaffe could not operate in all areas at the same time, so air support would be carried out according to schedule. For example, in the morning fighters from JG51 would operate near Bobruisk, in the afternoon over the Dnieper, and in the evening over the Western Dvina.

On this day, in the Rogachev and Ozarichi area, the troops of the 1st Belorussian Front launched offensives in the general direction of Bobruisk. In the morning, rainy weather with low cloud stood over the front line, which again prevented the first air attack against the German 9th Army, and also brought some confusion to further actions. Nevertheless, during the day, the 16th Air Army delivered almost the most powerful blow to the positions of German troops in the entire war. A total of 3,191 sorties were flown, including 1,109 ground-attack planes, 762 bombers and 1,320 fighters. In some periods, these armadas passed over targets in continuous alternating waves, and ground-attack strikes on individual objects continuously lasted for an hour and a half.

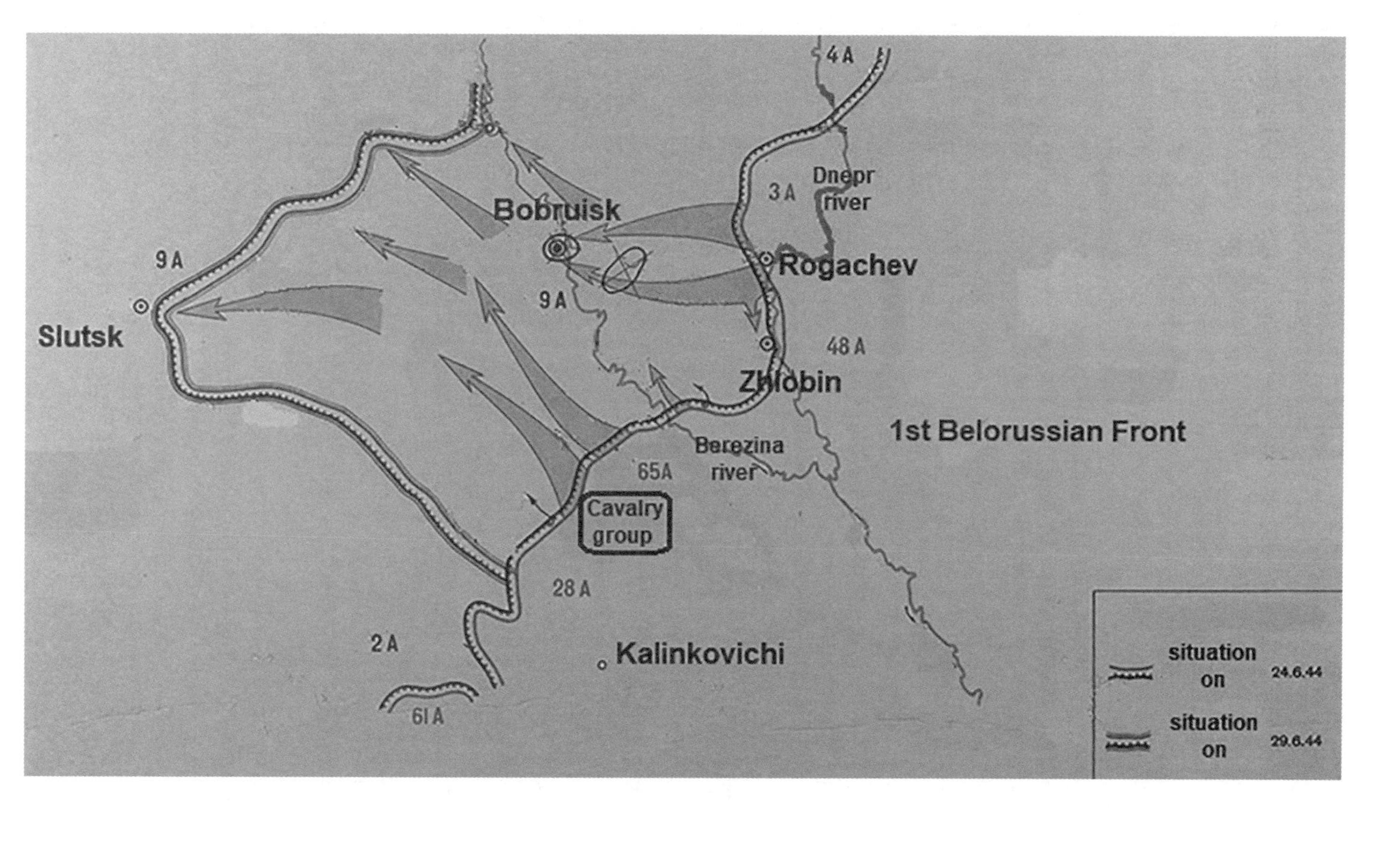
4 A
Dnepr
river
3 A
Bobruisk
Rogachev
9 A
9 A
Slutsk
48 A
Zhlobin
1st Belorussian Front
Berezina
river
65A
Cavalry
group
28 A
2 A
Kalinkovichi
61 A
situation
on
24.6.44
situation
on
29.6.44

Some 147,000 high-explosive bombs, 15,900 fragmentation bombs and 8,000 PTABs (anti-tank bombs) were dropped on enemy territory, and almost 2,000 rockets were fired at various targets. By the evening, the entire relatively small section of the front was shrouded in solid clouds of smoke and dust, rising hundreds of metres into the sky. Some crews attacked point targets, for example, the five most experienced Pe-2 pilots from the 301st Bomber Aviation Division dropped FAB-250 bombs on the Gestapo office in Bobruisk from an altitude of 1,700m, reporting direct hits to the building.

Such air support could not fail to lead to success, and by evening the units of the 3rd, 28th, 65th and 48th Armies were deeply wedged into the German defences, beginning a rapid advance on Bobruisk. In total, during the second day of the operation, the Soviet air force carried out a record number of sorties – about 7,000! In terms of scale, this was quite consistent with the actions of the American and British air forces on the Western Front. German fighters from JG51 'Mölders' were credited with twenty-seven aerial victories over Belarus. Lieutenant Anton Hafner from the 8th Staffel distinguished himself the most, shooting down three Il-2s and two Yak-9s in the Bobruisk area. The Russians lost a total of seventy-three aircraft, including forty-eight Il-2s.

Despite the clear threat of the collapse of the entire front of Army Group Centre, the Führer, as usual, forbade any 'significant' retreats. After long negotiations and disputes with the chief of the General Staff of the Army, Generaloberst Kurt Zeitzler, Hitler eventually decided that the evacuation from Vitebsk would lead to a 'general withdrawal'. Therefore, this city must be defended to the last possible opportunity. And the gaps that had formed in the defence, as had happened many times before, must be plugged with rear and consolidated units. In addition, the Germans urgently halted the large-scale anti-partisan Operation Kormoran, ordering all units involved in combing the forests to go urgently to the front line.

In Belarus and Western Ukraine, the front line was only of relative importance. Often, Soviet pilots, having made an emergency landing or parachuted into a remote area, became victims of Ukrainian nationalists and other militants. Many forest areas were controlled by Polish partisans from Armia Krajowa and Russian partisans. The Germans only conditionally controlled a huge area of the Pripyat marshes, especially north of the Gomel–Pinsk–Brest railway, which was called 'bandit territory' (Bandengebiet). It consisted mainly of dense forests and swamps stretching for tens of kilometres.

There is an interesting and characteristic episode in the Luftwaffe chronicles. On the night of 18–19 June, a damaged He 111 bomber made an emergency landing in a forest, about 50km south of Baranovichi air base. At first, the crew made their way north through the swampy wasteland, and then entered 'bandit territory'. When the Germans reached the vicinity of the village of Tukhovichi, they were discovered by the partisans. A 'forest safari' (as the participants themselves called this adventure) then lasted for several hours. The Germans, pursued by the partisans, fled, periodically firing back from a machine gun. At this time two He 111 bombers appeared above and began to drive away the Belarusians by firing their machine guns. The crossing of a 2km-long meadow was especially dramatic. When the pilots, running with their last strength, reached the middle of it, partisans appeared from the bushes to the right and behind and began shooting. However, a bomber circling above immediately dropped to a height of 20m and literally cut them down with its guns. Then there was the saving shrubbery again, through which the Germans made their way, crouching as low as possible. Bullets whistled over their heads, mowing down branches and leaves. Then the huge shadow of a descending He 111 swept over the area and somewhere behind them there was a loud roar of its machine guns, after which everything was quiet for a while. It was only with the constant support of German bombers that the crew eventually managed to escape from the Belarusian partisans. And it happened 100km from the front line, in the deep rear.

Numerous raids by SS men, including Ukrainian volunteers, which began back in 1941, had no effect. The brutal massacres, the destruction of entire villages, and the mass killings of residents suspected of collaborating with the partisans only increased the hatred of Belarusians towards the occupiers. By 1943, entire partisan armies were already operating in the rear of Army Group Centre, which carried out open attacks on German garrisons, railway stations and small groups of soldiers. The partisans cut telephone wires, blew up railway lines, oil storage facilities and warehouses, and shot at vehicles travelling on the roads. Often the Germans had to use their aircraft against the rebels. For example, pilot H. Hainert from the 10th Staffel KG27 recalled how he repeatedly had to participate in such raids in an He 111 bomber: 'After the German offensive of 1941, numerous surrounded Russian units retreated into rugged forest and swampy areas. There were organised partisan detachments that disrupted German train traffic. There were not enough troops to effectively comb large territories and eliminate banditry. There were small airfields in the partisan areas, where Soviet supply planes and couriers landed mostly at night. We increasingly shifted our night navigation flights to these partisan areas and, as a kind of "by-product" of our aerial reconnaissance, carried out high-explosive bombing at night. Several times we flew over these areas in the daytime and dropped our high-explosive bombs on previously explored strongpoints in forest clearings.'

By the summer of 1944, the Wehrmacht controlled only 50 per cent of the territory of Belarus. Now that the Red Army had broken through the front, the Germans faced the most terrible thing: to retreat to the west through forests and swamps teeming with partisans who knew no mercy to the occupiers. During the third day of the offensive, Soviet aircraft carried out 6,300 sorties, during the fourth 6,884. The air force actively supported the ground forces along the entire line of contact. Meanwhile, the troops of the 1st Baltic Front crossed the Western Dvina River on a front 35km away, capturing Beshenkovichi. All attempts by the Germans to gain a foothold on the defensive line 'Tiger' failed.

On 27 June, at barely dawn, Russian ground-attack planes and bombers from the 1st Air Army launched a massive raid on the German troops surrounded in Vitebsk, who were making a desperate attempt to escape from pocket to the south. Bombing attacks were combined with powerful shelling and strikes from hundreds of Katyusha rocket launchers. As a result, by lunchtime, the demoralised Germans agreed to surrender. So, another Hitler 'Festung' fell unexpectedly quickly, which until recently had been considered an impregnable stronghold. Only 200 soldiers from the 53rd Army Corps, which was completely defeated in a matter of days, managed to break out of the pocket.

Meanwhile, a dramatic situation had developed in the southern sector of the battle. By morning, units of the Russian 9th Tank Corps reached the Titovka area on the western bank of the Berezina River (south of Bobruisk). At the same time, the advanced units reached its western, northern and eastern outskirts. As a result, most of the troops of the German 9th Army ended up in two pockets: south-east of Bobruisk and in the city itself.

The headquarters of the 16th Air Army had to cancel most of the planned missions in the morning due to the lack of accurate data on the location of its own and enemy troops. In the forests surrounding Bobruisk, it was very difficult to see what was happening on the ground, as well as to determine the affiliation of armoured vehicles and infantry. In the afternoon, pilots of Soviet fighters flying at low altitude over the south-eastern environs of Bobruisk reported that the Germans were forming a large column in the area, pushing forward tanks and self-propelled guns, followed by trucks and fuel trucks, and in the tail, artillery and wagons. Realising the situation, the Germans began to concentrate in the area of Telusha and Kovalyi, south-east of Bobruisk, in order to first break into the city, and then move west with the troops remaining there. After lengthy clarifications, checks and approvals, at 18.00 an instruction came from the headquarters of the 1st Belorussian Front: at 19.00–21.00 to launch massive strikes against the encircled enemy troops (mainly units of the 41st Panzer Corps of General Hofmeister).

The commanders of the air divisions and air regiments were immediately alerted and called to the ST-35 devices, through which direct communication with General Sergei Rudenko was carried out. He personally set the tasks and conducted the briefing. A total of 526 aircraft were involved in the operation, including 217 Il-2s, 112 Pe-2s, 63 A-20s and 134 fighters.

P-39s and La-5s were the first to arrive in Bobruisk, which were assigned the task of aiming attack aircraft at the target. Lined up in long chains, they bordered the area of concentration of the German column, as if visually indicating the scope of the target area. At 19.15, the roar of twin-engined bombers was heard. Pe-2s and A-20s dropped bombs in level flight from 850–1,200m. Direct aiming was performed by the leading aircraft, and the rest of the crews pressed their reset buttons on their command. The ground-attack planes flew lower – at 400–600m, dropped their bombs, and then fired at the detected targets with rockets and cannon. At the same time, the intensity of the air attacks gradually increased, and a 'queue' even formed in the sky. Newly arrived groups of planes had to circle and wait for the previous aircraft to drop their bombs and expend their shells.

Meanwhile, something unimaginable was happening down below. After the first air strikes on the convoy, the forest caught fire, then several trucks burst into flames. After that, the road began to be filled with smoke, which had an unusually pungent smell. Someone shouted in panic that the Russians had used toxic substances, which the Wehrmacht had been afraid of for a couple of years, although this proved to be a false alarm. As a result, a terrible panic arose and officers and soldiers began to look for gas masks, some of which had previously been thrown away or lost on the way. Some in desperation, afraid of suffocating in chlorine, began to take them away from each other. Having put on these muzzles, entire units, abandoning their equipment and heavy weapons, fled in horror away from the road.

Meanwhile, the bombardment continued until dark. The last groups of Russian ground-attack planes were no longer aiming at specific targets, but simply at the central points of the chaos that had arisen. Huge clouds of smoke were rising everywhere. By nightfall, the breakthrough to Bobruisk turned into an uncontrollable, chaotic flight. Some Germans simply ran through the forest in groups and singly, others climbed through swamps, while the most desperate tried to climb a 5m-high railway embankment in trucks and move along it. At the same time, vehicles that slipped or got stuck were simply rammed and dumped. At night, the headquarters of the 41st Panzer Corps radioed a message that there was no connection with the neighbouring 35th Army Corps, the defeated divisions were retreating to Bobruisk, and combat groups were scattered around the area. The drama lasted all night and as a result, only scattered groups of Germans broke into Bobruisk, and the next day Soviet soldiers found hundreds of burned and abandoned vehicles, motorcycles, carts and other junk at the site of the air attack. The Russians were especially surprised by the huge number of gas masks scattered everywhere, and many corpses were wearing them. This successful operation cost the Soviet air force just eight aircraft, most of which were shot down by chaotic fire from the ground.

By the evening of 27 June, the 4th German Army had completely evacuated its last bridgehead on the eastern bank of the Dnieper and begun evacuating Mogilev. The section of the Panther line, which German propaganda often positioned as an 'advanced bastion' successfully repelling the 'attacks of the Soviets near Smolensk', finally ceased to exist. This event marked the beginning of a real catastrophe for the Germans. The entire 4th Army now had only one way to escape – through a wooded and swampy wasteland partially controlled by the partisans, located in the Bobruisk–Orsha–Minsk triangle. They had to run along several narrow roads and in conditions of complete air supremacy by the Soviet air force.

The only highway running from Mogilev to the west became the main target of Russian U-2 night bombers, Pe-2 dive bombers and Il-2 ground-attack planes for several days. The first air attack took place at noon on 28 June. The raids continued until the evening, after which the entire Minsk–Mogilev highway was shrouded in clouds of smoke. Many German units could not stand it and turned on to forest roads to advance under the protection of the tree canopy. However, this led to even more chaos and disorganisation. Captured Corporal Albert Kurd from the 12th Infantry Division said: 'West of Mogilev, our marching column was attacked by Russian ground-attack planes, which bombed and shelled the road in groups of 4 planes at different intervals, making two passes. During one such air attack, 5 vehicles were set on fire in our convoy, which consisted of 28 vehicles.' Artillery Lieutenant Hans Scholkman said: 'On the way from Mogilev to the west, our column was repeatedly attacked by Russian ground-attack planes, which in groups of 2 to 16 aircraft, bombed and fired at clusters of departing troops on the road with two approaches. Bombing attacks, as a rule, were carried out from an altitude of 800–1,000 metres, then the planes descended to 50–100 metres, firing at the column from cannon and machine guns. The panic was very great. Vehicles and horse-drawn carts drove off the highway in disarray, soldiers hid in the rye. Here and there, vehicles burned, set on fire by the Russian ground-attack planes.'

The only obstacle for the Russian planes was the indiscriminate firing of German infantry. In fact, the events of three years ago were repeated, when the retreating Soviet troops tried to avoid encirclement and retreated in complete disorder to Minsk, being subjected to endless Luftwaffe air attacks. Now it was the other way around, the Germans fled in panic to Minsk, fearing to get trapped in a pocket, and Soviet ground-attack planes chattered eerily above the trees.

The strongest resistance was provided by German troops in the northern sector, in the Lepel and Polotsk area. Using numerous lake defiles, which were difficult to outflank, they stubbornly defended them. Nevertheless, the troops of the 1st Baltic Front broke into the city of Lepel and at the same time continued to move towards Vilnius. At the end of the month, the last units of the German 9th Army that been trapped in the Bobruisk pocket surrendered. The rest fled in scattered groups through forests and swamps to the west and north-west, overcoming incredible difficulties and fighting with advanced units of the Red Army and partisans. Crowds of soldiers from the 4th Army, having barely crossed the Berezina River, were moving towards Minsk.

During the first eight days of Operation Bagration, the Red Army Air Force carried out more than 34,000 combat sorties. The total losses (including non-combat) of the four air armies amounted to 455 aircraft (approximately 9 per cent of those available at the beginning of the offensive), including 188 Il-2s. German fighters managed to shoot down only thirty-five to forty Russian planes, and this did not affect the overall situation in any way.

## Combat Work of Soviet Aviation in Operation Bagration from 23 to 30 June 1944

| Army | Sorties | Aircraft lost |
|---|---|---|
| 3rd Air Army | 8,676 | 99 |
| 1st Air Army | 9,880 | 109 |
| 4th Air Army | 4,998 | 137 |
| 16th Air Army | 10,705 | 110 |
| Total: | 34,259 | 455 |

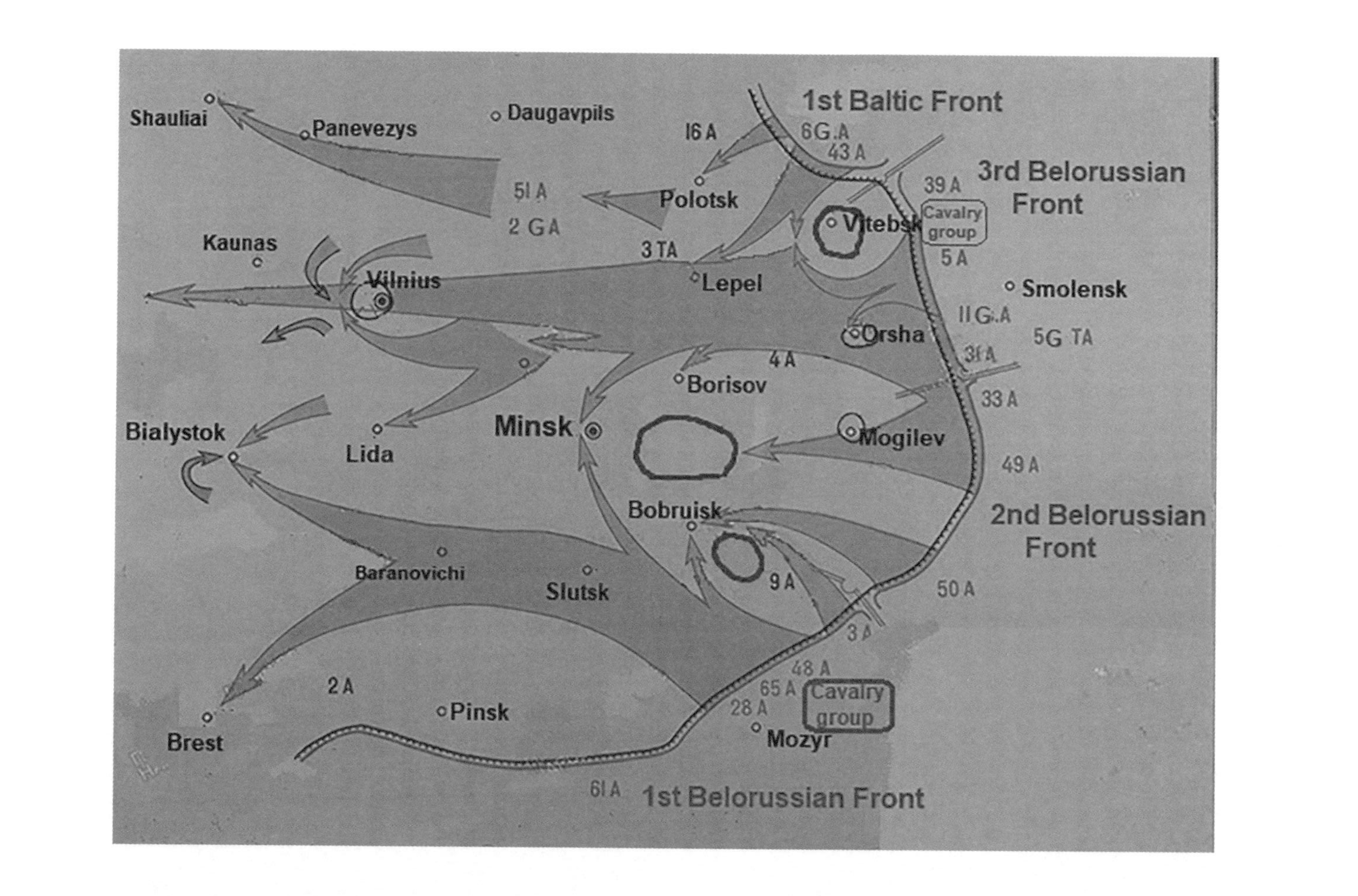
1st Baltic Front
3rd Belorussian Front
2nd Belorussian Front
1st Belorussian Front
Cavalry group
Cavalry group
16 A
6G.A
43 A
39 A
5 A
11 G.A
5G TA
31 A
33 A
49 A
50 A
3 A
48 A
65 A
28 A
61 A
51 A
2 GA
3 TA
4 A
9 A
2 A
Shauliai
Panevezys
Daugavpils
Polotsk
Vitebsk
Smolensk
Kaunas
Vilnius
Lepel
Orsha
Borisov
Minsk
Mogilev
Bialystok
Lida
Bobruisk
Baranovichi
Slutsk
Pinsk
Brest
Mozyr

On the evening of 28 June, an Si 204 passenger plane landed in the area of the headquarters of Army Group Centre, which had just moved to Lida (150km west of Minsk). Field Marshal Walter Model got out of it. He announced that, on Hitler's orders, he was assuming command, while retaining the leadership of the neighbouring Army Group Northern Ukraine. At this crisis moment for the Wehrmacht, Model led half of the German forces on the Eastern Front, while receiving almost carte blanche to transfer divisions from one sector to another, and to make decisions on the withdrawal of troops and subsequent counter-attacks.

The German command tried to plug the gaps in the crumbling front with the help of emergency reserves. The 5th Panzer Division of General Karl Decker was the first to arrive in the Borisov area on 26–28 June. This unit was staffed almost to full strength. It consisted of twenty-one tank destroyer Jagdpanzer IVs, seventy-eight Pz.IVs, seventy-nine Pz.Vs, forty-five Pz.VI Tigers and 250 armoured personnel carriers. On 30 June, Decker engaged the 5th Guards Tank Army of General Pavel Rotmistrov. The mechanic-driver of a T-34 tank, Semyon Kovalenko, recalled these events: 'To delay the Soviet tanks, they set up ambushes. In the thickets by the roads, especially at intersections or where it makes a sharp turn, there were "Tigers" or "Panthers", self-propelled guns. Their crews had already managed to aim at landmarks and opened amazingly accurate fire. They forced us to stop, while they themselves moved to a new position.' In one day, the Soviet tankers lost thirty-eight tanks, and another twenty-five were damaged. The total losses of Rotmistrov's army from 26 June to 2 July amounted to 143 tanks and sixteen self-propelled guns. However, Dekker's 5th Panzer Division also suffered heavy losses, and all the broken and easily damaged tanks had to be abandoned during the retreat.

The Russian cavalry was moving faster than anyone else through the Belarusian forests. The cavalry-mechanised group of General Issa Pliev crossed the Ptich River west of Bobruisk on 26–27 June, after which it again launched a raid into the German rear. Scout armoured personnel carriers and tanks rushed after the cavalry. The combat log of the 4th Cavalry Corps stated: 'Even small streams presented great difficulties for crossing due to the swampy terrain, especially for vehicles, tanks and artillery. These difficulties were overcome by great exertion of the physical strength of the entire personnel. At the crossings, Cossacks and officers literally carried artillery pieces, ammunition wagons and vehicles in their hands.'

By midnight on 28 June, the cavalrymen reached the outskirts of Slutsk (90km south of Minsk). As usual, the appearance of Russian troops in the deep rear caused a shock to the Germans. The city garrison requested urgent air support. The next day, Fw 190 fighters appeared over the forests and swamps and conducted several air attacks against the cavalry. However, this did not delay them for long. At dawn on 30 June, they rushed into the city from three directions at once. Having quickly disposed of the garrison, Pliev led his detachment further to the north-west. After a gruelling day-long march through forests and swamps, at dawn on 2 July, Russian cavalry suddenly appeared in Nesvizh, putting the local garrison and police to flight. On the same day, the riders reached the Minsk–Baranovichi highway. After walking 180km across a swampy wasteland in six days, Pliev's detachment again showed the impressive capabilities of the Russian cavalry. Then the cavalrymen had to repel numerous German attacks for two days as they tried to unblock the vital highway. However, only isolated groups of soldiers managed to break through to the west. Many Germans tried to bypass the cavalry positions through the forests, but it turned out to be the way to their grave. In the vast wasteland, hundreds of infantrymen fell victim to the partisans, while many others perished in the swamps.

On 5 July, the Red Army stormed into Minsk, cutting off all escape routes for the German 4th Army, which was still east of the city. About 100,000 men were caught in the forest pocket. Many of them died in fruitless attempts to break through to the west, the rest surrendered.

## The 'Potato War'

On 6 July, the Red Army approached the Vilnius–Lida–Slonim line, from which only 100km remained to the border of the Third Reich. Under these conditions, Model urgently tried to create a new line of defence from the retreating troops and divisions transferred from other sectors of the front. Vilnius, a major railway hub located 300km east of Königsberg, was to become the main stronghold on the Red Army's path to East Prussia. At the beginning of July, there were several thousand German soldiers in the city, which had recently been in the deep rear, and reinforcements were due to arrive soon. But even before the garrison had to fight with Soviet tanks, it was unexpectedly attacked by Polish rebels from Armia Krajowa.

The fact is that until 1918, Vilnius was part of the Russian Empire, then it was occupied by Poland during the Polish-Lithuanian War and renamed Vilna. In October 1939, in accordance with the Soviet-German Treaty of Friendship and borders, Vilna was transferred to Lithuania and changed its name to Vilnius. But the Poles still considered this city Polish and dreamed of returning it to Poland. On the night of 6

July, 5,500 Polish rebels led by Alexander Kryzhanovsky launched Operation Ostra Brama, which was an integral part of the Burza plan. It envisaged a series of local uprisings in the German-occupied territories of pre-war Poland. Poles attacked the eastern suburbs of Vilnius, as well as units of the Combat Group 'Tolsdorff' (Kampfgruppe 'Tolsdorff'), which were moving towards the city from the west.

For the Wehrmacht, this Polish uprising was completely unexpected and prevented the Germans from creating a strong defensive perimeter before the approach of Soviet troops. To repel the Polish attacks, the garrison had to request urgent air support. On the morning of 7 July, diving Ju 87 and Fw 190s struck the positions of Armia Krajowa in the eastern part of Vilnius, and an armoured train accidentally stuck in the city had to be thrown into battle. Meanwhile, the first Soviet tanks approached Vilnius, capturing the airfield and the suburb of Gurno, located on the eastern outskirts of the city. But at the last moment, the Germans managed to deliver reinforcements of 4,000 soldiers to Vilnius under the command of Generalmajor Rainer Stahl, who received orders to turn the city into a 'fortress' and defend it until the reserves arrived.

On the evening of 7 July, 200 paratroopers from the 2nd Battalion of the 16th Airborne Regiment (II./FJR16) were dropped from Ju 52s on the western outskirts of the city. On 8 July, fighting began on the north-eastern, southern and north-western outskirts. At 15.00, fifty Pe-2 bombers raided the south-western and north-western parts of the city, dropping 38 tons of high-explosive and fragmentation bombs. The attack was carried out from an altitude of 1,600–1,900m, and the crews did not notice any anti-aircraft fire or German fighters.

On 9 July, Vilnius was completely surrounded. The 72nd Rifle Corps of the 5th Army captured the entire northern bank of the Vilia River, while the soldiers of the 65th Rifle Corps broke into the central part of the city. The Luftwaffe carried out two air strikes on the positions of Soviet troops and Armia Krajowa in the eastern part of Vilnius, which involved twenty-seven Ju 87s and twenty-three Fw 190s. Soviet soldiers saw numerous flights of German transport planes over the western part of Vilnius and the dropping of cargo containers by parachute.

During the defence of the city, the garrison used up almost all the ammunition and food, so Stahel requested the delivery of goods by air. The operation was urgently assigned to the bomber air group III./KG27. The unit relocated from Milets airfield to Byala-Podlaska, 35km west of Brest. 'How long will this last? Now we are flying to the potato war again,' the staff doctor of III./KG27 Dr Keller aptly commented in a letter to his wife. By 'potato war' (*Kartoffelkrieg*), he meant that the highly qualified crews of German bombers were once again forced to divert from their usual missions to deliver food to another pocket. At first the supply missions passed without serious problems, and each He 111 usually dropped five 250kg cargo containers on the western outskirts of Vilnius.

On 10 July, the 5th Army captured the entire northern part of the city and entered the Old City. Two days later, only the north-western part of Vilnius and several blocks of the Old City remained in German hands. At the same time, the garrison was divided into two isolated parts – one on the banks of the Vilia River in the observatory area, the second in the Vingis Park area. At 12.49–13.09 fifty-four Pe-2s from the 1st Guards Bomber Aviation Corps raided the Old City, dropping 36.7 tons of high-explosive and incendiary bombs. Given that the Red Army already controlled most of the city, the soldiers actively marked their location with white flares. In the evening of that day, the Soviet air attacks on Vilnius were the fiercest. From 17.00 to 19.00, Il-2s appeared above the city at an altitude of 700–800m and bombed and shelled German strongholds (the observatory and quarters No. 269 and 273) from several approaches. At 18.05, a large group of Pe-2s from the 3rd Guards BAD dropped bombs on the same objects from a height of 1,000m. In the evening there was a thunderstorm, so the bomber crews could not clearly distinguish their targets. Many of them dropped bombs at random through gaps in the clouds. Nevertheless, these air strikes proved effective. A large fire broke out in the observatory building and the neighbouring quarter after the bombing, many vehicles were destroyed and several dozen horses were killed. The Soviet infantry was only 200m from the observatory building. The soldiers clearly saw bombs falling and exploding, buildings collapsing and the corpses of horses being blown to pieces.

The Germans benefited from the thunderstorm and the bombing. The downpour extinguished the fires and the entire area was covered with clouds of smoke and steam, creating a natural smokescreen around the strongholds. Then darkness fell, and the Red Army soldiers could not see what was happening in the enemy positions. In the evening, the head of the operations Department of the General Staff of the Army, Generalleutnant Adolf Heusinger, was able to convince Hitler of the futility of further holding Vilnius. Moreover, it was not possible to create a new line of defence at this line as the Red Army had already broken through far to the west of the city. The Führer reluctantly gave permission for a breakthrough, after which Generalmajor Stahel gave the order at 21.00 (immediately after dark) to move out in a north-westerly direction.

Meanwhile, III./KG27 had to complete the last pocket supply mission. At 19.10–19.25, a group of bombers took off from Byala Podlaska and headed for the target, the distance to which was about 350km. The planes were supposed to reach Vilnius over the valley of the Vilia River and drop containers from a height of 300m on to a small area that was still held by German troops. But by that time, the entire area around the city was filled with Soviet forces and their anti-aircraft guns of various calibres. Therefore, when the He 111s appeared over the Vilia valley and descended to the desired height, powerful fire was opened on them from all sides. Navigator A. Frank from 8./KG27 recalled: 'The whole mission was planned incorrectly. Our troops with tanks were in the pocket. We all came out of the valley from the same direction and had to drop the cargo at an altitude of 300m. On the way through the valley, we were met by insane anti-aircraft fire from the Russians. We already saw 2 He 111s lying in the pocket. At that time, I was stubborn as a tank, and, as navigator, I forced Hauptmann Winkler to stay at an altitude of 300m. He nervously flew through the explosions of anti-aircraft shells and kicked me in the ass. I was lying in front of the scope, and he was continuously screaming: "Finally drop the containers!" But I stubbornly held on and threw the containers at the target.'

In total, KG27 lost five aircraft in this risky 'potato mission', and four more were damaged.

On the night of 12–13 July, the Germans managed to break through the Soviet barriers and the inner ring of the blockade relatively easily. The smoke from the fires and the ongoing thunderstorm helped them escape into the forest almost imperceptibly. At the same time, German troops from the Tolsdorff Combat Group launched a counter-blocking offensive, which involved the 6th Panzer Division, a battalion of Tiger heavy tanks, an SS parachute jäger battalion and two airborne companies. As a result, by dawn, the unblocking group occupied Evye. At 13.00 on 13 July, 3,000 soldiers from the Stahel group entered the area.

According to Soviet information, not only infantry, but also at least 100 vehicles and twenty tanks were able to get out of the encirclement. Two hours later, the last German groups remaining in Vilnius surrendered. At the same time, most of the Russian collaborators (*khivi*) who served in the Wehrmacht preferred suicide to surrender. They knew that there would be no mercy for them.

For Armia Krajowa, this whole operation ended in failure. During the assault, the Soviet soldiers were quite friendly to the rebels. They went into battle together, ate food, exchanged souvenirs, and then jointly patrolled the streets of Vilnius. But soon after the end of the assault, NKVD troops led by General Serov arrived. They quickly dispersed and disarmed the Polish detachments, sending some of the fighters to the pro-Soviet Polish Army (Ludowe Wojsko Polskie).

For some Soviet units, the battle for Vilnius was very difficult. For example, General Pavel Rotmistrov's 5th Guards Tank Army, which provided the outer ring of the blockade and at the same time tried to advance towards Kaunas, was subjected to constant counter-attacks and air attacks starting on 8 July. On 11 July, the 3rd Guards Tank Corps lost eighteen tanks and self-propelled guns, including nine Shermans. As a result, Marshal Ivan Chernyakhovsky, commander of the 3rd Belorussian Front, removed Rotmistrov from his post (with Stalin's consent) and appointed General Vasily Volsky instead.

Chapter 7

# THE GRIFFINS ATTACK

The Luftwaffe tried to delay the Red Army's offensive in a proven way – by air attacks against the railway infrastructure. By the beginning of Operation Bagration, General Meister's Fliegerkorps IV was still an impressive force: about 220 He 111 bombers. In addition, in June, the 6th Air Fleet had another 'ace in their pocket' – He 177s from Kampfgeschwader KG1.

On the night of 25–26 June, KG1 and KG4 carried out a massive raid on the Smolensk railway hub, dropping 400 high-explosive and several thousand incendiary bombs. However, only a third of them hit the target and they mainly fell on the historical part of the city, where dozens of fires broke out. The Smolensk Pedagogical Institute, which housed the hospital, was destroyed. However, the railway hub was severely damaged. Some 3,470m of rails were destroyed along with 220 empty wagons, ninety other wagons and twelve steam locomotives, while a warehouse and other facilities were damaged. On the night of 26–27 June, the Luftwaffe attacked the Bryansk-II railway hub (German designation Bryansk-Sud). The tactics were typical. First, the pathfinders dropped coloured markers – incendiary bombs that gave off red and green colours when burning – to highlight the aiming point and the boundaries of the target.

However, heavy anti-aircraft fire prevented accurate aiming, and only a third of the bombs dropped hit the target. The following night, the Luftwaffe launched a second massive raid on Smolensk, which again involved He 177s from I./KG1. More than 200 high-explosive and about 1,000 incendiary bombs were dropped on the city. As a result, the station building, the home of the locomotive crews, was completely destroyed at the railway hub, while a steam locomotive was destroyed, along with forty wagons, a steam bath train, and two warehouses.

On the night of 3 July, fifteen He 177s raided Sarny railway station, as well as the bridge over the Sluch River. This time, not a single bomb hit the target. An air attack against Korosten station, carried out the following night, also proved unsuccessful. By this time, the Russian air defences had strengthened significantly and learned how to disrupt the Luftwaffe. The Russians actively used smoke, the creation of false fires and even the dropping of fake marker bombs by night fighters. In Korosten, nothing was visible because of the smokescreen, and as a result, out of 100 bombs dropped, only three fell on the target. On the night of 4–5 July, the Germans carried out a third consecutive raid on Smolensk. However, the Russians created such a strong smokescreen over the city that the bombers had to turn around and attack a back-up target, Krichev railway station.

The following nights, the Luftwaffe carried out bombing attacks against railway stations at Belokorovichi, Olevsk, Sarny and Korosten. From 10 to 18 July, Fliegerkorps IV did not conduct raids due to a lack of fuel and urgent relocation to new air bases. According to some reports, around this period, the commander of KG1, Oberstleutnant von Riesen, personally received a call from Reichsmarschall Hermann Göring. He ordered the use of He 177s for daytime air attacks on advancing Soviet tanks. There is no complete information about KG1's actions during this period, but some indirect evidence confirms that such attacks did take place. For example, on the afternoon of 18 July, in the Grodno region, a four-aircraft Yak-9 fighter formation led by Major Nikolai Spiridenko from the 172nd IAP flew in the Augustow area and the pilots saw an unusual sight. At an altitude of 200m, twenty-five bombers similar to Junkers Ju 88s were flying without fighter cover. Considering that the Ju 88A bombers were no longer used on the Eastern Front during this period, and the He 111 flew during the daytime only in emergency cases (mainly to supply the surrounded troops), it is likely that the Russian pilots saw He 177s, and these flew on to bomb Soviet tanks.

However, soon von Riesen had a new goal. At 23.30 on 19 July, Russian radar stations detected several targets approaching from the direction of Riga. At 23.42, the posts of the 107th Separate Battalion of the VNOS, located in the Wasteland area, reported the passage of several aircraft at an altitude of 4,000m heading east. At the same time, the leading bombers dropped green and white marker bombs, indicating the route for the remaining aircraft. At midnight, it became clear to the Russians that the target was probably the Velikiye Luki railway hub.

After midnight, the He 177s approached. The tactics of the raid were as follows. First, pathfinders dropped marker and incendiary bombs from a great height, clearly marking the target. Then, 20–30km before the target area, the leader of each group radioed the crews which target they were attacking and made sure that everyone saw the leader. After that, the He 177s set their combat course.

The Russians opened heavy artillery fire, but thirty anti-aircraft guns were not enough to repel such a massive raid. In addition, they scrambled nine night fighters. Since the sky was illuminated by many searchlights, a large number of marker bombs were burning in the air and fires were burning brightly on the ground, it was not difficult for the pilots to detect German aircraft. For example, Major Gennady Yakhnov saw an aircraft illuminated by a searchlight beam, which seemed to him similar to a Ju 88. The pilot attacked the target, after which the bomber turned sharply to the left and began to dive away. Interestingly, none of the pilots realised that they were looking at rare He 177 bombers. Most identified them as outwardly similar to the Do 215 and Do 217. Sixty to sixty-five He 177s participated in the mission, and it was perhaps the most massive and most successful raid involving these long-suffering aircraft – whose entry into combat was delayed by engine issues – in the entire war.

About 300 high-explosive and seventy heavy incendiary bombs were dropped on Velikiye Luki, of which about half hit the target. Some 108 railway wagons and platforms with vehicles, ammunition and other military equipment were destroyed, six steam locomotives were smashed and damaged, a depot and three station buildings were destroyed, ninety-three links on forty railway tracks. Eighty people were killed and 259 were injured. The railway hub was completely disabled for almost a day, and single-track through traffic was restored only by the next night. A total of 200 high-explosive and fifty incendiary bombs were dropped on the neighbouring Novosokolniki railway hub, as a result of which 190 railway wagons and platforms were burned or destroyed, including four wagons with ammunition, 141 links of the rail track and seven switches and ten buildings, including an artillery warehouse, while the water supply and communication lines were disabled. Some 134 people were killed in the bombing, including fifty soldiers, thirty-four civilians and fifty German prisoners of war. Another 254 were injured. Train traffic at the station was partially restored at 09.00 on 20 July.

Soon after the attack on Novosokolniki and Velikiye Luki, an event occurred that could well have changed the course of the war. At noon that day, an explosion occurred at Hitler's Wolf's Lair headquarters in East Prussia. According to von Riesen's memoirs, KG1 was indirectly involved in this event. He claimed that during the daytime flight, a pair of He 177s had engine problems, and therefore they accidentally dropped bombs into a swamp located in a no-fly zone, which fell next to the Wolf's Lair. As a result, there was a rumour that the Griffins had carried out an air attack against Hitler! However, from the author's research, it appears the incident was a work of fiction invented by Riesen.

On 20 July, the most critical situation for the Wehrmacht developed at the junction of the Army Groups Centre and North. A large gap formed between the two, into which the Soviet 51st Army and the 3rd Guards Mechanised Corps rushed. Since the potential breakthrough to the Gulf of Riga threatened to completely encircle the 16th and 18th Armies, and there were no ground forces to close the gap, it was in this direction that all available aircraft, including He 177 bombers, were thrown. It is clear that high-speed heavy bombers were not suitable for pinpoint strikes, so in the daytime the Griffins simply dropped bombs from horizontal flight on certain squares, and often just on the forests among which the Soviet troops were moving. However, the damage from such air attacks was small. For example, on 25 July, the 77th Infantry Division, which was bombed on the march in the Kupianu–Koruna–Korolyuna area, suffered the most, but lost four men killed and twelve wounded, as well as thirty horses. Without encountering serious resistance (mainly construction, security and aviation battalions were in their path), on this day the Soviet troops broke through to Šiauliai. The next day, after stubborn fighting, the city was taken. The Baltic Sea coast was only 140km away. At the same time, the right flank of the 51st Army reached Jelgava, reaching the approaches to Riga and the Gulf of Riga. On 28 July, the 51st Army continued its offensive in the north-western and northern directions. Instead of real troops, the Russians were confronted by all sorts of rabbles in the form of consolidated 'units' from the Riga police, Luftwaffe construction companies, the Königsberg air zone battalion, field training and security brigades, funeral platoons, etc. All the efforts of these improvised units turned out to be useless, and on 29 July, the advanced units of the 3rd Mechanised Corps reached the Gulf of Riga in the Tucums area, cutting off Army Group North.

Two weeks later, the German command, having secretly transferred several panzer divisions to Courland, was able to unblock the 16th and 18th Armies with an unexpected blow. But since Hitler categorically refused to leave the Baltic region, this success only delayed the final encirclement of Army Group North.

July 1944 was the last month when the Luftwaffe operated on all fronts to the full extent of its combat capabilities. In April, the Allies had launched a large-scale operation to destroy the fuel industry of the Third Reich. Oil fields (including in Romania, Austria, Hungary and Yugoslavia), oil refineries in the Ruhr and Silesia, as well as synthetic fuel production plants in the Czech Republic, Magdeburg, Lane, Lückendorf and Poliz were subjected to large bombing raids. As a result, starting in June, Germany was unable to produce enough aviation fuel. In a couple of months of fierce fighting, almost all its reserves were used up, and at the end of July, a fuel famine began. All units were ordered to save every barrel of fuel. It got to the point that air bases began to use horses, oxen and cows to tow aircraft from the dispersals to the take-off point and from the landing point back again. That is, fighters and bombers landed, turned off their engines, and then waited for the animals to arrive for towing.

First of all, the most 'voracious' aircraft, which consumed the largest amount of fuel, also became a victim of the economies. This included the He 177, which had received their name Griffin in honour of the mythological monster and fully justified it. In mid-July, fuel began to arrive at Vereen and Zeerappen airfields with long interruptions, and at the end of the month supplies stopped altogether. The combat work of KG1 was reduced to zero, and in August the unit was reorganised into the fighter Geschwader JG7. The He 177s, which had so much time and effort to design and build, were mothballed, and later most of them were sent for scrap. Later, a similar fate befell most of the Kampfgeschwader who flew the older He 111.

Soviet long-range bombers operated similarly to the German ones, mainly attacking railway infrastructure. For example, on the night of 4–5 July, thirty-four Il-4s from the 3rd Guards AD DD carried out a raid on the Baranovichi-Tovarnaya railway station, dropping 41½ tons of bombs on it. The crews reported numerous hits on the target, but aerial photography taken from a height of 4,200m showed that almost all the bombs fell north-west of the station in a field. The next night, thirty-five bombers flew to the Brest-Tovarnaya station. On the night of 7–8 July, thirty-one aircraft from the 3rd Guards Aviation Division again participated in a massive raid on Brest. This time, the target was the central station of this hub. Due to strong anti-aircraft fire, bombs were dropped from an altitude of 5,000–5,500m, while the Ilyushins were illuminated several times by marker bombs dropped from an even higher altitude by German night fighters. The crews clearly saw the silhouettes of several 'hunters', identified as Ju 88s and Bf 110s, but most of the bombers managed to escape in the dark. The next day, agents in Brest reported that as a result of an air attack, the central station building and the bridge over the Mukhovets River were destroyed, several warehouses had burned down and ten trains were damaged.

The next night, twenty-four Il-4s struck the Bialystok railway hub, dropping 34½ tons of high-explosive bombs on it. When approaching the target, anti-aircraft artillery opened a powerful barrage, and their explosions resembled a fiery umbrella suspended in the sky. Because of this, it was necessary to drop the 'cargo' from a high altitude – 5,000–5,500m, which reduced the accuracy of the Il-4s' bombing. The sky over Bialystok was patrolled by a large number of night fighters and one Il-4 was shot down by them. On the night of 9–10 July, Russian bombers bombed Brest-Tsentralny station again; on the night of 14–15 July, Kobrin station; on the night of 15–16 July, Brest station; on the night of 18–19 July, Sedlce station; on the night of 22–23 July, Sedlce again; and on the night of 24–25 July, Demblin station. In the report of the 3rd Guards AD DD on the air attack against Demblin, it was reported: 'As a result of the bombing, up to ten fires broke out, presumably fuel tanks and trains burned, three large explosions, trains and ammunition depots were blown up. Fires were observed at a distance of 100km from the target.' Aerial photographs taken at the end of the raid showed that the Polish city was indeed engulfed in fires.

On the evening of 25 July, the crews of long-range bombers received orders to strike at the outskirts of Warsaw Praga, on the eastern bank of the Vistula. At 20.40, engines roared at the Belaya Tserkov airfield, after which the heavily loaded Il-4s began to taxi one by one to the start and rise into the gloomy sky. A total of thirty-eight aircraft took part in the raid, two of which carried FAB-1000 high-explosive bombs. After reaching the Vistula, the planes turned to the north-west, guided by the riverbed. However, a real surprise awaited the Russian bombers ahead. On the approach to the target, there were several dozen explosions of anti-aircraft shells, then about 100 searchlights cut through the sky. Over Warsaw itself, the Ilyushins received the most powerful fire from many guns at once. At the same time, peaceful life continued in the Polish capital itself and its suburbs. Street lights were shining on the streets, and many vehicles were driving with their headlights on brightly. When viewed from above, Warsaw was very different not only from the usual occupied cities in Belarus, Ukraine and the Baltic region but also from the cities of Central and Western Europe, where they had been used to living in the dark for a long time. It was obvious that the people of Warsaw did not yet know what night bombing raids were.

For a significant part of the city's residents, the hum of Russian aircraft engines and subsequent bomb explosions became a signal that the Red Army was already close and it was necessary to prepare for long-planned actions ...

For Stalin's Falcons themselves, the raid was unsuccessful. Due to the intense anti-aircraft fire, only thirteen to fifteen aircraft were able to pass directly over the target, and just some of them were able to drop bombs from a height of 5,600m. Five more unloaded before reaching the goal, the rest generally randomly. Two Il-4s did not return from the mission. On the night of 27–28 July, the crews of the 3rd Guards AD DD carried out a second raid on Praga, a suburb of Warsaw. This time, the bombing height was increased to 6,300m, which was the limit for this type of aircraft with a minimum bomb load of 1 ton. This made it easier to complete the task, but reduced the accuracy even more. The headquarters of the aviation division modestly assessed the results as 'satisfactory'. One Il-4 was attacked by a Ju 88C-6 night fighter on departure, but the crew managed to fight it off by using the latest weapon for the first time, AG-2 remote grenades. It was a pretty original weapon. The AG-2 was a cast-iron ball weighing 2kg, filled with 80g of explosives. A braking parachute was attached to the balloon in a cylindrical container. At the moment of the drop, the lid of the parachute box was pulled off and the fuse was cocked at the same time. After two to three seconds, the grenade exploded 100–150m behind and 20–25m below the aircraft. Of course, the pilots did not need to lean out of the cockpit and throw it with their hand as special holders were attached to the fuselage.

For two years, the Il-4 was a real 'workhorse' of Soviet long-range bomber aviation. From the Volga and Kuban to Romania and Poland, from the Moscow region and the Valdai Upland to the Baltic region and Finland, all operations of the Soviet troops were invariably accompanied by night raids of these aircraft (nicknamed the 'flying basket' by the Germans) on railway stations, air bases, bridges and other objects. They were not very beautiful and equally unreliable, but still beloved by their crews, Ilyushins became the same personification of the 'nightlife' over the Eastern Front as their He 111 counterparts. In this regard, it is symbolic that the mass combat use of both aircraft ended almost simultaneously.

After the raids on the outskirts of Warsaw, the pilots of the 3rd Guards AD DD, like the entire Red Army, were enthusiastic (Germany was already nearby!) and they were ready to continue to smash railway hubs in the enemy's rear. However, at the end of July, the Red Army Air Forces, like their main opponent, faced a serious fuel shortage. And if the Luftwaffe had suffered it due to the bombing of fuel factories and oil fields in Romania by American aircraft, then the Russian shortage was explained by rather banal reasons. Firstly, the excessive growth of the number of aircraft itself and the enormous consumption of fuel during Operation Bagration. Secondly, there was a clear discrepancy between the capabilities of the oil refining industry and the increased needs of the armed forces. As a result, both the Germans and the Russians had a fuel shortage that almost killed off the most voracious aircraft, the bombers.

This fate did not pass by the 3rd Guards AD DD, which has mentioned many times so far. From 1 to 28 August, not a single flight was carried out due to the complete lack of fuel at Belaya Tserkov airfield. By the end of the month, some fuel had been was delivered, and on the night of 24 August, a raid was carried out on Tilsit. Then, on 5 September, the division relocated to Lutsk and Shepetin airfields. The crews thought that combat work would resume soon, but during September only seven raids were carried out (including three on Budapest), and the following month just two. In December, the 3rd Guards Air Division was renamed the 13th Guards Bomber Division. Later, until the end of the war, the unit continued to fight on in the old Il-4, but they were used, like the He 111, only occasionally.

It was the shortage of fuel, and not the 'iron will of Model', as Hitler claimed, that slowed the Soviet offensive west of Minsk. On 8 July, the troops of the 1st Belorussian Front liberated Baranovichi, and on 16 July they reached the city of Pruzhany, from which 225km remained to Warsaw. There, Rokossovsky's tanks and armoured personnel carriers finally stopped due to the lack of diesel fuel and petrol. To deliver fuel, the Russians had to organise an air bridge from south-eastern Belarus to south-western Belarus. Starting on 11 July, barrels of fuel were delivered by transport planes from warehouses in the Gomel and Kalinkovichi areas to Brianchitsy airfield (18km south of Slutsk). There they were loaded on to U-2 biplanes from the 271st NBAD, which took them to the small Valokhva airfield, 7km south-west of Baranovichi. From there, fuel and lubricants were transported by trucks to tank units and to the front-line airstrips. On the first day, biplanes performed 155 transport sorties, and on 12 July, fifty-five. In some cases, barrels were delivered directly from Valokhva to the tank positions. However, the volume of supplies was far from even the minimum requirements. It was not yet possible to use railways for cargo delivery due to the fact that they were thoroughly destroyed during the retreat by German railway 'worms' and 'scorpions'.

Chapter 8

# THE BATTLE OF THE VISTULA

## The Bloody Path and the Collapse of the Ukrainian SS

The Armia Krajowa remained an active player throughout Operation Bagration and subsequent battles, although it did not have a serious impact on the course of the whole campaign. For example, on 15 July, Polish rebels attacked Biala Podlaska air base, where the 8th Staffel KG27 was based. One pilot was killed in the shootout and an aircraft mechanic was seriously injured. This action reminded the Germans that they were not at home in Poland, but in occupied territory. And the very next day, III./KG27 relocated to Milets air base, from where it had to supply another pocket by air. 'All Russian successes are due only to banditry. We felt something today too. Soon this will come to an end, and the spit will be turned over again,' Dr Keller, a staff doctor III./KG27, complained to his wife. The doctor, figuratively speaking, was referring to the next offensive of the Red Army, which began on 14 July on the 300km front from Kovel to Stanislav. Marshal Ivan Konev's 1st Ukrainian Front struck north-east and east of Lviv. Two Soviet tank armies quickly broke through the German defences and rushed into Galicia. From the air, this offensive was supported by 1,500 aircraft of the 2nd and 8th Air Armies.

On the ground the situation quickly took on the 'crisis' character already familiar to the Wehrmacht. Since the order to retreat, as usual, was not given in time, on 18 July, the 13th Army Corps of General Arthur Hauffe was surrounded near the city of Brody. The new pocket included six divisions, including the 340th, 361st, 349th and 454th Infantry, the Ukrainian SS Division 'Galicia' and Corps Group C (Korpsabteilung C). The latter included the combat groups of the 183rd, 217th and 339th Infantry Divisions.

The 'Galicia' Division was a typical international unit under the auspices of the SS that was formed in the summer of 1943 in Galicia. Most of the Ukrainian volunteers came from poor peasant families who succumbed to Nazi propaganda. During the long training, the recruits were introduced in detail to 'racial theory', the ideas of anti-Semitism, and the conspiracy theory of 'Jewish Bolshevism' (the theory of the communist conspiracy of Jews, invented by Hitler). The division received its baptism of fire in February 1944, when the 4th 'Galician' Regiment, together with the Ukrainian Insurgent Army (UPA), conducted a punitive expedition to the Polish village of Huta Penyatska, whose inhabitants participated in the partisan struggle and helped Armia Krajowa. At dawn on 28 February, the village was surrounded by Ukrainians and completely destroyed. A total of 172 houses were burned down, and more than 500 civilians were brutally murdered. After that, soldiers from Galicia participated in numerous actions to destroy the Polish villages of Barysh, Ganachevka, Plotycha, Chernitsy, Polska, Budka and others, as well as in mass raids on Jews in the city of Brody. Thousands of civilians were brutally killed, including being burned alive.

And now, at the end of July, the bloodstained 'Galicia' Division entered the battle in the same area where all these war crimes had previously been committed.

On 19 July, Air Group III./KG27, which had not yet managed to recover from its dangerous missions to the semi-surrounded Vilnius, received an order to urgently supply German troops in the Brody district. The mission looked to be in the spirit of the recently completed one and was just as risky and adventurous. The bombers were supposed to reach the target area during daylight hours (before dusk), descend to 300m and drop cargo containers at the location of German and Ukrainian troops in the Ozidov area (70km north-east of Lviv). The results also turned out to be similar to the mission to supply the garrison of Vilnius, and the losses were even greater. Walter Stampf from 9./KG27 recalled: 'It was a hell of a flight! During the flight in that direction, I had already received several hits, but despite this, we flew on. In the forest valley where our surrounded comrades were, Russians were sitting on the hills and firing from all barrels: down, from above, from all sides!' But Stampf's bomber nevertheless managed to complete the 'impossible mission' and return back. However, three planes from the 8th Staffel did not return from the flight to Ozidov.

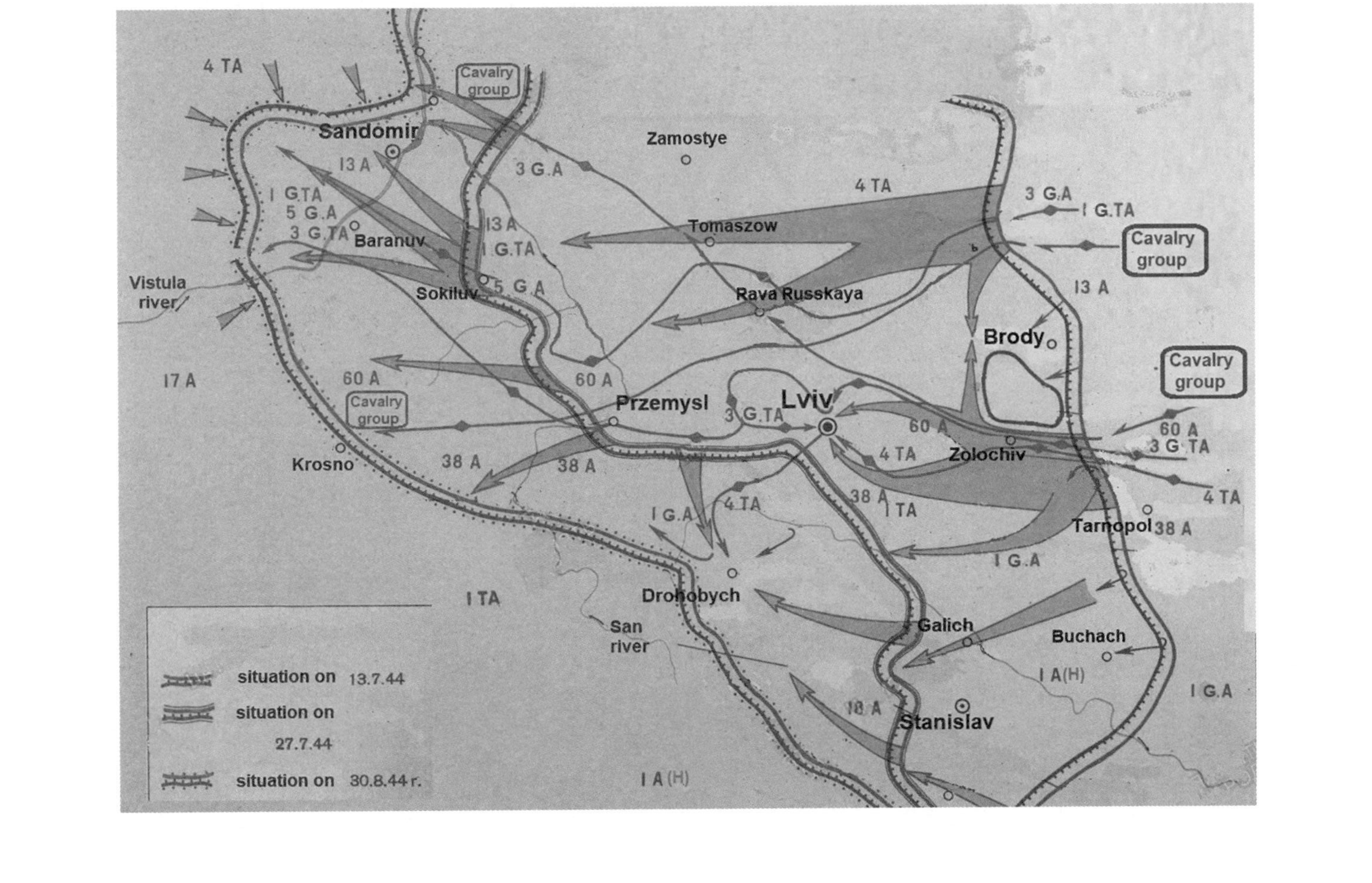
4 TA
Cavalry group
Sandomir
13 A
3 G.A
Zamostye
4 TA
3 G.A
I G.TA
I G.TA
5 G.A
3 G.TA
Baranuv
13 A
I G.TA
Tomaszow
Cavalry group
Vistula river
Sokiluv
5 G.A
Rava Russkaya
13 A
Brody
17 A
60 A
60 A
Cavalry group
Cavalry group
Przemysl
Lviv
3 G.TA
60 A
60 A
3 G TA
Krosno
38 A
38 A
4 TA
Zolochiv
4 TA
38 A
I TA
I G.A
4 TA
Tarnopol
38 A
I G.A
I TA
Drohobych
San river
Galich
Buchach
I A(H)
I G.A
18 A
Stanislav
I A (H)
situation on 13.7.44
situation on 27.7.44
situation on 30.8.44 r.

Meanwhile, the headquarters of the 13th Army Corps hastily developed a plan to break out of the pocket in a southerly direction. Corps group 'C', as the most powerful unit, became the shock link for the attack. At dawn the next day, the troops were supposed to cross the Western Bug River in the Bely Kamen area, then cross the Slonovka River further south and break into the area between Skvartsva and Khilchitsa. At the same time, no one really knew what was really happening in the south. Those in the pocket only knew for sure that the 1st Panzer Army was still in Lviv, and the 8th Panzer Division was fighting somewhere south of Zolochiv.

The breakthrough began at 03.30 on 20 July. However, unlike the events in Vilnius, here the Soviet troops managed to unravel the plans of the Germans and create a layered defence in the Bely Kamen area. As a result, there was a fierce battle involving a large number of tanks and artillery. Simultaneous attacks by the German 8th Panzer Division from the area south of Zolochiv were unsuccessful; thus, it was not possible to break through the corridor for the exit of the surrounded troops.

In the afternoon, bombers from III./KG27 flew to the pocket again with the task of delivering ammunition and fuel for tanks. To escape early detection, the He 111s flew directly over the treetops. As they approached the target, the bombers gained an altitude of 300m, the minimum possible when dropping such dangerous goods. Having found the right clearing and a drop site marked with a white cloth cross, the planes dropped the containers and turned back on their course. After that, the bombers switched back to low-level flight, almost knocking down the tops of the trees with their wings. First, the group flew over the frightened peasants peacefully cultivating arable land, and then over a Soviet anti-aircraft gun. Despite the suddenness, it managed to fire a volley and He 111H-20 '1G+IR' was shot down after its right engine caught fire. This was the main danger of low-level flights: it was impossible to climb to a safe height with one engine, and it was also impossible to fly far away. The pilot, non-commissioned officer Alfred Jobst, tried to keep the bomber in the air as long as possible, and then made an emergency landing on a grain field in the Rava Russkaya area. There, the crew found themselves in the thick of things: nearby German tanks were fighting the advancing Red Army. Soon, the pilots had to retreat to the west in a truck with soldiers.

On 21 July, the climax came in a short battle in the Brody area. Having failed to break out of the pocket in an organised manner, the Germans split into separate groups that tried to infiltrate through the blockade ring one by one. In the afternoon, aircraft of two Soviet air armies (2nd VA and 8th VA) conducted three massive air attacks against the encircled troops, as well as against the 8th Panzer Division in the area of Zolochiv. A total of 1,225 aircraft took part, including 495 Il-2s, 290 bombers and 440 fighters. The planes attacked from a low altitude, dropping bombs literally on the heads of German and Ukrainian soldiers and shooting them at point-blank range with their cannon. Semyon Donchenko, the deputy commander of the 9th Guards SHAD, recalled: 'Having made a U-turn, ground-attack planes go on the attack. The first group strikes guns and mortars, the second tanks and vehicles. Ground-attack planes dive at targets from a height of three hundred metres. It can be seen how enemy soldiers rushed, ran, and opened fire indiscriminately. The crews repeat the calls, act slowly, methodically, for sure.'

Ivan Drachenko from the 140th Guards SHAP said: 'We crossed the front line at a low level and began to go deeper into the enemy's rear. An impressive panorama opened before my eyes: tanks were burning down, all sorts of baggage was lying on the roads, armoured vehicles were lying upside down, guns were pointing their barrels at the sky.' And none of this was an exaggeration. After these air attacks, accompanied by simultaneous heavy artillery shelling, the units of the 13th Army Corps were completely disorganised and demoralised.

On the night of 21–22 July, the encircled launched last desperate attacks. As a result, only a few German units managed to break out of the cauldron to the south in the direction of Gologora and Zolotaya Lipa, where the 48th Panzer Corps still held positions east of Lviv. The Catholic chaplain of the 217th Infantry Division, Bade, recalled these events: 'When the sun turned blood red on 22 July 1944, the 13th Army Corps was eliminated. About 25,000–30,000 German soldiers were killed on the battlefield. Several thousand people fled to Hungary for several more days. The great night of the deep silence of the Russian captivity fell on the remains … Such an end is bitter as death, and terrible as the end of the world.'

On 23 July, Red Army soldiers discovered and captured the headquarters of the 13th Army Corps led by General Hauffe in the forest near Bely Kamen. However, he was not destined to go to the USSR and meet there with the previously captured generals of the Wehrmacht. While being escorted to the rear, the car containing the prisoners was blown up by a land mine, laid under the road by the Germans themselves. As a result, Hauffe and some of his staff officers were killed. According to Soviet information, 17,000 soldiers were captured, while about 5,000 managed to escape. A large amount of military equipment was seized, including 719 guns, 1,100 mortars and 3,900 vehicles. For the German army, this was another defeat and another loss of many experienced troops and expensive equipment. The Ukrainian SS 'Galicia' Division died ingloriously in this brutal battle. Its losses in the Brody pocket amounted to about 10,000 dead and missing. And only a few managed to escape.

Field Marshal Model was largely to blame for this defeat, and he clearly could not cope with the command of two army groups at once.

Kampfgeschwader KG27 sacrificed five aircraft and twenty-one pilots in this mission. Interestingly, when the assassination attempt on Hitler and the military coup in Berlin took place on 20 July, many young German pilots, upon learning about it, were shocked to the core. Exposed to Nazi propaganda, they considered this act a 'vile betrayal of traitors'. And at the Milec airfield, located north-east of Krakow, a rumour seriously spread that KG27 would soon participate in air attacks against the putschists in Berlin!

Meanwhile, the events in Lviv, which Soviet tanks were already approaching, developed according to the Vilnius scenario. On 22 July, when Soviet troops were approaching the city, 7,000 Armia Krajowa rebels led by Vladislav Filipkovsky began an uprising code-named 'the Storm in Lviv' ('Burza we Lwowie'). Two days later, the first Russian tanks entered the city, but they were met not by Germans, but by AK fighters who declared that it was 'already free Lviv'. Although this was a strong exaggeration, the rebels controlled only part of the city. After 27 July, when Lviv was finally liberated, the leaders of the uprising were arrested and the infantry were sent to replenish the Wojsko Polskie.

## Russians Enter Poland

To the north, the Soviet offensive was also developing successfully. On 18 July, Soviet troops launched an offensive in the Kovel area. The objective of the grouping, which included the 8th Guards, 47th, 70th Armies and the 2nd Tank Army, was Warsaw. From the air, they were supported by the 6th Air Army of General Fyodor Polynin, which consisted of 1,117 aircraft, including 560 fighters and 438 ground-attack planes.

As had happened more than once, the first massive air attack on German territory at dawn on 18 July was thwarted by bad weather. Nevertheless, Polynin was ordered to act according to the plan, regardless of the risks and losses. Many missions took place in the most difficult conditions, and on the way to the targets and back, the planes sometimes found themselves in the clouds, then passed through a solid wall of rain, where they were literally flooded with water, then again, they found themselves in 'clean' air. And then they dived into the fog again. Inexperienced crews lost sight of the leaders, could not

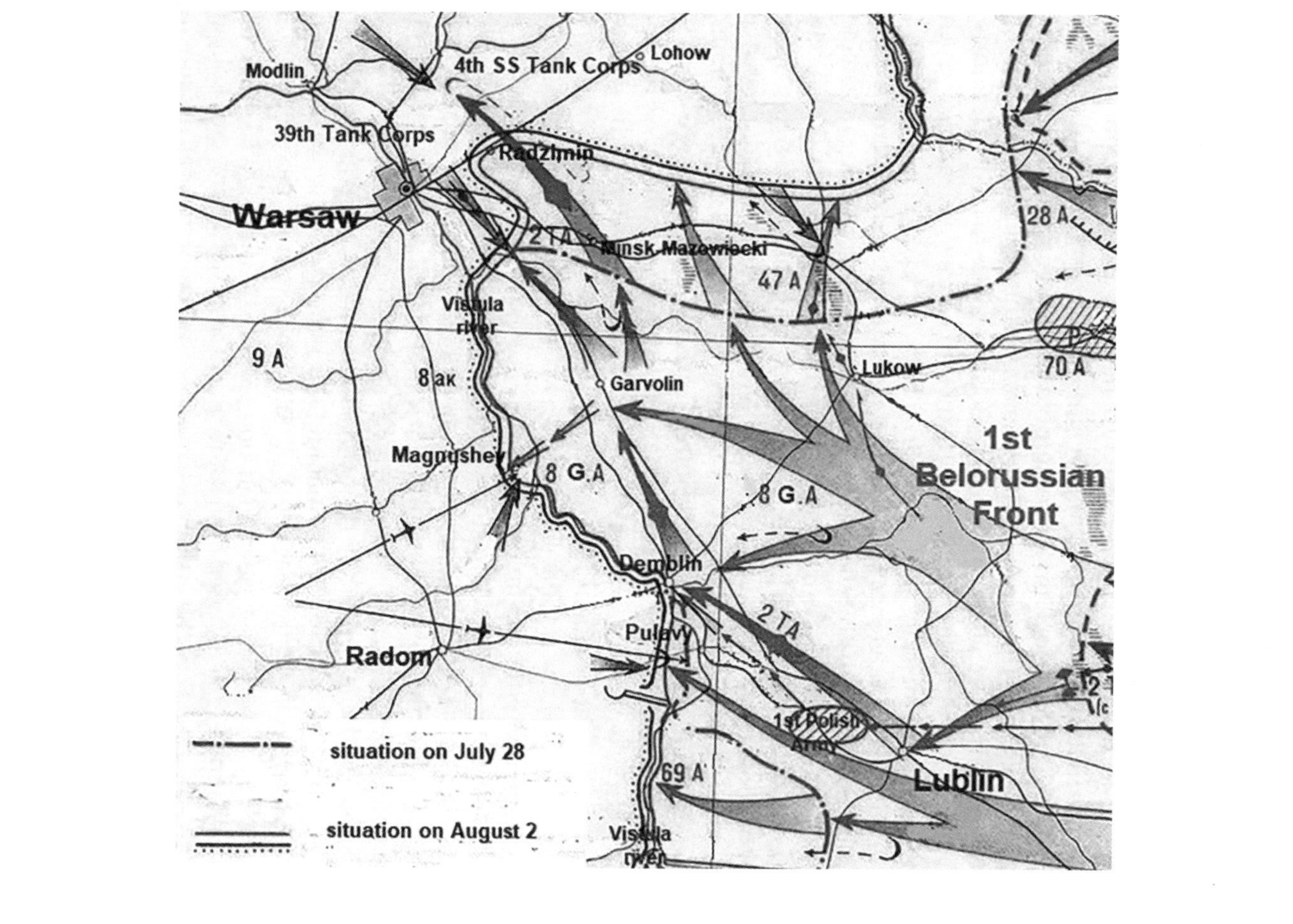
Modlin
4th SS Tank Corps
Lohow
39th Tank Corps
Radzimin
Warsaw
2 TA
Minsk Mazowiecki
47 A
28 A
Vistula river
9 A
8 ak
Garvolin
Lukow
70 A
Magnushev
8 G.A
8 G.A
1st Belorussian Front
Demblin
2 TA
Pulavy
Radom
1st Polish Army
Lublin
69 A
Vistula river
situation on July 28
situation on August 2

cope with orientation and then returned to their base on their own. Often, after taking off and completing the task, the groups could not find sufficient landmarks to reach their airfield. Sometimes the pilots had to descend to ground level to at least see something, but this was fraught with the danger of coming under fire, crashing into a tree or ramming your own comrades. For example, in the 299th SHAD, one of the Il-2 groups travelling to the target almost collided with another Il-2 formation returning to base. To restore orientation, the leader of the first group dropped to a height of 50m, and the leader of the second dropped to 40m. At some point, both groups swept towards each other over the trees, literally one above the other. As a result, the 6th Air Army managed to carry out 930 sorties due to its heroic efforts. However, the losses were also great: thirty-three aircraft, of which twenty were missing.

The German defences quickly collapsed, and by the evening of 21 July, Soviet troops reached the Western Bug River and began forcing this water barrier, along which the border with the Third Reich had previously passed. As usual, cavalry and the 2nd Tank Army were introduced into the breakthrough, which began a rapid offensive towards the Vistula. Three days later, Russian tanks reached Lublin, where Armia Krajowa raised another uprising.

The liberation of Lublin, the first major Polish city, played an important role. This event allowed Stalin to form the Polish Committee of National Liberation, in fact, a new Polish government headed by Edward Osubka-Morawski. PKWN was formed as a result of negotiations involving primarily the main Polish communist organisations – the Union of Polish Patriots (ZPP) and the Polish Workers' Party (PPR). At the same time, the actions of the rebels from Armia Krajowa, who had organised uprisings in cities before the arrival of the Red Army, were perceived very cautiously by Stalin.

The old Polish–Soviet border arose as a result of the wars waged by Poland in 1918–21. By the decision of the Versailles Peace Conference, the territories of the eastern regions of Austria-Hungary and the western provinces of Russia became part of the newly formed state, the Republic of Poland. At the same time, the eastern border of Poland in the context of the Russian Civil War was not formally defined. The head of the Polish state, Józef Piłsudski, took advantage of this. While still a student, he hated Russia and joined the ranks of the revolutionaries. In 1887, Piłsudski's brother was sent to carry out hard labour for participating in a conspiracy against Emperor Alexander III, and Józef himself was exiled to Siberia for five years. After returning to his homeland, he joined the Polish Socialist Party and continued the fierce struggle against Russia, which became the main goal of his whole life. After the end of the First World War and the formation of the new Polish state, Piłsudski headed it, setting about creating a strong army. Now he had a new idea for a fix – the creation of a Polish–Lithuanian–Belarusian–Ukrainian federation called Mezhdumorie, or Intermarium in the West. In fact, it was concerned with the revival of the Polish–Lithuanian Commonwealth, a Polish state that ceased to exist at the end of the eighteenth century. Piłsudski dreamed of a Great Poland that would throw Russia back to its former borders.

During the Polish–Ukrainian, Polish–Lithuanian and Russian–Polish wars, the Poles partially succeeded in implementing this ambitious plan. Piłsudski's army annexed large territories of Belarus, Ukraine and Lithuania, populated mainly by non-Polish people. For Soviet Russia, the defeat of 1921 was very humiliating, and the established Soviet–Polish border was perceived as a forced compromise. For the Russians, this was the same unfair annexation as for the French the annexation of Alsace and Lorraine by Germany in 1871. Just as the French had dreamed of reclaiming their territories for forty years (in August 1914, the slogan 'To Alsace! Lets go to Alsace faster!' was the main leitmotif during the mobilisation), and the Russians also dreamed of annulling the terms of the 1921 treaty imposed on them.

At the same time, Ukrainians, Belarusians and Lithuanians in Poland were subjected to outright discrimination and humiliation, and Warsaw pursued a strict colonisation policy in the eastern lands. Therefore, many of the locals welcomed the arrival of the Red Army in September 1939. As a result of the Soviet–German treaty (the Molotov–Ribbentrop Pact), the new border of the Soviet Union passed along the 'Curzon Line', a boundary that was proposed as a demarcation line by the Entente countries and personally by British Foreign Minister Lord Curzon back in 1920. After Lithuania became part of the USSR, the city of Vilna (Vilnius) was annexed to this republic.

After the invasion of the German army in the USSR, the issue of the Soviet–Polish border lost its relevance for a while. For the first time, Stalin and Churchill discussed this problem during the Tehran Conference (in November–December 1943). After lengthy discussions, the British leader agreed to the 'Curzon line', offering to transfer part of German territory to Poland as compensation. That is, in fact, to move Poland to the west. US President Roosevelt also agreed with this project.

When, in July 1944, Armia Krajowa raised the first uprisings before the arrival of the Red Army, Stalin quickly learned that the rebels' goal was to restore the Polish Empire within the borders of 1939. It was the uprising of the Polish rebels in Vilnius that the red leader took particularly painfully. 'Where is Poland located and where is Vilnius located?' he raged. At the same time, he knew that Armia Krajowa was receiving instructions from the Polish emigrant government in London. Stalin decided that the uprisings were being secretly inspired by Great Britain and considered this a gross violation of previously reached agreements. This explains the Kremlin's hostile attitude towards Armia Krajowa.

On 24 July, the Russian advance detachments had already reached the Vistula in the Demblin area. In parallel, T-34 tanks entered the town of Siedlce, located about halfway between Brest and Warsaw. Brest was surrounded on 27 July. The Führer, shocked by his recent assassination attempt, did not have time to give the traditional order to defend another 'fortress', and the Luftwaffe did not have time to send their 'potato bombers' there, as the next day the city had already surrendered. At the same time, Soviet troops reached the Vistula River south of Warsaw on a wide front. On 1 August, units of the 8th Guards Army crossed the river in the Magnushev area and established a bridgehead on the west bank. Within four days, it was enlarged to 15km wide and 5km deep. Four ferry crossings were organised in a short time across the river, the width of which was 400–600m in this section, and the depth from 3 to 15m. Initially, seventeen ferries, two barges and seventy boats of various designs (including Polish fishing boats captured nearby) were used to service them.

Meanwhile, south-east of Magnushev, the 69th Army also crossed to the west bank of the Vistula and seized a bridgehead in the Pulavy area. In the shortest possible time, three ferry crossings were organised, which were serviced by six ferries with a capacity of 9–16 tons and 144 boats of different designs.

The Germans launched their first strong attacks against the Pulavy bridgehead on 2 August. 'Soldiers of the 11th Police Regiment rushed to the attack, throwing on their satchels, overcoats and uniforms on the move, throwing off their jackets and rolling up their sleeves. In hand-to-hand combat, the Soviet soldiers broke the onslaught of the enemy and put him to flight,' the 69th Army combat magazine said. The next day, with the support of self-propelled artillery and artillery, the Germans (no longer rolling up their sleeves) launched an offensive again and were able to push out units of the 61st Rifle Corps in the Barychka and Borovets area.

The 6th Air Army was assigned to cover the Pulavy and Magnushev bridgeheads, which received the unofficial name 'Southern' and 'Northern' from the Russians, respectively. However, the Soviet air force was still experiencing an acute shortage of fuel and engine oil. Fighters often had to go on a mission with a half-filled fuel tank. However, the Luftwaffe concentrated six fighter aircraft groups and the entire Geschwader of direct support for troops – SG77, which had forty-seven Ju 87s and thirty-three Fw 190s – on a narrow section of the front. In addition, the entire 'strategic' Fliegerkorps IV was used against the Russian bridgeheads on the Vistula.

On the evening of 4 August, sirens were heard over the Magnushev bridgehead, after which three groups of Stukas fell one after another on the positions of the 57th and 74th Guards Rifle Divisions. When the smoke and dust from the explosions dispersed, the Germans launched their first strong attacks at dusk. They managed to retake the village of Rychivud and push the Soviet troops to the river bank. Only the urgent introduction of tank reserves into battle allowed the situation to stabilise by morning.

On 5 August, the Luftwaffe heavily bombed both bridgeheads, their main target being a bridge under construction in the Pulavy area. As a result of direct hits, fifty piles were destroyed and another twenty-five damaged, eleven soldiers of the engineering troops were killed, and six more were injured.

On the night of 6 August, German planes continuously bombed Soviet positions on the west bank of the Vistula, and in the afternoon the Russians recorded 340 overflights of German aircraft. The Stukas' attacks began early in the morning, then they were replaced by small groups of Fw 190s, then Ju 87s arrived again, etc. On 6 August, the combat operations magazine of the 8th Guards Army reported: 'Enemy aircraft in groups of 12–18 aircraft continuously bombed and shelled the positions of our troops and ferry crossing across the Vistula River.' A particularly powerful air attack took place at 17.40 on the positions of the 227th Guards Rifle Regiment. As soon as the smoke from the explosions cleared, and the infantrymen shook themselves off, several German tanks went on the attack, followed by infantry. By nightfall, the Germans again managed to push back the Red Army and retake two more villages. In other areas, the Russians barely managed to hold on. During the air attacks, 254 high-explosive bombs and seventy-eight containers with fragmentation bombs were dropped on the Pulavy bridgehead.

During 7 August, German aircraft continuously bombed and shelled the Northern bridgehead, the roads leading to it and the ferry crossing across the Vistula. The Southern bridgehead was not bombed that day, which allowed the engineering and bridge-building battalions to calmly complete the construction of a bridge across the river in the area of Lucimi. The bridge, built in just a week, had a length of 386m, a width of 4m and a load capacity of 30 tons. In the early hours, the first 182 vehicles and seventy-five horse-drawn wagons passed across.

On 8 August, all the Luftwaffe's available forces were thrown against the Magnushev bridgehead, over which 340 bomber and ground-attack plane overflights were recorded. At 07.10 from the Rogozhek area, a battalion of German infantry, supported by self-propelled howitzers, launched an offensive in a northern direction. Units of the 57th Guards Rifle Division were forced to retreat. At 15.00, after another air attack, another strike group with fifteen tanks attacked the positions of the 39th Guards Rifle Division. By evening, the Germans managed to capture the village of Zvezhinets and break through to the eastern outskirts of the village of Kozelka. Only in the area of Maryampol and Mikhaluv did the Soviet infantry manage to hold their positions. But at 21.30, having regrouped, one German strike group resumed the attack and occupied the whole of Mikhaluv, while another from the village of Khodkovskaya Volya crossed the Radomka River and attacked the village of Khodkov. And by morning, the Germans had captured Zenkov and Grabovskaya Volya, significantly reducing the size of the bridgehead.

On the night of 8–9 August, He 111 bombers hit the Magnushev bridgehead several times. In the afternoon, massive air attacks continued. Groups of twelve to twenty-five He 111s and Ju 87s escorted by fighters bombed and shelled positions of the 8th Guards Army and ferry crossing across the Vistula several times. The southern bridgehead was shelled intensively by German howitzers. At 16.00 on 8 August, two sections of the newly erected bridge over the Vistula were damaged by explosions. During the night, engineer battalions heroically restored the bridge. However, as soon as it was light, the whistle of 150mm shells was heard again, after which powerful explosions shook the river, tearing out whole pieces of the bridge. Traffic on it was paralysed until the next night. In the following days, the bridge was regularly damaged by artillery. In addition, the Germans launched floating mines with a clockwork mechanism along the river.

On the night of 9–10 August, marker bombs were continuously dropped over the Magnushev bridgehead, and it was as bright as day in the trenches and villages occupied by Soviet soldiers. The roar of planes bombing the Vistula crossings was heard continuously in the sky, complemented by the roar of anti-aircraft batteries firing on both banks of the river. As a result of the bomb attacks, a ferry and a 140-ton barge were sunk, a pontoon bridge was destroyed, and access roads were severely damaged.

From dawn until 18.05 on 10 August, the Luftwaffe bombed the bridgehead and ferry crossing almost continuously, with air attacks by large groups of ground-attack planes and bombers alternating with pinpoint strikes by single aircraft. Soviet air surveillance posts (VNOS) recorded almost 600 overflights of German aircraft during this time. At 07.15, after a heavy artillery bombardment, a strike group consisting of thirty tanks and self-propelled guns launched the first attack. It was followed by a second attack at 08.00, and a third attack at 08.30. Then there was a lull, and at 19.30 after another Stuka strike on Soviet positions, the Germans launched the most powerful offensive from several directions at once. The main role in it was played by the Luftwaffe 'Hermann Göring' division.

Until that day, the crossings of the Vistula River were practically not covered by anti-aircraft artillery. Only on 10 August, were batteries of three anti-aircraft artillery regiments from the 24th Anti-Aircraft Artillery Division (ZenAD) stationed in the Tarnov area on both banks.

On the morning of 12 August, a thick fog descended over the Vistula, which had completely dissipated only by lunchtime. At 13.40, Stukas launched another air attack. As soon as the smoke and dust from the explosions cleared, the strike group consisting of an infantry battalion and eleven tanks again rushed to the offensive against the positions of the 79th Guards Rifle Division. The Germans managed to capture the villages of Dembnyak and Grabina. In the late afternoon, the main targets of the air attacks were the bridge over the Vistula. At 14.30, engineering units completed the construction of a wooden bridge across the river west of Tarnow. But at 17.25 the first group of Ju 87s approached the Vistula, and then they began to take turns diving on to the bridge. After a while, a second group of bombers appeared, followed by a third. Anti-aircraft batteries were firing furiously, and the sky above the bridge was coloured with hundreds of black clouds from explosions. Several bombs fell near the bridge, its structures swayed from the explosions, but resisted. Finally, at 19.00, the largest group of Stukas appeared. Despite powerful fire from the ground, their pilots did not turn off course and dived directly on to the bridge, after which they brought the planes out of their dives over the water itself. This time, the Germans managed to achieve several direct hits at once and destroy three sections of the bridge out of six.

As it turned out, the events of 10–12 August were the culmination of the battle for the Magnushev bridgehead. Although the Germans failed to eliminate it, with their fierce attacks they exhausted the units of the 8th Guards Army, did not allow them to expand their positions and bought time to build a new defensive line. The Germans were greatly helped by nature. In early August, a strong flood began on the Vistula, during which the water level in the river rose significantly. The area around the bridgehead was covered with lowlands and swampy floodplains, which led to the flooding of roads and entrances to the ferry crossing and heavy mud.

On 15 August, Rokossovsky ordered the 8th Guards and 69th Army to prepare a new offensive against the city of Radom in order to combine both bridgeheads into one and create conditions for a further advance into Poland. For this purpose, units of the 1st Polish Army and the 16th Tank Corps were transferred to the Magnushev bridgehead. However, the attacks that began on 19 August led only to local successes, and on 21 August the Germans counter-attacked General Chuikov's army and drove it back to its original positions. The fighting continued with varying success until the end of the month. Similarly, all attempts by the 69th Army to expand its bridgehead in a western direction also choked.

The losses of the 8th Guards Army in August amounted to more than 24,000 men including 4,624 killed and 19,000 wounded. This is despite the fact that by the beginning of the month its combat strength numbered about 72,000. The 69th Army lost more than 12,000 people during the same period, including 3,149 killed and missing. Similarly, the Red Army failed to expand the bridgehead captured in early August in the Baranuv area. By autumn, the Vistula front had stabilised.

It remains to add that the massive air attacks against the Magnushev and Pulavy bridgeheads, during which the Luftwaffe achieved some success, became the last operation of the Second World War in which the old He 111 and Ju 87 bombers were used in a major way. At the end of August, the process of reorganising most of the Kampfgeschwader bomber units into fighter staffel began.

## Godzina 'W'

Due to the slow development of the offensive on Warsaw from the east, Stalin ordered the 2nd Tank Army to be sent from the south-east. On 27 July, its commander, Major General Alexei Radzievsky, was ordered to move along the Lublin–Warsaw highway in order to seize the Praga suburb of the Polish capital and then the crossings over the Narew River, north of the city. The situation seemed to favour a breakthrough. The German divisions that retreated to the west bank after the fall of Lublin expected a further offensive by Soviet tanks bypassing Warsaw from the south, and the shortest path to the capital from the south-east was practically open. By the beginning of this raid, the 2nd Tank

Army had almost 500 tanks and self-propelled artillery pieces in its composition

On 30 July, the 103rd Tank Brigade broke into Radzymin, and by the morning of the next day Minsk-Mazowiecki was occupied. These cities were located north-east and east of Warsaw respectively. Meanwhile, the 3rd Tank Corps was already moving directly towards Warsaw and the estimated time for reaching the eastern outskirts was indicated as 12.00–13.00. But in the evening of that day, two key events occurred simultaneously. The underground headquarters of Armia Krajowa in Warsaw learned from their agents that Russian tanks were already on the way to the city. After that, it decided to launch a long-planned uprising.

In short, the plan was as follows. Approximately twelve hours before the approach of the Red Army, rebel detachments were to simultaneously attack buildings and neighbourhoods occupied by the Germans, then establish control over the city for three to four days, after which they created conditions for the air landing of the 1st Polish Parachute Brigade from England. They would then announce the transfer of power into the hands of the emigrant government headed by Tadeusz Komorowski. It all looked like a repeat of the Vilnius and Lviv scenarios, only on a larger scale. The uprising was supposed to begin exactly one day after the decision was made, at 'Godzina W' ('Hour In' – from the Polish wybuch, 'explosion'). That is, at 17.00 on 1 August.

At about the same time that Komorowski was giving his fateful order, a group of four German panzer divisions secretly concentrated in the forests east of Warsaw began a counteroffensive against Radzievsky's 2nd Tank Army. The most formidable force was the Luftwaffe's 1st Fallschirm-Panzer Division Hermann Göring. From 1943 to the first half of 1944, this elite unit, subordinated to the Reichsmarschall personally, fought in Italy and in many cases saved the situation there. On 15 July, the division commander, General Wilhelm Schmaltz, received an unexpected order to urgently move to the Eastern Front. At the same time, Göring promised Hitler that his elite division would quickly correct the critical situation on the Vistula, which, in his opinion, was the result of 'military betrayal'. The Reichsmarschall was referring to the recent assassination attempt on the Führer.

On 1 August, Radzievsky ordered his tankers to move to a circular defence and wait for the infantry to approach. But the next day, the Germans knocked out the 103rd Tank Brigade from Radzimin, and on the morning of 3 August, the Tigers and Panthers literally hit the Russians from all sides – from the west, from the north and from the east. A forest tank battle unfolded. Having suffered heavy losses, the 3rd Tank

Corps was forced to break out of the pocket, abandoning equipment and artillery pieces. This is how the combat magazine of the 50th Tank Brigade described these events: 'The enemy pulled up a large number of anti-tank guns, put them on the flanks, covered by machine gunners. Infantry regiments are encircling our tanks from all sides. Our tanks and anti-tank guns are repelling the onslaught of the enemy. At the same time, they organise an exit from the pocket. At 21.30, two red flares were fired, the infantry went on the attack. Every tank coming out is hit by enemy artillery.'

It was the 50th Tank Brigade that suffered the greatest losses in this battle. After leaving the forest near Volomin, only twenty-three tanks and one artillery piece remained in its inventory. Brigade commander Major Isaac Fundovny, commander of the 51st Tank Brigade, Hero of the Soviet Union Colonel Semyon Mirvoda and 120 soldiers were missing. Both Mirvoda and Fundovny were experienced tankers who had been fighting since 1941. And if the fate of the first one subsequently became clear (he died on 6 August while trying to cross the front line), then the fate of Fundovny is still not known for certain.

In total, during the two weeks of the offensive, the 2nd Tank Army irretrievably lost 243 tanks (including 175 T-34s and 48 Shermans), 197 vehicles, 102 motorcycles, 11 armoured vehicles and 53 artillery pieces. A significant proportion of the armoured vehicles were damaged or abandoned on the road due to technical malfunctions. The army's losses amounted to 4,484 men. An important point is that the Soviet air force, due to the reasons described above (a lack of fuel and difficulties with relocation to new air bases), could not provide serious support to either its tankers or the rebellious Poles and, moreover, overlooked the concentration of 300 German tanks in the forest. In addition, Russian intelligence did not know that the Germans had created a heavily fortified defensive strip on the eastern bank of the Vistula.

However, the rebels themselves in Warsaw had no way back. By 4 August, Armia Krajowa and the organisations cooperating with it had managed to capture almost the entire central part of Warsaw and some suburbs. However, the operational plan was still not executed. The resistance fighters were unable to occupy such key facilities as the citadel in the northern part of the city, the Warsaw University building complex, the royal Palace in the Old Town, Danzig railway station, the SS barracks on Narutovich Square, the main water pumping station, the Gensyuvka concentration camp, etc. But the main failure was the fact that the Germans retained control of the bridges over the Vistula. At the same time, many detachments of Poles, unable to complete their tasks, retreated to the surrounding forests.

However, the ranks of the rebels were quickly replenished by those who joined them after a speech made at the start of the uprising: emigrants who settled in Warsaw before the war, fugitives from numerous concentration and labour camps, deserters from German auxiliary units, etc. Even citizens of Australia, South Africa and Nigeria could be found in the AK units! Numerous armoury workshops worked in the basements of houses, which produced not only small arms, but also flamethrowers, grenades and mines.

On 7–8 August, the German garrison, which had recovered from the first shock and had received reinforcements by that time, began the first raids, which were accompanied by savage massacres and atrocities. In parallel, artillery shelling and bombing of the neighbourhoods occupied by Armia Krajowa began. However, they did not bring the expected effect. The most vulnerable objects of the rebels (headquarters, armoury workshops, hospitals and food warehouses) were located either in the basements of ancient buildings or in the city sewers, whose branched tunnels and shafts became the main form of communication and at the same time a reliable shelter from bombs and shells.

Chapter 9

# WASHING AWAY THE ROMANIAN SHAME

While the fierce battle continued on the Vistula, where the Wehrmacht command had transferred all its reserves, another collapse for the German army broke out in the south. Shortly after the start of the Soviet offensive in Belarus, the headquarters of Army Group South Ukraine began to fear a strike by the Red Army in its sector. Generaloberst Schörner watched with dismay as all the best divisions were withdrawn from him one by one and sent north to plug the gaps in the crumbling front. The German 6th and 8th Armies were gradually losing all their reserves, and the morale of the Romanians watching this, already extremely tired of the hopeless war, was falling exponentially. However, Hitler relieved Schörner of these worries by appointing him commander of Army Group North on 25 July.

The leaky Romanian inheritance went to Generaloberst Johannes Friessner. The Führer considered this general to be another specialist in 'stubborn defence'. Arriving in Romania, Friessner quickly became convinced that Army Group Southern Ukraine was in a deplorable state, while the forces of the Red Army opposing it were strengthening constantly.

German pilot Paul Langer, from the bomber group I./KG4 (based in Romania for a long time), compiled a visual description of how poor this backward country was, which entered the war for the sake of conquering new territories in the east. The pilots and technical staff lived in the primitive mud huts of poor local peasants. While sleeping, they were constantly 'attacked' by fleas and bedbugs, and they had to lie on empty bomb crates, from which the Germans made bunk beds. Lindner wrote: 'The lifestyle of poor corn and grape farmers in Romania was probably the most primitive one could imagine at that

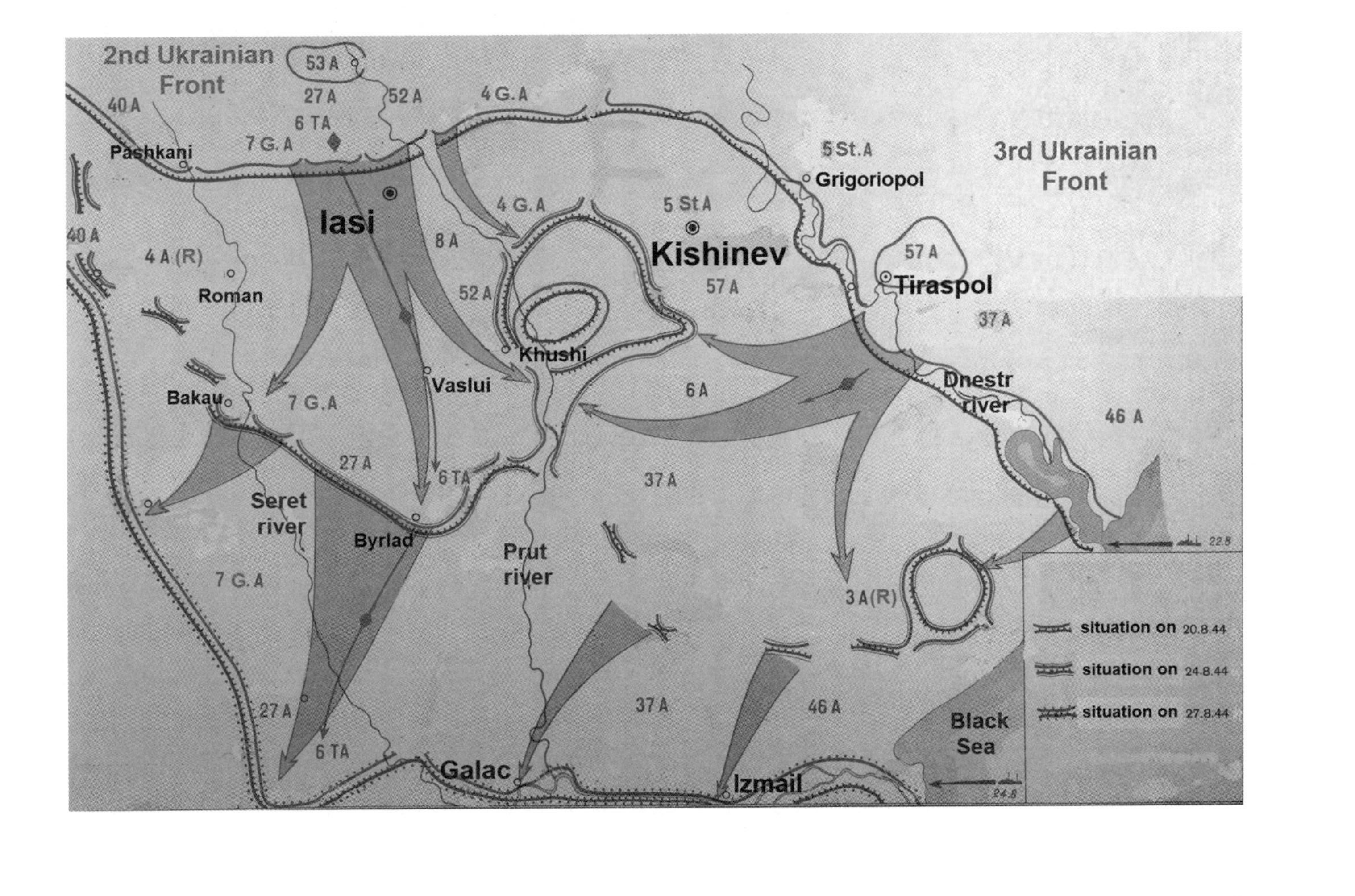
2nd Ukrainian Front
53 A
27 A
52 A
4 G.A
40 A
6 TA
7 G.A
Pashkani
Iasi
8 A
4 G.A
5 St A
5 St.A
Grigoriopol
3rd Ukrainian Front
40 A
4 A (R)
Roman
52 A
Kishinev
57 A
57 A
Tiraspol
37 A
Khushi
Vaslui
Bakau
7 G.A
6 A
Dnestr river
46 A
27 A
6 TA
37 A
Seret river
Byrlad
Prut river
22.8
7 G.A
3 A(R)
situation on 20.8.44
situation on 24.8.44
situation on 27.8.44
27 A
37 A
46 A
Black Sea
6 TA
Galac
Izmail
24.8

time. They lived in small adobe houses built of untreated acacia wood. The walls were made of woven branches smeared with clay. The floor consisted of a mixture of clay, cow dung and sand, and the roof was covered with straw, reeds or wooden tiles. There was a raised veranda in front of the house, where the whole family slept on summer nights. The sleepers wrapped themselves in home-made carpets or blankets. Romanian peasants had a barn directly adjacent to the house, covered with reeds or straw, which usually contained a cow and several sheep. There was an open clay hearth in the courtyard, in the centre of which was a round recess in which stood a corn pot. Empty ears of corn, rice wood, dry cane or corn straw served as fuel. In winter, a large "sleeping stove" was used for cooking and heating the premises, which was located in a large room … The peasants' equipment consisted of a primitive plough made of wood and upholstered with iron. Semicircular corn hoes were used as farmers' hand tools. The main food of the Romanians was various types of corn porridge, which was cooked from morning to evening by peasant farmers.'

It is not surprising that the Romanian soldiers (mostly those 'corn farmers') were engaged in continuous looting. According to the author's grandmother, who lived for two years under occupation in Ukraine, Romanians stole from houses and loaded into their carts everything they could get their hands on, including iron cups, dirty rags and torn towels! When the Romanian army entered the war, Marshal Antonescu promised the people that due to new conquests the country would be fabulously enriched, and an endless stream of trophies would flow from the east into the country. In fact, the peasants began to live even poorer, and meat and sausage became real delicacies. Now, in August 1944, the Red Army stood on the threshold, and no one had any illusions about the future prospects.

German intelligence and Marshal Antonescu had heard rumours that a military coup was brewing in the country. Under these conditions, the frightened dictator flew to the Wolf's Lair on 4 August, which was already almost at the front line. Hitler tried to reassure his ally by telling him about the 'emerging exhaustion' of the enemy, about the 'miracle weapons' that would change the course of the war and promised that the Germans would defend Romania as their homeland. Antonescu told Hitler: 'I have given the order to mobilise the entire nation. We are going through an all-out war, and no one should spare their lives.' That was the last time the dictators saw each other.

By mid-August, the Russians had concentrated 1.3 million soldiers, 16,000 artillery pieces and 1,800 tanks and self-propelled guns against the weakened Friessner divisions. The 5th and 17th Air Armies consisted of 1,900 aircraft, including 731 Il-2s, 743 fighters, 121 bombers, 193 night bombers (Po-2s[1] and R-5s) and 86 artillery fire spotter aircraft and reconnaissance aircraft. The total advantage in the air allowed the Soviets to launch an offensive with powerful air attacks.

On the first day of the offensive – 20 August – Soviet aircraft carried out 3,220 sorties, of which about half, 1,546, fell to Il-2s. In parallel, the Russians launched a powerful artillery attack on the German and Romanian defences. Russian gunner Ivan Novokhatsky recalled: 'When we moved forward, the area was black to a depth of about ten kilometres. The enemy's defences were practically destroyed. Enemy trenches, dug to their full height, turned into shallow ditches, no more than knee-deep. The dugouts were destroyed. Sometimes there were miraculously surviving dugouts, but the enemy soldiers who were in them were dead, although there were no signs of wounds. Death occurred from high air pressure after shell explosions and suffocation.'

This is how Friessner described these events in his memoirs: 'In the early morning, the roar of volleys from thousands of guns heralded the beginning of the decisive battle for Romania. After the strongest one-and-a-half-hour artillery preparation, the Soviet infantry, supported by tanks, went on the offensive, first in the Iasi area, and then in the Dniester sector of the front. Many of the enemy's rifle divisions were reduced to shock wedges. A huge amount of manpower and equipment allowed the Soviets, albeit with heavy losses, to break through our front in many areas. However, the reason for this relatively rapid success is not the numerical superiority of the enemy, but above all the insufficient resistance and unreliability of many Romanian formations.' This was the last occasion of many when the Germans blamed the Romanians for the defeat (it was the same in Stalingrad).

Meanwhile, Soviet naval aircraft dealt a crushing blow to the German Black Sea Fleet, concentrated in Constanta. At 11.00, an armada of 106 Il-4s, Douglas A-20s and Pe-2 bombers appeared over the harbour, accompanied by seventy-seven fighters. A total of 234 bombs were dropped on the target, which fell surprisingly accurately. According to Soviet information, more than forty ships were destroyed. In fact, thirty-eight different ships and vessels were sunk and severely damaged in Constanta, including three submarines (*U-9*, *U-18* and *U-24*), nine torpedo boats, three patrol ships, three minesweepers, five patrol and rescue boats.

---

1 On 30 July 1944, aircraft designer Nikolai Polikarpov died. Soon after, the U-2 was renamed the Po-2.

The huge German–Romanian fleet on the Black Sea, mainly consisting of small ships, boats, landing barges, lighters and tugs, had been annoying the Russians for several years. It constantly prevented them from landing troops and supplying their garrisons, and it ensured that the Germans held the Kuban bridgehead and the Crimea for a long time. And now all this motley flotilla had been driven to the western coast of the Black Sea and trapped.

The joint offensive of the 2nd and 3rd Ukrainian Fronts was led by Generals Rodion Malinovsky and Fedor Tolbukhin. By the end of the second day of the operation, they managed to surround the main forces of the German 6th Army in the Leuseni area, as well as block most of the Romanian 3rd Army on the Black Sea coast. On 22 August, an artillery salute was traditionally fired in Moscow from 240 anti-aircraft guns, which fired a total of twenty volleys. By the end of 24 August, Soviet troops had advanced 130–140km, encircling eighteen enemy divisions. Two days later, the entire territory of Moldova was completely liberated, and the way to Bucharest was opened.

Realising that further war with the Soviet Union had lost its meaning, the Romanian conspirators, led by King Mihai I, decided to launch a long-planned military coup. On the afternoon of 23 August, dictator Ion Antonescu was summoned to the Royal Palace in Bucharest 'to report on the current situation' and immediately arrested. A new government was immediately formed, which quickly agreed with Moscow on a ceasefire. At the same time, German troops stationed in Romania were asked to leave its territory.

It is clear that the Romanian military, who had fought side by side with the Germans for three years, found themselves in a somewhat unpleasant situation, but Hitler himself eased their conscience. He heard about the incident at 23.00 from Friessner. After listening to the latest news, the Führer ordered: 'Immediately eliminate the clique of traitors and create a new government!' In addition, Hitler hinted at the possibility of bombing Bucharest as an 'additional argument'.

At the same time, anti-aircraft units under the leadership of the commander of the Luftwaffe forces in Romania, General Gerstenberger, who occupied positions in the Ploieşti area, 50–60km north of the Romanian capital, were ordered to capture Bucharest. Friessner himself delayed the start of decisive action in every possible way, fearing that if the Romanians declared war on Germany, German troops, as well as rear institutions, would find themselves in a very difficult situation. He later recalled: 'I ordered my chief of Staff, General Grolmann, to try again to draw the attention of the headquarters of the Supreme Command to the reservation in the communique of the new Bucharest government, which was distinguished by loyalty and allowed all German troops to withdraw unhindered from Romania. At the same time, I asked you to pay attention to the fact that in the event of our bombing of the Romanian capital, Romanian troops will inevitably begin military operations against all German troops and rear institutions – hospitals, ammunition depots, military equipment and food depots. In order to delay the execution of the bombing order, I gave the order to the 4th Air Fleet to first find out the prerequisites for this.'

However, Hitler did not wait. Realising that Friessner was at a loss, on the evening of 24 August he directly addressed Göring and ordered him to launch an air strike on the government quarter of Bucharest.

Incidentally, these events were in many ways a repetition of the past for Romanians. Something similar had already happened exactly twenty-eight years before the events described. On 14 August 1916, Romania entered the First World War on the side of the Entente. This happened against the background of the Entente's military successes, including the 'Brusilov Breakthrough' – a relatively successful offensive by Russian troops on the South-western Front. In Romania itself, the decision of King Ferdinand I caused national rejoicing, thousands of people filled the streets and squares, wore portraits of the monarch and sang patriotic songs. And in the Entente countries, in general, this insignificant event of Romania's joining them (due to a general feeling of hopelessness and lack of good news) was perceived as a symbol of the coming turning point in the war. In Bucharest, this celebration lasted until 25 August, when the city was suddenly shaken by powerful explosions. Three German Zeppelins carried out the first air attack on the city, dropping high-explosive bombs on the royal palace and the government quarter and simultaneously killing many civilians. The bombing then continued for several days, and the terrifying sight of the airships hovering over the capital, reminiscent of scenes from fantasy books like H.G. Wells' *The War of the Worlds*, caused unimaginable horror and panic among the population. And so, it all happened again in August 1944, and almost on the same date!

The first on the night of 24–25 August, the raid on Bucharest was carried out by He 111s of the 'railway hunters' from 14.(Eis)/KG27. After covering a distance of 750km from their airfield near Krakow, they dropped bombs on the building of the Romanian government (Haus des Ministerprasidenten), located in the city centre. Then in the morning, He 111 bombers from I./KG4 and Stukas from I./SG2 carried out a second air attack. The residential part of the palace of Mihai I was completely destroyed, as was the government building. However, the king and his ministers, apparently expecting such a reaction from

Hitler, fled the capital in advance. In response to this hooliganism, Romania declared war on Germany on 25 August and the situation got completely out of control. On the night of 27 August, the new government issued an address to the people. 'The war is coming to an end. Germany is collapsing. All Hitler's armies are being defeated. The victory of the allies is obvious. Considering this situation and taking into account the Molotov statement approved by President Roosevelt and Prime Minister Churchill, which guaranteed the sovereignty of Romania and the independence of our state, we made it possible for our country not to appear at the peace conference among the defeated states with the prospect of complete defeat ... We must wash away the shameful traces of cooperation with Hitler from our face in order to embark on a new path that will ensure a secure future for us,' it said.

In addition to 'washing away the shame' and other moral incentives, Stalin provided Romanians with material and patriotic motivation: the retaking of Transylvania. This historic province had been annexed by Hungary with Hitler's approval in 1940.

The German troops had to hastily flee through the mountain passes towards Hungary and create a new line of defence there. Not everyone escaped as 56,000 men, including fourteen generals and 1,200 officers, were captured by their former allies.

The German Black Sea Fleet suffered no less a disaster. At the end of August, most of the ships that had survived the air attacks were evacuated to the Bulgarian port of Varna, where about seventy vessels were abandoned or sunk during 29–30 August, including thirty high-speed landing barges, twenty patrol ships and eleven minesweepers. Part of the fleet surrendered in the Izmail and Galatz area. Several dozen more ships were trying to break through the Danube into Serbia in groups and singly, and it was a very long and winding route of several hundred kilometres that passed close to the Romanian capital, then along the Bulgarian border. Many ships and other vessels were shot at by artillery from the coast, captured by the Romanians and the advancing Red Army. For example, on the evening of 30 August, south of Bucharest, the Romanian monitor *Bessarabia* boarded the German tugboat *Kreuzenstein*, the river tug *Kronburg*, the ferry DDSG *Semering* and the oil barge *Galaz*. On the same day, in Giurgiu (50km south of Bucharest), the Romanians captured the river steamer *Berlin*, the tugs *Bremen* and *Wotje*, two patrol boats, the Italian submarines *SV-1*, *CB-2*, CB-3 and CB-4, and three lighters. And on 6–7 September, in the Prahovo area (in south-western Romania), an entire flotilla consisting of fourteen high-speed landing barges, ten tugboats, three minesweeper boats and several more steamships were destroyed.

On 14 September, in the area of Brza Palanka (160km south-east of Belgrade), as a result of air attacks, seven high-speed barges were sunk at once, which had previously managed to travel 1,500km along the river. As a result, only the pitiful remnants of the former huge Black Sea Fleet were able to reach the territory that remained under the control of the Wehrmacht.

This disaster coincided with Finland's withdrawal from the war. The Hitler coalition had begun to rapidly collapse.

Chapter 10

# THE LONG ROAD TO THE DUNES

The situation in the northern sector of the Eastern Front was also developing dramatically. On 4 July 1944, after the capture of Rezekne and Daugavpils (the eastern part of Latvia), the troops of the 2nd Baltic Front under the command of General Andrei Yeremenko were tasked with advancing in the general direction towards the capital of Latvia. The city was intended to be liberated by 10 August.

On 17 July, the troops of the 3rd Baltic Front under the command of General Ivan Maslennikov went on the offensive to the north. They were successful, and on 23 July the Russians liberated Pskov. Soon they reached the territory of Estonia. Then the Leningrad Front struck its blow. Narva was liberated on 30 July. Yeremenko's offensive on Riga started on 1 August and initially developed quite successfully (although not at all according to plan). On 13 August, after a fierce assault, the city of Madona, located 120km from Riga, was captured. By this time, the Wehrmacht troops in neighbouring Belarus were almost defeated, Soviet troops reached the Vistula, and it seemed that soon Army Group North would simply be dumped into the Baltic Sea.

After a short respite, the offensive resumed on 17 August. Yeremenko placed special hopes on the 5th Tank Corps under the command of Colonel Mikhail Sakhno. As soon as the first German line of defence was breached, this unit was thrown into a deep breakthrough into the enemy's rear. On 19 August, the corps, was rapidly advancing around Lake Kala and smashing the rear units and baggage trains of the Germans. At 14.30 it captured the crossings over the Ogre River, after which it crossed it. At 17.30 Russian tanks broke into the town of Ergli and captured the railway station of the same name, which was a major hub. 'A passenger train that has just arrived from Riga, several military trains and warehouses

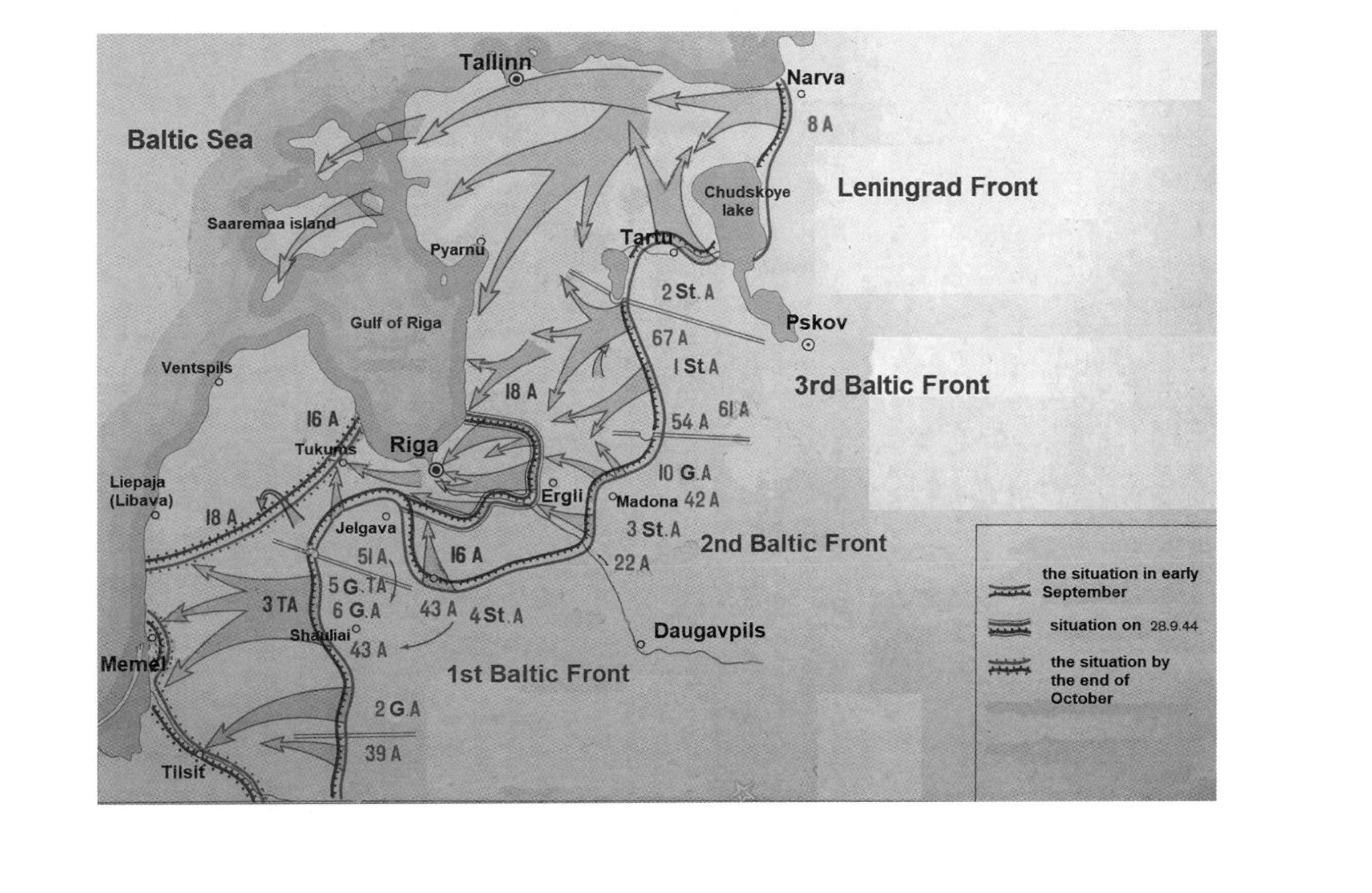

Tallinn
Narva
Baltic Sea
8 A
Leningrad Front
Chudskoye lake
Saaremaa island
Pyarnu
Tartu
2 St. A
Pskov
Gulf of Riga
67 A
1 St A
Ventspils
18 A
3rd Baltic Front
61 A
16 A
54 A
Tukums
Riga
Liepaja (Libava)
10 G.A
Ergli
Madona
42 A
18 A
Jelgava
3 St. A
2nd Baltic Front
51 A
16 A
22 A
5 G. TA
3 TA
6 G.A
43 A
4 St. A
Shauliai
43 A
Daugavpils
Memel
1st Baltic Front
2 G.A
39 A
Tilsit
the situation in early September
situation on 28.9.44
the situation by the end of October

with military equipment have been seized at Ergli station,' the journal of military operations of the 2nd Baltic Front reported.

The next day, Yeremenko ordered Sakhno to capture the intersection of 'Tauruna's' roads (It was actually Taurupe) and then advance in the direction of Suntazhi, that is, to Riga. However, these plans turned out to be overly optimistic. By that time, the Germans had transferred reinforcements to the Baltic States. In addition, tanks and motorised infantry had to operate in impassable swamps, where they got bogged down.

As a result, on 20 August, the 2nd Motorised Rifle Battalion of the 5th Motorised Rifle Brigade, advancing in the vanguard under the command of Major Korney Dityuk with forty-five tanks and self-propelled guns was suddenly attacked from the forests and almost defeated. Being subjected to air attacks, the next day the Russians were forced to hastily retreat back to the eastern bank of the Ogre River. 'The fighting in the Ergli area was so heavy that sometimes the attacking units themselves went on the defensive, and sometimes fought with superior enemy forces surrounded,' Yeremenko himself wrote in his memoirs. The Russians were constantly suffering from German air attacks. 'Enemy aircraft throughout the day with Ju 87 aircraft, 24 of them, and Fw 190s, 12–25, bombed our combat formations in the areas of Rauseni, Grude, Ergli ...' in the journal of combat operations of the 5th Tank Corps recorded on 22 August. After the defeat on the Ergli–Taurun road, the main forces of the corps did not participate in the battle, and by 28 August all Yeremenko's units had already gone on the defensive. To the rear of the Germans, the 4th and 6th Companies remained in the forest pocket, as well as a mortar battery of the 2nd Motorised Rifle Battalion under the overall command of the Deputy Chief of Staff of the 5th Motorised Rifle Brigade, Captain Semyon Romanov. On 22 August, he received an order to withdraw these units from pocket in the area of the village of Past. But it was not possible to complete the task since all the escape routes were blocked by German forces, and the breakthrough route from pocket was fired with mortars and machineguns. In addition, according to a hastily drawn-up plan, the breakthrough was supposed to be supported by artillery, but the battery of the only surviving radio had no charge. Therefore, at a crucial moment, it was not possible to contact the brigade headquarters to clarify the coordinates of the targets. Then Romanov, after consulting with his comrades, decided to hide the surviving equipment and fighters in the forest thicket north of Ergli.

Front-line correspondent A.D. Kochetkov wrote: 'The Nazis did not climb into the thicket, and the battalion managed to break away from its pursuers. In the deep forest, among the spreading firs and pines, a camp was equipped: huts were built, they were covered with fir twigs, the floors were covered with moss. And a sharp-sighted, sensitive life, like that of hunters, began. It was necessary to observe the enemy, identify his weaknesses, gather strength. It was necessary to take care of the weapons.'

The Russian soldiers, who became partisans for a while, were lucky: among them was 22-year-old scout, Gennady Myakshin. He fought in a partisan unit for more than two years, where he gained extensive experience of such actions. After the liberation of the Pskov region in July 1944, Myakshin joined the ranks of the 5th Motorised Rifle Brigade, and a month and a half later he was again surrounded by forests ... At a critical moment, the veterans did not lose their heads and began to act according to the situation. The adventurous raid in the German rear lasted for sixteen days, while the battalion repeatedly attacked enemy units and rear offices. For example, on 1 September, an attack was carried out on the headquarters of the 329th German Infantry Division in which several prisoners were captured. In addition, several disparate groups of soldiers from other units were discovered and attached to the battalion. At the same time, the scouts and commanders were preparing for a breakthrough, studying the terrain and the system of German code signals.

After careful reconnaissance, it was possible to identify the most poorly covered area in the German defence – the forest north of Lake Yumurda. They decided to go for a breakthrough shortly before dawn, in order to pass through enemy positions in the dark, and go out to their own at dawn. At the same time, the operation took place in the spirit of adventure films about the war. This is how the front-line correspondent Kochetkov described it: 'On the evening of September 6, the battalion left the camp. It was already quite dark. It was raining. The swampy soil squelched underfoot. Having covered 9 kilometres during the night, the battalion reached the highway – the place of the breakthrough. Major Dityuk and Captain Romanov, with several soldiers, moved to the road and, hiding in a ditch, began to observe. A little ahead there were enemy dugouts, 100–150 metres apart from each other. Further behind them was the enemy's defensive line. Despite the early hour, vehicles and horse-drawn carts were moving along the road – life went on as usual. As planned, our soldiers, dressed in German raincoats, with German machine guns and red flashlights, came out on the highway. They stopped traffic from both directions. And at the same moment, Captain Romanov and other fighters crossed the road. And suddenly a German sentry shouted: "Stop!" Grenades flew into the dugouts. Two of them were immediately blown up, while others, neighbouring ones, were hit with machine guns. Screams were heard, a commotion began – it was the Nazis running in. Meanwhile, the battalion was rushing to no man's land.'

The group managed not only to break through the German positions, but also to take out twenty-three wounded, and drag away twelve captured Germans. On the same day, Yeremenko, who had learned about the incredible details of the raid, arrived at the scene. On his instructions, Major Dityuk, Captain Romanov, and scouts Myakshin and Mashkov were immediately presented with the title of Hero of the Soviet Union. However, the operation itself actually failed without reaching its goal.

Meanwhile, the 3rd Baltic Front began its offensive on 10 August. After heavy fighting, the Soviet troops managed to advance to Tartu. Despite the threat of encirclement, Hitler demanded that the commander of Army Group North, Ferdinand Schörner, hold the Baltic region at all costs. Having regrouped its forces and received reinforcements, on 14 September the Red Army launched a new offensive from several directions at once. This time Yeremenko's troops were successful. Two days later, in the face of another collapse, Schörner barely managed to persuade Hitler to allow a retreat from Estonia. Within ten days, the 18th Army reached Riga. By the end of the month, Schörner had managed to stop the Red Army's advance towards that city.

But on 5 October, the 1st Baltic Front under the command of Ivan Baghramyan went on the offensive. The Russians attacked the 3rd Panzer Army of General Erhard Raus with superior forces. As soon as the first line of defence was breached, Baghramyan led the 5th Guards Tank Army of General Vasily Volsky into the breakthrough. By the beginning of the operation, there were 440 tanks and self-propelled guns. By this time, the Soviets had accumulated a lot of experience in such blitzkrieg raids and now they were cruelly taking revenge on the Wehrmacht for the defeats of 1941–42. Baghramyan's tankers simply drove around the villages where the Germans were sitting, avoided major battles and constantly moved forward. In three days, they managed to advance 90km. On 8 October, Raus was forced to bring his best reserve, the Grossdeutschland Division, into battle. In addition, the 58th Infantry Division was quickly delivered from Riga to this sector. However, these desperate measures could no longer save the situation. At 14.00 on 10 October, the first T-34 tanks left for the Baltic Sea coast near Memel (now Klaipėda). The remnants of the defeated German divisions fled in panic to this city and only the timely arrival of the German heavy cruiser *Prinz Eugen* prevented its fall. On

11 October, this ship approached the harbour of Memel and opened fire at the advancing Russians with its eight 203mm guns. Firing 700 shells in two days, the cruiser allowed the German soldiers to gain a foothold on the defensive perimeter.

This operation was another stunning success of the Red Army. Moreover, this time their losses turned out to be minimal. For example, the 5th Guards Tank Army lost eighty tanks and self-propelled guns, and forty-nine more were damaged. Soon the Russians expanded the corridor, finally cutting off Army Group North in Courland.

Note that in 1944, the Russians very quickly repaired damaged and broken tanks and put them back into operation. When historians talk about the losses of armoured vehicles of the Red Army and the production of tanks in factories, they do not take into account that tanks were not disposable products. Many T-34s, KV-1s and IS-2s were used several times. Due to their simple and cheap design, Russian tanks, unlike German ones, were easily repaired in the field. Those tanks that could not be repaired in army workshops were sent by train to the deep rear. There, in different cities of the country, there were about a dozen repair bases. The scale of their productivity is amazing. Suffice it to say that even a small repair base No. 6 (Bogorodsky Mechanical Plant), in the Gorky region, repaired 3,500 T-34 tanks! This is despite the fact that most of the workers at this plant were women and teenagers.

## Chapter 11

# THE FIERY SKY OF WARSAW

In mid-August, having pulled up its main forces, the Red Army launched a new offensive against Warsaw. Units of the 70th Army, despite fierce German resistance, approached the town of Tłuszcz, north-east of the Polish capital. On 18 August, the 1st Belorussian Front launched a decisive offensive. The main attack was carried out on the right flank by the forces of the 65th and 70th Armies in order to bypass the city from the north, and the auxiliary one was carried out in the centre by units of the 47th Army. The air force received orders at the new 'H' hour to support the offensive with massive air attacks against German troops and supply lines.

After persistent fighting in early September, the leading Soviet units reached the approaches to Warsaw for the second time. The pilots of Russian fighters were surprised to see that the Germans' Stukas, instead of bombing the approaching Red Army, were dropping bombs on their own territory, on Warsaw, every day. 'Apparently, Polish rebels are fighting German troops in some quarters, holding certain areas of the city in their hands,' the intelligence summary of the 16th Air Army said.

On 3–4 September, the 70th, 65th and 47th Armies launched a new offensive north of Warsaw (Serock and Pułtusk) in order to cross the Narew River and enter the rear of the German troops holding the Polish capital. On 5 September, the 16th Air Army carried out 1,064 sorties. The next day, 509 sorties were carried out, and for the first time the Wojsko Polskie Air Force took part in them. The aim of the eight Polish fighters involved was to intercept German aircraft over Warsaw. 'The lack of fuel does not allow the increasing of the power of air attacks, although ground troops need the support of ground-attack planes and fighters,' General Rudenko complained. Then the sharply deteriorated weather intervened in the situation. As for the ground forces, after small initial successes, the offensive again encountered stubborn German defences.

At 11.45 a.m. on 10 September, the most powerful shelling began in the 47th Army sector, which lasted for an hour. When the smoke from the explosions cleared, several ground-attack aircraft formations appeared over the German strongholds around 13.00. After that, the infantry, shouting 'Hurrah', rose to the attack and began to advance towards the suburb of Praga.

Meanwhile, in Warsaw itself, events unfolded according to a dramatic plot. When in August it became clear to the Germans that it would not be possible to quickly suppress the uprising, the Combat Group 'Von dem Bach' (KGr. Von dem Bach) was formed under the command of SS Gruppenführer Erich von dem Bach-Zelewski. This included several assault, infantry, grenadier battalions, SS regiments, volunteer battalions and other troops, including Luftwaffe units. At the same time, a special role was assigned to the Ukrainian units. And it wasn't accidental. Relations between Poles and Ukrainians in the occupied territories were very tense. Ukrainians fiercely hated the Poles for oppression during the era of the Second Polish Republic (II Rzeczpospolita) of 1921–39 and considered Western Ukraine, Volhynia and Galicia to be native Ukrainian territory. Poles dreamed of returning these provinces to Poland and hated Ukrainians for their cooperation with the Germans. Thousands of Poles joined the ranks of Armia Krajowa to fight against Ukrainian nationalists.

The first massacre took place in January 1943 in Galicia. Poles killed 400 representatives of the rural Ukrainian intelligensia and clergy and 2,000 civilians, and several thousand more became refugees. The massacres were accompanied by robberies and rapes. In response, Ukrainian nationalists began the massacre of Poles in Volhynia (south of the Pripyat marshes). The first act of genocide was the destruction of the Polish settlement of Paroslya near the city of Sarny on 9 February 1943. Having gathered all the residents in one place, the Ukrainians brutally hacked 173 people to death with axes. In the spring and summer of 1943, the Ukrainian Insurgent Army (UPA) began systematic ethnic cleansing in Volhynia, destroying one Polish village and its population after another. The attempts of the Armia Krajowa to defend these settlements (in order to stake out territory for post-war Poland) only embittered the Ukrainians. The punishers preferred to use pitchforks, axes, shovels, and sledgehammers against civilians, not small arms. Women and children were often burned alive. According to the calculations of modern researchers, there were 50,000–60,000 Polish victims of Ukrainians, while dozens of villages were completely burned down. The Polish partisans killed 3,000 to 15,000 Ukrainians.

Obviously, after such 'successes', the Germans could fully trust the Ukrainians in the fight against Armia Krajowa. Even before the uprising began, two police companies from the 14th Grenadier Division 'Galicia' were in Warsaw, and one of the prisons was also guarded by Ukrainians. These detachments took part in the unfolding massacre from the very beginning. Soon, the 34th Police Regiment (it included two German–Ukrainian battalions), the Volyn Legion of 400 people, and several Ukrainian 'Cossack' detachments from the so-called 'Russian Liberation Army' were sent to Varshava. Finally, many Ukrainians served in the SS Dirlewanger Brigade, famous for its incredible brutality.

Since mid-August, KGr. 'Von dem Bach' had begun a methodical assault on the rebellious neighbourhoods. At the end of the month, the leadership of Armia Krajowa came to the conclusion that further retention of all occupied areas was impossible and it decided to retreat from the Old City. The evacuation of this territory, which consisted of narrow streets densely built up with four- to five-storey stone houses, took place at night and ended on 2 September. The rebels also realised that the Red Army was unlikely to cross the Vistula River in the near future, and the prolonged struggle would lead to more major casualties. In turn, the German command realised that the final conquest of the vast city could take months, at the same time it was obvious that the German bridgehead on the eastern bank of the Vistula could fall at any moment.

As a result, on 7 September, Gruppenführer von dem Bach-Zelewski proposed to start negotiations, which were entrusted to General Günther Rohr. Rohr had a rather intelligent appearance, did not belong to the SS and, accordingly, should have aroused greater confidence among the Poles. The next day, a truce was imposed, thanks to which about 20,000 civilians were evacuated from rebel-held neighbourhoods. Rohr promised to grant all AK fighters the status of prisoners of war (previously they were considered 'partisans' and mercilessly shot). However, on 11 September, the Poles learned about the new offensive of the Red Army on the outskirts of Praga, as well as the fact that Polish troops were preparing for the attack. As a result, a split arose in the ranks of the rebels, and further negotiations were disrupted.

After heavy fighting on 13 September, units of the Soviet 47th Army finally broke into Praga. The next day, by lunchtime, the suburb of the Polish capital was liberated. Hastily retreating to the west bank, the Germans were able to blow up only two of the three bridges across the Vistula. Russian soldiers managed to capture the southern bridge in the area of the river harbour in a damaged but usable condition.

If the roar of hundreds of guns and bomb explosions east of Warsaw caused horror and panic for the Germans, then for the soldiers of Armia Krajowa it was rather a soul-warming melody that revived the fading hope of victory. Despite the setbacks, by this point the rebels still controlled about a quarter of the city's territory and occupied four sectors that were isolated from each other. The largest rebel sector was in the central part between the Old Town and the railway hub, while to the south and east of it the Poles defended part of the port warehouses and southern workers' settlements. In the northern part of Warsaw, the area around Lelewela Square and the park were defended in isolation.

On 13 September, several Russian Il-2s flew over rebel-held neighbourhoods and dropped several pennants with letters. They contained instructions to equip platforms for dropping cargo from the air and designate them with triangles of bonfires or lanterns. The next night, Po-2s from the 2nd Guards NBAD and the Wojsko Polskie Air Force made their first sorties to supply the Armia Krajowa. GD-1 soft cargo containers with cartridges were dropped without parachutes from a height of 100m, and GD-2 bags with mortars and automatic weapons were parachuted from a height of 150m.

On the afternoon of 14 September, the fighters of the 6th IAK were assigned for the first time to cover the rebel-occupied areas of Warsaw from the air. The Russian pilots were informed that the Polish people, at the signal of the London emigrant government, had rebelled against the occupiers, but had been deceived and left without any significant outside help. In this regard, after a month and a half of gruelling fighting, the starved rebels turned to the troops of the 1st Belorussian Front for help. The mission to protect rebel neighbourhoods from the air was a failure. Diving Ju 87 bombers carried out six air attacks against the south-eastern part of the city during the day. At the same time, none of the Stukas were detected by the Redut radar station located on the east bank of the Vistula. The solution to this 'invisibility' was soon revealed by the commander of the 273rd IAD, Lieutenant Colonel Nikolai Isaev. On the afternoon of 15 September, Isaev patrolled over Warsaw for a long time in his Bell P-39 and watched what was happening. Thanks to his very sharp eyesight, the pilot saw that four Ju 87s were based at the small Rakow airbase 8km south-west of the city. The Stukas flew to the target at a very low level, then abruptly rose up, dived, dropped bombs on various buildings and left for the base at low level. Immediately after landing, all the planes were so carefully camouflaged that they were practically invisible from above.

On the night of 14–15 September, Po-2 biplanes carried out 295 sorties to supply Armia Krajowa, dropping 495 machine guns, 50 mortars, 7,000 mines, 800,000 rounds of ammunition, 6.3 tons of biscuit and 3,000 cigarettes. Another ninety-six flights were flown by the 1st Aviation Division of Wojsko Polskie, which dropped 8 tons of biscuit on Warsaw. Polish pilots were not trusted to deliver other cargoes. 'Poles should not be allowed to drop weapons, because they are poorly prepared and will throw them in the wrong place,' Rudenko told Colonel Rasskazov, commander of the 9th Guards NBAD, on this occasion.

On the night of 15–16 September, Soviet and Polish aircraft carried out 238 sorties to Warsaw, although the Poles did not drop cargo but bombed German strongholds in the city. Meanwhile, units of the 1st Polish Army crossed the Vistula and captured a small bridgehead on the west bank in the Sekerka area. The air defence of the Soviet troops on the eastern bank of the Vistula was entrusted to the 24th Anti-aircraft Artillery Division. It had eighty-three anti-aircraft guns. On 17 September, the division was subordinated to the 1st Polish Army, and its main task was to protect the only surviving bridge over the Vistula (Koz-Południowy).

On the night of 17–18 September, eighty-seven Po-2s flew to Warsaw, of which six were unable to drop cargo due to a lack of light signals from the ground. The remaining biplanes successfully completed the mission, delivering 102 anti-tank rifles, 400 grenades, 504 mines, 3.5 tons of food, 4 tons of tobacco and other supplies to the rebels. In addition, the crews of light night bombers carried out a particularly important mission to deliver three officers of the intelligence office of the 1st Belorussian Front to the city by parachute. This was necessary for better coordination with Armia Krajowa, including in the problem of cargo delivery and a more accurate understanding of the situation in the city. Prior to that, communication with the rebels was one-sided: daily ground-attack planes Il-2 dropped pennants with letters, to which, obviously, no answers came.

This mission was extremely risky and even suicidal. The scouts had to jump out over the city, most of which was controlled by the enemy, at risk of shelling from the ground, and then parachute among the ruins into the sector where the rebels were located. And even if it could be done safely, there was a reasonable question: how to get back in case the uprising failed? After careful study of the mission, the Po-2 arrived at the drop point (Wilson Square) at dawn, 05.50–06.10. To disguise and disorient the Germans, cargo bags were parachuted from a high altitude at the same time. The scouts themselves jumped from a height of 150m on semi-automatic parachutes. Two of them successfully landed in a given sector, but the third, who jumped out prematurely, went down to no one knows where.

Meanwhile, the Western Allies were also making efforts to support the uprising. Since August, RAF cargo planes, as well as B-24s and Halifaxes from 1586 (Polish) Special Duties Flight, had periodically flown to the city. Back on 14 August, President Roosevelt appealed to Stalin with a request to organise a transit flight of B-17 Flying Fortress bombers to supply Warsaw, followed by a landing on Soviet territory. However, the president received a rather harsh response, which stated that operations to support the rebels were a matter for Great Britain and America. The Soviet government had no right to interfere with them, but British and American aircraft would not be provided with any landing sites.

Stalin still considered the premature uprising to be a British adventure and a violation of existing agreements. The Soviet leader was convinced that the true purpose of the uprising was borne out of a desire to plant representatives of the Polish emigrant government in Warsaw to force Stalin to negotiate with them and bargain over the future eastern Polish border. In a secret telegram addressed to Roosevelt and Churchill, he wrote: 'Sooner or later, the truth about a bunch of criminals who started the Warsaw adventure for the sake of seizing power will become known to everyone. These people exploited the credulity of the Warsaw people, throwing many almost unarmed people under German guns, tanks and aircraft. A situation has arisen where every new day is used not by the Poles for the liberation of Warsaw, but by the Nazis, who are inhumanly exterminating the inhabitants of Warsaw.'

On 30 July, a few hours before the uprising began, the head of the Polish emigrant government, Stanislav Mikolajczyk, visited Moscow. Mikolajczyk first met with British Ambassador to the USSR Archibald Clark Kerr. The diplomat advised him to accept Soviet demands: remove anti-Soviet ministers from the government, agree to Soviet proposals on the border, stop accusing the USSR of shooting captured Polish army officers in Katyn and reach an agreement on the future government of Poland with the Polish National Liberation Committee.

However, instead Mikolajczyk began to bargain with Stalin over the eastern border of Poland. For example, he offered to give him Lviv in exchange for the Polish government stating – falsely as it later turned out – that the Polish officers in Katyn were shot not by Russians, but by Germans! Of course, Stalin came to the conclusion that the fact Mikolajczyk's visit coincided with the beginning of the uprising was not a coincidence but instead was a planned provocation. All this led to the first serious crisis in relations between the Allies in the anti-Hitler coalition. In fact, Mikolajczyk achieved what Hitler dreamed of, hoping for the collapse of the coalition due to internal contradictions. Only on 9 September, after three weeks of negotiations and persistent pressure from Churchill, did Stalin finally agree to a transit flight of American bombers.

Operation Frantic VII took place on 18 September. The headquarters of the Soviet 16th Air Army received advance notification of the upcoming mission, as well as instructions to study it in detail. In this regard, General Rudenko organised an entire operation in the Warsaw area. First, almost all planned ground-attack planes and fighter sorties over the Polish capital and its environs were cancelled. Secondly, the pilots were tasked with recording the tactics of the B-17 Flying Fortresses and the results of their actions in as much detail as possible.

On the morning of 18 September, 107 B-17s from the 95th, 100th and 390th Bomber Groups, as well as 137 P-51 fighters from the 355th FG, took off from British airfields. Having gathered in battle formation, they headed east. Over Pomerania, seventy-three P-51 Mustangs from the escort turned around and headed back to England, while the remaining sixty-four continued their journey together with the Flying Fortresses. At 14.15 Moscow time, the headquarters of the 16th Air Army received a message that a formation of American bombers had passed over the North Sea, crossed the Oder near Stettin and was heading for Warsaw. At 14.40, a pair of La-5 fighters from the 286th IAD took off and headed towards the city, gradually gaining altitude. Five minutes later, Captain Aidarov's Il-2 took off from the headquarters of the 2nd Guards SHAD, on board which was the cinematographer of the Red Army Air Force film group, Major L.B. Mazrukho. Accompanied by four Yak-1s, he flew to Warsaw, keeping to an altitude of 500m. Another movie camera was turned on on the ground in the Praga area.

At 14.45, the pilots of the La-5s, who at that moment were patrolling at an altitude of 3,000m over the eastern bank of the Vistula, saw an impressive sight. From the west, at an altitude of 4km, the first groups of Flying Fortresses were approaching Warsaw, their fuselages flashing brightly in the sun. Just above, small silhouettes of American fighters could be seen. Soon, flashes of German anti-aircraft guns flashed on the ground, and the sky was painted with the black blotches of many explosions. When approaching the target, the bombers changed course: some to the northern part of the city, others to the south. At 14.50, the first batch of cargo containers separated from them. The B-17 groups flew at a distance of about 1½km behind each other, while the cargo was discharged synchronously on command from the leading aircraft.

By 15.00, about 300 parachutes were hanging in the sky over Warsaw at the same time, and many of them were hit by small-calibre anti-aircraft artillery, exploded or fell to the ground already burning. The fantastic and epic picture was complemented by a downed Flying Fortress, which, burning and falling apart, crashed in the northern part of the city.

The German air defences, accustomed to dealing with small groups of Soviet bombers and ground-attack planes, was clearly not ready for such a number of 'guests', so the middle and final groups of B-17s were practically not fired on. The last American planes flew over Warsaw at 15.10, and two hours later the Flying Fortresses and Mustangs landed at the Soviet air bases of Poltava and Mirgorod.

Soviet pilots and ground observers counted approximately 1,000 dropped cargo containers. However, only 2 per cent of them fell on rebel-controlled neighbourhoods, and the same number fell on the eastern bank of the Vistula. Some of the cargo fell in the Mińsk Mazowiecki area, 30km from Warsaw. In fact, 96 per cent of the dropped cargo went to the Germans. The navigators of the Flying Fortresses simply did not take into account a correction for the wind, as a result of which the containers were blown away to the south-west, and the leaders of the closing groups of aircraft, who saw perfectly that the cargo was falling past the target, stubbornly continued to keep the set course. According to American information, 1,284 containers were dropped, of which 288 fell into the territory controlled by the Armia Krajowa. It was not food and cigarettes that fell into the hands of the Germans. Machine guns with cartridges, mortars with ammunition, explosives in an iron stopper, machine guns and pistols, grenades, fuses were found in the cassettes opened by the Red Army. As well as chocolate, canned meat, biscuits, coffee and other yummy things. In short, the Americans did a good job of supplying the SS and Ukrainians with weapons and food!

The Soviet command described the American raid as a failure. However, the next day, communication was established with the scouts who had previously landed in the city. They reported that a significant part of the ammunition that had been dropped by the Po-2s had been destroyed on impact, half of the PPSh submachine guns were in an unsuitable condition, and a significant part of the bags fell on German territory. For example, of the fifty-eight anti-tank rifles dropped on the night of 18–19 September, only twenty-four were found, and only forty-four out of 207 submachine guns. But there were also positives. Firstly, now the 16th Air Army could strike targets in Warsaw at the request of the rebels, and secondly, the boundaries of the sectors under their control were precisely established.

On 20 September, Soviet and Polish aircraft carried out air attacks on the city for the first time daylight. Polish Il-2s bombed and shelled the hippodrome and the Botanical Garden, and twenty-three Pe-2 dive bombers from the 3rd Guards BAD bombed the Citadel and the Slodovets railway station. By this point, the distribution of support for the uprising between the Red Army and the Wojsko Polskie had finally been determined. The Russians gave priority to helping the isolated northern rebel group defending around Wilson Square, and it was there that the best part of the cargo was dumped. The Poles had their contacts in the central and southern sectors, and the Wojsko Polskie Air Force flew primarily to these quarters.

Meanwhile, a turning point had finally come in the battle. All attempts by Soviet troops to cross to the west bank ended unsuccessfully. Meanwhile, the bridgehead in the southern part of the city, occupied by the 1st Polish Army, was quickly blocked by the Germans and cut into pieces. At the same time, some Polish detachments were destroyed almost completely, and the crews of aircraft regularly sent to investigate could not see anything below because of the constant fires. In the report of the crews of the 2nd Guards SHAD, flying over Warsaw on the evening of 21 September, it was reported: 'Blocks No. 514, 513 are covered with solid smoke and can hardly be seen. Visibility in this area is less than a kilometre. There are no troops in the trenches and trenches in the area from the southern highway bridge to block No. 520 on the west bank of the Vistula River, the block is covered with smoke … Block No. 412 is engulfed in fires and smoke. When flying over blocks 524, 533, the planes were fired at by mortar fire from the roofs of houses.' Having lost about 5,000 soldiers in heavy street fighting, Wojsko Polskie units evacuated back to the eastern bank.

German artillery intensified the shelling of rebel-held neighbourhoods, as well as the eastern bank. Self-propelled Karl mortars, which were in position in the south-western part of the city, also fired several terrifying 600mm shells at the positions of the Russian 47th Army. Even anti-aircraft gunners suffered serious losses from German shells. From 17 to 23 September, as a result of shelling in the 24th ZENAD, thirty-two anti-aircraft gunners were killed and wounded, while five guns were disabled.

Meanwhile, the headquarters of the 16th Air Army began an operation to deliver a 45mm M1937 (53-K) anti-tank gun to the rebels. This mission was not only difficult, it was unique. The gun weighed 560kg and had a rather long thin barrel; it is clear that it was not possible to simply attach it to the fuselage of an aircraft and drop it by parachute. But a way was found. The cannon was disassembled into six parts: barrel with recoil device (113kg), carriage (90kg), bed (85kg), wheels (50kg), shield (55kg) and assembly tools and sight (43kg). The most difficult item to deliver was the barrel. It was suspended by straps under an R-5 biplane and the drop was carried out by cutting a halyard carried into the navigator's cabin. The carriage was secured in a similar way. Calculations showed that for guaranteed delivery of the gun barrel in an undamaged state, a parachute with an area of 500 sq m would be required! But there were simply no such parachutes in the arsenal of the Red Army Air Force. Therefore, the cargo had to be dropped on two parachutes with an area of 75 sq m each.

The remaining parts were packed in special bags in three sets. In total, four R-5 aircraft took part in the unique mission. On the night of 23–24 September, the parts were dropped successfully on target No. 1 (Wilson Square) and landed on rebel positions. There, the first set of 100 artillery shells was dropped from Po-2s in cargo bags. However, the Poles apparently failed to assemble the gun as the planned delivery of 45mm shells the following night was cancelled, as were the planned missions to deliver new sets of guns.

Meanwhile, the Luftwaffe continued to bomb rebel-held neighbourhoods on a daily basis. On 24 September, two groups of fifteen Ju 87s dropped bombs on the south-eastern districts of Warsaw. The next morning, at 09.15, another raid was carried out on the positions of Armia Krajowa in the south-eastern part of the city. First, eleven Ju 87s bombed them, then five Fw 190s. On 26 September, Stukas and Fw 190s again bombed and shelled buildings occupied by Poles in the south-eastern part of the city. On 28 September 28, the eastern part of Warsaw became the targets of German bombers. From the opposite side, Russian anti-aircraft artillery fired furiously at the diving planes, firing more than 700 shells. During 29 September, the Stukas bombed the north-eastern part of the city (Wilson Square) three times.

On the night of 24–25 September, 94 sorties were carried out, and a Russian lieutenant from the intelligence office with a radio operator and a radio station were dropped on target No. 3 (Bagno and Krucha Streets in the southern part of the city). The device itself landed safely, but the radio operator hit the destroyed roof of the building, fell inside and was seriously injured. The unfortunate man was found by Polish soldiers, but died in hospital three days later.

On the night of 25–26 September, the Russians carried out 127 transport flights, 123 on the night of 27–28 September, and 98 the next. If at the beginning of the operation the slow-moving Po-2s flew over Warsaw almost without interference, then by the end of the month the German air defences had noticeably strengthened. Searchlights, automatic anti-aircraft guns and machine guns were installed in the rebel-cleared neighbourhoods, and several barrage balloons were raised. Because of this, biplane pilots had to fly several laps and drop cargo from a higher altitude.

In total, from 13 September to 1 October, Soviet aircraft dropped 156 mortars, 505 anti-tank rifles, 1,478 submachine guns, 1,189 carbines and rifles, 41,780 hand grenades, 518,000 mortar mines, 8 million rounds of ammunition, 55 tons of food, 1 ton of tobacco, 6,000 books of smoking paper, 9.6km of cable and etc. Seven people were also landed. Russian losses amounted to eight Po-2s.

On 30 September, the final part of the Warsaw drama began. In the morning, after heavy shelling, assault groups of SS and Ukrainian forces launched a decisive offensive against Armia Krajowa. Pilots of Soviet fighters flying over the city reported that there were many tanks and self-propelled guns on the streets, firing directly at buildings, howitzers continuously shelling the city from the south-west, and fires and smoke were visible everywhere. Soon, the Poles defending themselves in the area of Wilson Square radioed that some of them would break through to the eastern bank of the Vistula, and they asked for maximum support. At 10.00, Soviet artillery opened fire on the Citadel area and the port facilities occupied by the Germans. Then eight Il-2 groups from the 2nd Guards SHAD struck at these targets. At 13.20, the air attacks and shelling were stopped, after which the rebels received permission to break through. However, it was too late, by this time German self-propelled guns were already standing in Wilson Square and finishing off the last pockets of resistance. At 18.15, the northern rebel group of about 1,300 people surrendered. On the night of 1 October, a group of twenty-eight rebels (including six wounded) managed to break through to the Vistula and cross to the eastern bank.

Realising that the uprising could be about to end in collapse, on the night of 1 October, Soviet and Polish aircraft made a record 414 sorties in support of Armia Krajowa. Most of them were aimed at bombing various targets in the city. There were no flights on the following day due to bad weather. On the night of 2–3 October, the 9th Guards NBAD received orders to drop supplies to Warsaw again, but all missions were cancelled again due to heavy clouds, fog and almost zero visibility.

At 17.00 on 3 October, the headquarters of the 1st Polish Army received the last message from Warsaw, and the next day it became clear that the rebels (with the exception of some small groups) had surrendered. In total, about 15,000 people surrendered, who went to prison camps in various parts of Germany. Another 5,000 to 6,000 resistance fighters mixed with the civilian population, hoping to continue the fight later.

However, soon the entire civilian population of Warsaw was expelled from the city and sent to the Durchgangslager-121 transit camp in Pruszków.

During August and September, the Luftwaffe carried out 1,408 sorties to bomb rebel-held neighbourhoods, dropping 1,580 tons of bombs.

The fate of the city turned out to be tragic. Warsaw was completely devastated, and its beautiful streets and buildings were purposefully destroyed. In addition to the Germans themselves, foreign soldiers, including Ukrainians, took an active part in this vandalism. The official website of the Warsaw Uprising Memorial Association (Stowarzyszenia Pamięci Powstania Warszawskiego 1944) says: 'The Ukrainian soldiers behaved extremely cruelly, they committed many monstrous crimes, especially against the civilian population. Ukrainians also took an active part in the destruction and looting of Warsaw after the surrender of the Warsaw Uprising in the period from October 1944 to January 1945.'

Meanwhile, on the morning of 4 October, the Wehrmacht launched a major offensive against the Soviet bridgeheads on the Narew. As a result, on the first day, the Germans broke through the front and significantly pushed the units of the 65th and 70th Armies to the bank. Further, the fighting in this sector continued with varying success until the end of 1944. As these events showed, the Red Army in this area was seriously weakened by continuous fighting and could not launch a powerful offensive for the next three months.

Chapter 12

# THE SLOVAK UPRISING

## The Uprising in the Mountains

Since the emergence of the Slovak Republic and the puppet pro-German regime of Jozef Tiso in 1939, an insurgency had been forming gradually in Slovakia. And in 1942, the first groups of partisans, mainly pro-communist, began to appear in the mountains. They were in active contact with Moscow, and in the summer of the following year, Stalin had the idea to organise an uprising in the country. In July 1943, one of the leaders of the Communist Party of Czechoslovakia, Carol Schmidke, was taken from Moscow to Poland. With the help of Polish partisans, he was able to cross the border of Slovakia and settle there illegally.

In addition, the Soviet leadership took care in advance of the creation of the Czechoslovak Army, which was supposed to be an alternative to the Czechoslovak units formed in Great Britain at the initiative of the leader of the Czech government in exile, Edvard Beneš. In December 1943, in the Melitopol area, the 1st Slovak Infantry Division deserted and defected to Soviet territory in almost full force. On the basis of this unit, as well as with the involvement of previously captured soldiers – Czechs and Slovaks by nationality – Stalin decided to form an entire unit, which, when the Red Army approached the territory of Slovakia, it was planned to throw into the enemy's rear. On 7 January 1944, the formation of the Czechoslovak airborne brigade led by Colonel Vladimir Prikril began in Efremov near Moscow. Soon, the soldiers completed a three-month course of combat and special training for operations in the enemy's rear. The training included group night parachute jumps from Li-2 transports. On 17 April, the brigade was named the 2nd Separate Czechoslovak Airborne Brigade. It was then incorporated into the previously created 1st Czechoslovak Army Corps under the command of Brigadier General Jan Kratohvil.

As the situation at the front worsened for the Third Reich and its allies, opposition sentiments began to grow in the Slovak army, as well as in the industrial and financial circles of the country. However, at the same time there was an important nuance that had a noticeable impact on all subsequent events. Stalin and the members of the Communist Party of Czechoslovakia who were in the USSR intended to recreate a single state of Czechs and Slovaks after the war. The Slovak military and political elite were divided into two groups. One dreamed of an independent post-war Slovakia, and the majority of the local population held the same opinion. The other part of the opposition, led by Brigadier General Jan Golian and Divisional General Rudolf Viest, on the contrary, sought to restore the country to its pre-war borders. At the same time, some of them believed that Slovakia should become the main part of the federation, and the state should be renamed Slovakoczechia! Some of the generals of the Slovak army maintained illegal contacts with the Beneš government. In the spring of 1944, this group began to prepare its own uprising.

At the same time, in a country divided by mountains and deep river valleys and gorges into many isolated regions, there was no single centre, and Bratislava, located on the south-western outskirts, was the capital, in fact, only nominally. Culturally and economically, the Slovaks gravitated more towards Vienna, located 50km away, than to the far eastern provinces. For these reasons, the Slovak insurgency was extremely diverse, with each group pursuing its own goals. Perhaps the only dream uniting everyone was the desire to prevent the destruction of the country as a result of large-scale hostilities.

On the night of 24–25 July, a partisan detachment of eleven people under the command of Senior Lieutenant Peter Velichko was landed by a Soviet aircraft in the Kantor Valley (in the northern part of Slovakia). The group was tasked with organising regular partisan detachments and equipping a reception area for following groups. Subsequently, the 1st Slovak Partisan Brigade grew out of this unit, which included both Czechs and Slovaks, as well as Russians and even French (mostly escaped prisoners of war). In total, in July–early August 1944, twenty-four partisan detachments with a total strength of more than 400 people were landed in Slovakia. In addition, in August, by order of the central headquarters of the partisan movement, about a dozen partisan detachments that had previously operated on the territory of Belarus and Ukraine were transferred to Slovakia through the front line. Having penetrated into the eastern regions of Slovakia, the partisans began to blow up railways, attack German commandants' offices and patrols, and disorganise the German rear. In parallel, two bodies were formed: the Defence Committee of Slovakia and the pro-Soviet Main Headquarters of the Slovak partisan movement. In the future, they coordinated their actions as necessary (mainly it concerned the 'division of spheres of influence', i.e., the distribution of controlled territories). But on occasion they interfered with and harmed each other.

As a result of this action, on 23 August, Tiso appealed to Hitler with a request to provide military assistance to combat the saboteurs. Despite the difficult situation on the fronts, the Führer, fearing a repeat of the Romanian scenario in Slovakia, ordered the necessary number of units to be allocated from the Reserve Army. At first they were located in villages along the railways.

Meanwhile, on 29 August, Jan Golian gave an official order to start the uprising, which was already in full swing. The next day, the radio station in Banská Bystrica (the second city of the country) addressed the population of the country with a call for universal action against the Germans and their accomplices. On 1 September, the Slovak National Council came out of hiding in the city and adopted a declaration on the restoration of the Czechoslovak Republic and the overthrow of the Tiso government. Later, Banská Bystrica, located in the wide valley of the Gron River, between the Low Tatras and Slovak Ore Mountains, became the main centre of the uprising. By early September, the rebels had about 60,000 soldiers, 18,000 partisans, 200 artillery pieces, 24 tanks, 4 self-propelled guns, 3 armoured trains and 34 aircraft in service. At the same time, a significant proportion of the troops were fugitive French prisoners of war, Jews released from three labour camps in the country, and representatives of other nationalities.

In turn, the Wehrmacht began the occupation of Slovakia on 27 August, and the next day the Germans captured the Dukelsky Pass, through which lay the closest route to this mountainous country for Soviet troops. On 30 August, the country's Defence Minister, Ferdinand Chatloš, announced on the radio that German troops were beginning to fight 'communist rebels' and 'traitors'. On the 31st, Hitler entrusted the suppression of the rebellion to SS Obergruppenführer Gottlob Berger, but just two weeks later he was replaced by Gruppenführer Hermann Hoefle. The Führer ordered him to act without hesitation, destroying all the rebellious villages.

As for the aviation part of the uprising, it began like this. On the evening of 1 August, a single He 111 bomber appeared in the Tarnopol area, making mysterious circles in the sky. It was hit by anti-aircraft fire from a Russian armoured train parked near Volochisk station and made an emergency landing in a field near the village of Solovtsy.

The Russian soldiers who arrived on the scene were surprised when six people got out of the plane: a general, a colonel, a captain, two engineers and two lower ranks of the Slovak army! They said that with the approach of the Red Army to Slovakia, anti-Nazi sentiments had intensified there, and the Slovaks were ready to massively side with the Soviets. The officers said that a conspiracy had matured in the Slovak Air Force, and a group of pilots were preparing for a mass flight to Soviet territory. At the same time, they asked to make an agreement on the time and conditions.

On 4 August, an Fw 58S aircraft with five people on board took off from Mokrad airfield. Having successfully crossed the front line, it landed in Chertkov. The next flight took place on 20 August. A Junkers W34 from the 41st Flying Squadron with seven people on board took off from Poprad and landed at Lviv airfield. On 27 August, a Klemm Kl 35D training aircraft flew there from the Three Oaks (Tri Duby) airfield.

The following flights were less successful. On 29 August, a Praga E-39 biplane from the 12th Flight crashed in the Carpathians and both pilots died. And on 30 August, in the area of Debica (south-east of Milec), the pilot of a Yak-9, Second Lieutenant N.G. Minin from the 85th Guards IAP, shot down an Fw 189 reconnaissance aircraft that he identified as Hungarian. In fact, it was a Slovak Fw 189W-2 from the 1st Reconnaissance Squadron. Moreover, in addition to the two pilots, there were four other passengers on board.

Immediately after the outbreak of the uprising, a Slovak mixed squadron (Slovenské povstalecké letectvo) was formed at Tri Duby airfield, which eventually had five Avia B-534 fighters, twelve Letov S-328 light bombers, two Bf 109E-4s, two Bf 109G-6s, six Fw 189As, two SM bombers-84, one Bk-534, one Fw 58 and several Kl-35s and He 72 training aircraft. On 30 August, Slovak pilots carried out the first combat sorties in the interests of the rebels. That evening, fearing German air attacks against the air base and its sudden capture, the rebels decided to relocate most of their aircraft to Soviet territory.

At dawn on 31 August, twenty-eight aircraft (eight S-328s, six Fw 189s, four B-534s, two Bf 109G-6s, two Kl 33Ds, one Kl 35, one Fw 44, one FW-58C, one E-39, one Fi-156C and one W34) took to the air and flew east. According to Soviet information, at about 07.07 the group safely crossed the front line and at about 09.30 most of the aircraft landed at the Soviet airfields of Lviv, Sambor, Rava-Russkaya and Zolochev. A total of twenty-eight people arrived in only six Fw 189s, and the absolute record was set by Captain O. Golka of the 1st Squadron, who landed with six people on board! The relocation took place on schedule, just in time for the Luftwaffe to begin operations against the uprising.

Air support for the punitive operation was entrusted to Lieutenant General Hans Seidemann's Fliegerkorps VIII, whose headquarters were located in Tarnow. Since by this time the Luftwaffe was not in the best condition, the aviation group had to be created in a spirit of improvisation. First of all, the Henne Combat Group (Gefechtsverband Henne, GVH) was formed on the basis of the 2nd Aviation School of Bomber Navigators (Kampfbeobachterschule 2, III./KBS2). It was headed by the commander of this school, Rudolf Henne. It was also decided to involve SS aviation in the operation – the special aviation squadron Fl.G.z.b.V.7 (Fliegergeschwader z.b.V.7) under Oberstleutnant Heinz Hansius. This unusual unit was formed in 1942 to serve the SS and police forces. At first, it was equipped with old aircraft such as Ar 95s, He 60s, Ju 52s and Hs 126s. These were used for courier transportation, delivery of urgent cargoes and transportation of important prisoners, as well as fighting against partisans. In February 1944, the staff of the Geschwader was significantly increased and then consisted of seven conventional staffels (squadrons), one experimental staffel (Erg.Sta./Fl.G.z.b.V.7) and several other small units. The main strike force in the SS aviation was Einsatzgruppe I./Fl.G.z.b.V.7, which flew Ju 87Ds, Fw 58s, Fw 189s and Hs 129s.

The most exotic unit was Erprobungskommando 204, which was engaged in testing the twin-engined Siebel Si 204E-0 as a light night bomber.

First of all, the Germans took control of the Slovak aviation infrastructure in the areas unoccupied by the rebels. While the GVH units, which also included the Luftwaffe infantry battalion, quickly captured airfields in western Slovakia (Piešťany, Vainory, and others), landing troops on them, the troops of Army Group Northern Ukraine occupied air bases in Prešov, Poprad, Mokrad and Spisska Nova. As a result, the Germans captured 192 aircraft (mostly training types), as well as warehouses of engines, fuel and other materials.

At 6 p.m. on 31 August, GVH conducted the first bombing raid against the rebels. Seven Ju 88A-5s from III./KBS2 raided the Tri Duby air base, then Bf 109 fighters fired at the target from a low level. As a result, four aircraft were destroyed (S-328, Fw 58, SM.84 and Bf 109E-4) and two more were damaged. The Germans also began to carry out air strikes on villages occupied by the rebels. For example, on 2 September, training bombers dropped bombs on the village of Zahradne (8km north of Prešov). As a result, half of the houses were destroyed and nine civilians were killed.

On 10 September, a large group of aircraft from GVH and SS I./Fl.G.z.b.V.7 carried out a repeated air attack against the Tri Duby air base. As a result, seventeen aircraft were destroyed and three were damaged. Twenty people were killed and seventeen others were injured. The air attacks on 31 August and 10 September caused irreparable damage to the Slovak Mixed Squadron, which lost most of its planes.

## Operation Zvolen

When Stalin was informed about the flight of Slovak pilots to the USSR and the beginning of the uprising, he immediately ordered Marshal Ivan Konev, commander of the 1st Ukrainian Front, to present his thoughts on possible assistance to the rebels. Konev proposed to strike with the forces of the 38th Army across the Carpathians in the direction of Dukla and Prešov, involving the 1st Guards Cavalry Corps and the 1st Czechoslovak Army Corps in the first echelon.

A separate operation was prepared by the People's Commissariat of State Security (NKGB). It provided for the mass transfer of specially trained agents and saboteurs, as well as instructors to train the rebels, to different regions of Slovakia.

The commander of the Long-range Aviation, Marshal Alexander Golovanov, was also instructed to immediately organise the delivery of weapons and ammunition to the Slovaks. The commander of the 4th Guards Aviation Corps ADD, General Georgy Stchetchikov, received an order on the night of 3–4 September to drop cargo at the Tri Duby air base. The commander of the 5th Guards Long-range Aviation Corps, General Ivan Georgiev, received a similar instruction. At the same time, Stalin demanded that the results of the missions be reported to him personally in the form of special reports.

On the night of 4–5 September, the first thirty Lisunov Li-2s took off to drop cargo to Slovakia. Then, on the night of 5–6 September, forty aircraft completed the mission, and the next night the same. This is how the air operation started, which was given the code name 'Zvolen'.

On 7 September, the 15th Guards AP DD received an order to fly missions in the interests of the Slovak uprising. At that time, the unit was based at Uman airfield and had thirty-two North American B-25 Mitchell bombers. At night, twelve planes took off on a mission, with one of them acting as a pathfinder. First, eighteen marker bombs were dropped over the Tri Duby air base, after which the rest of the crews parachuted fifty-eight PD-MM cargo bags. On the night of 8–9 September, six B-25s flew to Slovakia, but due to bad weather none of them could reach the target. In the following days, rebel supply missions were not conducted due to difficult weather conditions, as well as a shortage of fuel at air bases.

Meanwhile, the Soviet troops, without any serious preparation, launched an offensive, the purpose of which was to quickly break into the territory of Slovakia and join the rebels. On the morning of 4 September, the commander of the 1st Guards Cavalry Corps, Lieutenant General Viktor Baranov, was summoned to the headquarters of the 38th Army, where he received an oral order from Konev: to advance to the front line in the Markoshov–Mala Krasnaya Pokrovka area. To the left, the Czechoslovak Army Corps was concentrated. According to the plan, the 38th Army was to advance in the general direction towards Prešov, and the cavalrymen in the second echelon were ordered to reach the Poprad River in the area of Stara Lyubov and Plavnitsa on the third day of the operation, capturing bridgeheads on the southern bank. That is, to cover a distance of 80–85km from the starting positions. By early September, Baranov's cavalry corps numbered 18,466 men, 13,400 horses, 978 vehicles, 45 tanks, 310 artillery pieces and mortars, and 38 anti-aircraft guns.

This optimistic plan did not take into account many factors, both military (a lack of own forces and an underestimation of enemy forces), and weather (the beginning of autumn weather with heavy rains and limited visibility), as well as geographical conditions. This is how Soviet pilot Ivan Drachenko described Slovakia: 'Gloomy, winding gorges with the eternal roar of violent rivers, steep cliffs, gloomy oak, beech and coniferous wilds, violent winds tearing off the main ridge – that's what the Carpathians are! Rows of trenches and trenches stretched along the slopes of the heights. On the opposite side of the slopes are the positions of the Nazis. The enemy literally dug into the ground, built many bunkers, girded the heights with wire fences, laid thousands of mines and land mines in ravines, gorges, on trails. The Carpathians were an area extremely convenient for defence and very difficult for any attacking actions.'

On the morning of 8 September, after a powerful artillery bombardment, the 38th Army of General Kirill Moskalenko went on the offensive. It managed to push the Germans back a little, but the fighting immediately became fierce, and the operation itself did not go according to plan. In the evening, Baranov's cavalry was launched into a breakthrough through a 2km gap, but it had to fight off numerous counter-attacks and could barely make its way towards the mountains. Nevertheless, on 11 September, Konev categorically ordered the cavalrymen to immediately go for a breakthrough, without looking back at the main army forces. By the end of 13 September, Baranov's corps was able to reach the village of Ciechania with advanced units, from which 1½km remained to the Polish–Slovak border.

However, the next day, the battalions of the German 97th Jäger Division that arrived in the breakthrough area cut off the communications of the cavalrymen. At the same time, several more units were transferred there, which began to surround the Russian cavalrymen from all sides. 'As a result, the corps units were isolated and cut off from the 38th Army, the corps' rear communications were lost, and the supply of all types of combat support was discontinued,' the journal of combat operations of the 1st Guards Cavalry Corps reported. Entrenched on several hills and intersections of roads, the cavalrymen took up a circular defence. They quickly used up almost all the ammunition for the guns and mortars, after which they requested supplies by air.

A cargo dump site was urgently equipped in the area of Krempka. The first flights of Po-2s from the 208th NBAD took place on the night of 15–16 September. Bags of ammunition and food were dropped from a height of 300–400m. The planes could not go lower because of the mountainous terrain. A day later, Po-2s delivered 17 tons of ammunition and 400kg of food to Baranov's cavalrymen. In addition, thirteen Li-2s dropped cargo containers. On the night of 17–18 September, Po-2s dropped 16 tons of cargo to the cavalrymen. In three days, they received about 3,000 shells, more than 2,000 mines (shells) for mortars, 1,100 hand grenades, etc.

In parallel with the operation to supply the rebels, Russian Li-2 transports used as bombers attacked various targets in Slovakia. For example, on the night of 16–17 September, ninety-nine Li-2s from the 53rd and 54th AD DD raided the Chop railway hub (25km south of Uzhgorod). Another twenty Li-2s performed various special missions. One dropped cargo and parachutists near the village of Zazriva (in northern Slovakia), the other landed at the Tri Duby air base. A total of 900kg of weapons and ammunition, a radio station, and five people were unloaded there. The Li-2, piloted by Lieutenant Colonel Boris Yezersky, commander of the 7th Guards Aviation Regiment of Long-range Aviation, delivered a group of officers there, including Colonel Boris Chirskov, assistant commander of the 53rd Aviation Division.

By this point, it became clear to the Soviet command that the operation to link up with the rebels had failed. In this regard, it was decided to transfer the 2nd Separate Czechoslovak Airborne Brigade to Slovakia. At the beginning of the operation, the brigade had 1,855 officers and men. According to the initial plan, after the transfer of all personnel, Soviet airborne units were supposed to land in Slovakia (both by landing and by parachute). Chirskov was supposed to organise the reception, unloading and dispatch of aircraft.

Considering that the Tri Duby air base was small in size and was surrounded on all sides by forested mountains, some of which reach a height of up to 2,500m, simultaneous landing, parking and unloading of a large number of aircraft there proved impossible. Chirskov decided to organise the work in a conveyor-belt manner. The bombers were supposed to approach the airbase in groups of fifteen to twenty aircraft, circle in the waiting area and land one at a time from the south. At the same time, the engines were not turned off, and the Slovaks formed several rapid ground handling groups, which were given no more than ten to fifteen minutes to unload. After unloading, the plane immediately took off, and another one appeared in its place. For camouflage purposes, only two lights of different colours were turned on during landing – at the beginning and at the end of the runway. Pilot Alexey Vasiliev, who served in the 340th AP DD, recalled: 'There was nothing here that even remotely resembled a real air base. There was no specially equipped runway, no planes, no office buildings. There was only a small plateau, more or less level, surrounded on almost all its borders by mountain spurs.'

On the night of 17–18 September, the 53rd and 54th Air Divisions of the ADD conducted the first major mission to supply Slovak rebels and Soviet cavalrymen surrounded in the foothills of the Carpathians. Forty-three aircraft participated. Taking off from their rear aviation base in Uman, the transports followed the front line, where they landed at the advanced airfields of Krosno, Yasenki and Rudnomala. Loading was carried out at these sites, after which, in the dark, the Li-2 flew to their targets according to the schedule. Thirty-two aircraft dropped cargo from a height of 400m to units of the 1st Guards Cavalry Corps in the Polyanka area. Another forty Li-2s landed at the Tri Duby air base, delivering 56 tons of cargo and 123 people. Four more Li-2s dropped containers and parachutists in different regions of Slovakia (Pinchuk, Zhirnovets, Ustron, Mologosch). Alexey Vasiliev recalled: 'Ahead, a winding mountain range looms indistinctly against the sky. We gain altitude, go beyond the clouds, spreading below, like a vast foaming sea. Reminding us that the terrible Carpathians are below, the mountain peak, illuminated by the moon, loomed threateningly through the clouds. At the site of the Three Oaks, everything is ready to receive the first group of landing aircraft. Kerosene lanterns are lit along the borders of the runway. They also represent the landing "T". We flew in groups of five planes each. While another group of troops was on the way to the air base, Chirskov managed to release unloaded planes into the air. It looked like a kind of conveyor belt, on which three operations were performed: landing, unloading, take-off.'

After that, on the night of 18–19 September, an operation was launched to deliver Czechoslovak troops to the Tri Duby air base. At the same time, Russian bombers continued to bomb the Chop railway station, supply their surrounded cavalrymen by air and drop NKGB agents in different areas of Slovakia.

When London and Washington learned about the beginning of the Slovak uprising, they also decided to provide all possible assistance. On 17 September, the same day that American Boeing B-17s were dropping supplies for Polish rebels in Warsaw, two B-17s from the 483rd BG, which took off from Italy, headed for Slovakia. The bombers were escorted by forty-one P-51 fighters from the 52nd FG. After flying over Yugoslavia and the eastern part of Hungary along the front line, they turned north-west and, avoiding a meeting with German fighters, landed safely at the Tri Duby air base. The Flying Fortresses delivered a group of six OSS[1] agents led by Lieutenant James Green, as well as twelve Bazooka M1 60mm rocket launchers and 192 missiles. Some Mustangs also landed at the airfield and two of them – a P-51B from the 4th FS and a P-51C from the 5th FS – were severely damaged while doing this. Both planes had to be abandoned on the outskirts of the airbase. After picking up the pilots of the Mustangs and twelve pilots from the crews of American bombers previously shot down over Slovakia, both B-17s took off in the late afternoon and returned safely to Italy.

On the evening of 18 September, a Halifax from 148 Sqn RAF took off from Brindisi Air Base to deliver a group of British communications and intelligence officers to Tri Duby. In the dark, the plane reached the set point, but the pilot, despite visible signals from the ground, could not determine the landing trajectory. As a result, a group of SOE[2] agents led by Major John Seymour parachuted, then on the second pass the Halifax parachuted twelve containers with equipment and medicine, and on the third pass it dropped eight bales of bandages.

At noon on 20 September, 111 B-24 bombers from the 449th, 450th, 455th and 456th BG, accompanied by 103 Mustangs from the 52nd and 332nd FG, raided Malacky airfield. It was located 30km north of Bratislava, and it was there that the German aviation group used against the rebels was mainly based. Liberators dropped 24,886 9kg

---

1 The Office of Strategic Services was the main US intelligence service during the war and the predecessor of the CIA.

2 The Special Operations Executive was the British intelligence and sabotage organisation.

cluster bombs on the target, which literally ploughed through the airfield and hangars. American pilots reported twenty-six destroyed and eight heavily damaged aircraft. In fact, of the forty-six German aircraft at Malacky, twelve were completely destroyed, twenty-nine were severely damaged and only five remained intact. In addition to the air base, the railway station was damaged, and several houses in the village of Malacky were destroyed. Six civilians were killed and fourteen others were injured.

## The Empire's Retaliatory Strike

Meanwhile, the situation at the front was unfavourable for the uprising. The 1st Guards Cavalry Corps remained in the pocket in the Ciechania area. The offensive of the remaining troops allocated for the operation developed extremely slowly. Realising that the breakthrough to Preshov had clearly failed, Marshal Konev ordered Baranov to move south-east, to the Dukelsky Pass. There was an ancient road from Poland to Slovakia, the most suitable for the movement of troops and opening the way inland, bypassing the mountain ranges. From the north, troops of the 38th and 1st Guards Armies were approaching the pass, located at an altitude of 500m above sea level.

On 20 September, the 2nd Guards Cavalry Division was able to break through the Polish–Slovak border through forest trails and reach the vicinity of Korejovce (47km north-east of Prešov) by the end of the day. At the same time, the 7th Cavalry Division also managed to penetrate Slovakia and capture the village of Krajná Porúbka, on the western spur of the Dukelsky Pass. At this time, the weather improved dramatically, which led to a temporary surge in aviation activity on both warring sides, which had previously had almost no effect on the course of the battle. Soviet bombers and ground-attack planes were ordered primarily to strike communications, preventing the transfer of German troops to the pass.

On 20 September, almost at the same time as the USAAF bombed Malacky airfield, a Pe-2 reconnaissance aircraft from the 81st Guards BAP flew over the city of Prešov, located on the other side of Slovakia. He found six trains at the railway station. Despite the fact that by that time the rebels controlled most of central Slovakia, the Nowy Sącz (Southern Poland)–Stará L'ubovňa–Prešov–Košice railway line, which crossed the country from north to south, remained under German control. And there were regular trains running along it.

The message from the reconnaissance aircraft was reported to the commander of the 2nd Guards Bomber Aviation Corps (BAK), Major General Ivan Polbin. At 13.50 he ordered a strike on the station by the forces of the 81st Guards BAP (bomber aviation regiment). At 14.55, a Pe-2 bombers squadron of 'snipers' led by Captain Pavel Gusenko took off from Yasenki airbase. Nikolai Gapeenok, who served in the unit, recalled: 'At 15.00, the squadron took off and headed for the target in a wedge formation, accompanied by fighters. After 34 minutes, the aircraft began to move to the right bearing. When each aircraft entered the combat course, the crews clearly saw the station and the trains standing on it. It was calm at an altitude of 2,500 metres. The appearance of bombers turned out to be unexpected for the enemy, and the first explosions of anti-aircraft artillery shells appeared after dropping bombs from the leading aircraft. The squadron commander was the first to dive from a height of 2,500 metres, followed by the rest of the aircraft after a few seconds at a distance of 400 metres. At the same time, each crew chose an aiming point for themselves, dropped one FAB-250 bomb each and rapidly gained altitude to enter the second round of attack.'

According to the combat log of the 2nd BAK, ninety-three FAB-100 high-explosive bombs were dropped on the station, as a result of which forty-five wagons, five warehouses and a railway bridge were destroyed. According to the Prešov police station, the railway station was completely destroyed and, in addition, the salt factory located next to it was severely damaged, as well as the central street of the city, where seven houses burned down. The next day, a repeated air attack was carried out against Prešov railway station.

Due to the acute shortage of ammunition, Russian cavalrymen could not hold on to the mountains, and on 23 September, General Baranov received orders to break out of the pocket in a north-easterly direction. On the night of 24–25 September, in the area of Tylyava, the Red Army managed to break through the German lines and connect with the troops of the 38th Army. The next day, all units, including rear wagons and artillery, went out through the breached corridor to their territory. During the heroic raid into Slovakia, the 1st Guards Cavalry Corps lost 2,232 dead and wounded, 2,864 horses, 88 guns and mortars, and 24 tanks.

Meanwhile, another participant, Czechoslovak aviation, played a role in the battle. Back in autumn 1943, an agreement was signed between the Beneš government and the USSR on the creation of a Czechoslovak fighter aviation regiment. After negotiations, it was decided to send twenty pilots from the RAF's 310, 312 and 313 (Czechoslovak) Squadrons to the Soviet Union. The Soviet side was to provide aircraft and ground technical personnel. The detachment, under the famous ace staff captain František Fajtl, set off in spring 1944. In May, the 129th Czechoslovak Separate Air Squadron was formed at Ivanovo air Base, north-east of Moscow, which received a specially assembled batch of La-5FN fighters from Gorky Aircraft Factory No. 21. Later, the unit relocated to Kubinka and was renamed the 1st Czechoslovak Separate Fighter Aviation Regiment (1st CHOIAP).

The personnel of this unit consisted of various colourful personalities, the most unusual of which was the 29-year-old commander of the 1st Squadron, Lieutenant Josef Stehlík. Until 1939, he worked as an instructor pilot of the 3rd Aviation Regiment, based in Spišská Nová Ves in eastern Slovakia. After the country was occupied by the Germans, on 5 June, Stechlik fled to Poland, and from there went to France. There he fought in the French air force. After the surrender of France, the Czechoslovak pilots flew to England, where they were enrolled in the RAF volunteer reserve. Stehlik flew Hurricane and Spitfire fighters, winning several aerial victories. When, in early 1944, the pilot learned about the formation of the 1st CHOIAP, he gladly agreed to join it and lead the squadron. And now Stehlik's long, winding, adventurous battle path continued in Slovakia, from where he had escaped five years before!

On 15 September, the first four La-5FNs from the 1st CHOIAP flew to Tri Duby air base. Two days later, seventeen more La-5s arrived there. The very next day, Czech pilots conducted their first successful mission, attacking Piešťany air base 95km west of Zvolen. Having flown up to the target at low altitude over the valleys, the fighters suddenly appeared above it, after which they fired at hangars and planes from several approaches. According to German information, three aircraft were destroyed, and ten more were severely damaged. Later, the squadron, which the Germans called the 'Bandenluftwaffe', constantly fought air battles against the Luftwaffe and attacked various ground targets.

The Germans also conducted several air operations during this period. For example, on the night of 2 October, three Si 204E-0s from Erprobungskommando 204 raided railway facilities near Banská Bystrica station. There were several railway sections in the hands of the rebels, and the stretches between the stations of Brezno, Banská Bystrica, Zvolen and Krupina were actively used to transport soldiers and ammunition. In addition, the IPV-I 'Stefanik' armoured train plied along this line, firing at German troops. German planes hunted for this train for a long time, but it always managed to hide in the tunnels.

Meanwhile, the air bridge to Slovakia was working with great interruptions. From 22 to 26 September, flights were not carried out at all due to bad weather. On the evening of 26 September, thirty-five Li-2s from the 53rd AD DD flew from Uman to Krosno. At night, twenty-seven of them went to Slovakia, but due to difficult weather conditions, only thirteen planes were able to land. They delivered 123 people and 11 tons of cargo. From 30 September to 6 October, there was again non-flying weather over Slovakia, accompanied by heavy rains and dense fog. On the night of 6–7 October, forty-seven Li-2s from the 53rd and 54th AD DD delivered 42 tons of cargo and 326 personnel to the Tri Duby air base. Seventy wounded rebels were taken out on return flights.

On the afternoon of 7 October, help came again from the West. A large formation of Flying Fortresses took off from southern Italy to attack various targets in Hungary and Austria. In the area of Lake Balaton, six B-17s from the 483rd BG separated from the group, which, accompanied by thirty-two Mustangs from the 52nd FG, headed for Tri Duby air base. The Americans managed to land safely on the territory of the Third Reich for the second time. The bombers delivered 150 Bazookas with 2,800 rockets for them and other cargo. Also, twenty employees of the American special services OSS and SOE arrived in Slovakia. On the way back, the B-17 took out twenty pilots from the crews of previously downed bombers and a Slovak delegation of three people (they were heading to London for talks with Churchill). These missions were supposed to be just the beginning of large-scale Allied assistance, but subsequent events, as well as deteriorating weather conditions, put an end to the operation.

On the night of 7–8 October, sixty-eight Li-2s from the 53rd and 54th AD DD flew to Slovakia, but only forty-four of them were able to reach the target. The following night, sixty-eight Li-2s were able to land at Tri Duby air base, which delivered 63 tons of cargo and 453 people to the rebels. A total of 144 personnel were taken out on return flights, including ninety-four wounded. In total, during the three nights from 7–9 October, the ADD performed 305 flights to Slovakia, delivering 1,076 people and 344 tons of cargo. On return flights, the bombers took out 405 personnel, including 94 wounded.

On the night of 9–10 October, the operation was again disrupted due to non-flying weather over Slovakia. On the night of 12–13 October, twenty Li-2s from the 53rd AD DD reached the rebel airfield. On the night of 13–14 October, sixty-nine Li-2s landed in Slovakia, delivering 58 tons of cargo, two Willis jeeps and 473 soldiers. The bombers took out family members of the Slovak Government and officers of the Slovak army.

Russian transport planes were regularly attacked by German night fighters and suffered losses. This time, five Li-2s went missing.

According to German information, two of them were shot down by Ju 88C-6-night fighters from I./NJG100. On the night of 14–15 October, the transports of the 53rd Division did not fly due to weather conditions. Twenty-nine planes from the 54th AD DD flew to Slovakia, but only nine of them were able to land at the rebel airfield. Captain Penkin's Li-2 was chased by a night fighter in the Poprad area for fifteen minutes, with the German even turning on his landing lights in an attempt to illuminate the target in the fog. But the experienced pilot managed to evade him.

From 17 to 23 October, Russian bombers did not fly due to bad weather, as well as artillery attacks on advanced air bases carried out by German long-range artillery. On 17 October, the last raid to support the uprising was carried out by the Allies; a group of high-speed Mosquito bombers from the Canadian 418 Squadron that took off from Italy and carried out an air attack against Piešťany airfield. The raid was not very successful, with only three aircraft damaged on the ground. However, the German air defences shot down the bomber of Flying Lieutenant Stuart May flying at low level. The Mosquito made an emergency landing on its belly near the village of Brunovce (not far from the target). The crew were able to escape to the mountains, find the partisans there and hide.

The political situation in the rebel area was changing as fast as the weather. Back in mid-September, despite some difficulties and the delay of the Red Army offensive, the rebel leaders felt quite confident. Suffice it to say that democratic elections were even held in all the areas they controlled. After that, the Slovak People's Rada became the main civilian governing body, which managed to hold a couple of meetings. And on 16 September, a congress of the Communist and socialist parties was held in Banská Bystrica.

But the worse the situation became, the more contradictions between different groups and detachments became apparent. Thus, at the end of September, the Soviet partisan headquarters in Kiev ordered controlled sabotage groups to conduct operations independently of the Slovak rebel army and avoid any coordination. At the same time, disputes and conflicts on the subject of command flared up between Beneš, the partisans and various Slovak groups. They did not forget about the Western Allies. Since Churchill advocated the restoration of Czechoslovakia, in order to please him, on 1 October, the rebel army was renamed the '1st Czechoslovak Army of Slovakia'. This in turn caused discontent among some of the Slovak military. All this in the end only accelerated the inevitable outcome of events.

On 18 October, the Germans launched a general offensive against the rebels, whose main forces were now located in the Brezno–Zvolen–

Banská Bystrica triangle. The SS Schill Battle Group advanced from the south-west, the Tatra Panzer Division[3] from the west, the SS Dirlewanger Brigade from the north, and the Wittenmeyer battle group from the north-east. At the same time, SS-Freiwilligen-Panzergrenadier-Division 'Horst Wessel' unexpectedly began advancing from the southern direction, from the territory of Hungary. Ukrainians again played an important role among the punishers.

After almost complete destruction in the Brodsky pocket in July, the 14th SS Grenadier Division 'Galicia' was hastily rebuilt. Its staff was replenished at the expense of training units, as well as volunteers from Galicia who had escaped from the Red Army. The combat training of the recruits was of poor quality, and they could not resist the Red Army. But for the war with the partisans and civilians (especially together with the Germans), the Ukrainians were quite suitable. Soldiers from Galicia were assigned to the Tatra panzer division and entered Slovakia from the west.

On the first day, the punitive offensive was supported by about forty aircraft. Three of them were shot down by Czechoslovak pilots from the 1st CHOIAP, which flew out to intercept.

On 24 October, punitive troops captured Brezno and the strategically important pass, which opened a direct road to Banská Bystrica from the east. Meanwhile, all attempts by Soviet troops to break through to the rebels failed. Although on 6 October, units of the 1st Czechoslovak Army Corps and the 38th Army captured the Dukelsky Pass, when occupying the village of Visny Komarnik the advancing troops again encountered fierce enemy defences. The Soviet 18th Army liberated Mukachevo on 26 October, and Uzhgorod the next day. But even from this direction (from Transcarpathian Ukraine), it was not possible to break into the central regions of Slovakia.

On 24 October, Czechoslovak pilots completed their last missions to attack ground targets and patrol. The regimental commander, Staff Captain František Fajtl, decided the next day to evacuate the remaining twelve La-5s to Soviet territory. After a difficult and dramatic flight, which took place in cloudy weather in conditions of zero visibility, most of the fighters managed to fly to Soviet territory. The ground technicians and 'horseless' pilots went to the mountains and joined the partisans.

3 It was formed in the summer of 1944 from various motorised units specifically to suppress a possible uprising in Slovakia. The division had only one tank battalion, which had twenty-eight Pz.IIIs and Pz.IVs, as well as three Tigers.

Despite the impending collapse, the air bridge to Slovakia was still operating. On the night of 23–24 October, eighteen Li-2s from the 53rd and 54th AD DD landed at Tri Duby air base. On the way back, German night fighters shot down two planes. A crew member of one of them, Sergei Utkin, recalled: 'It was the second half of the night. It was still raining. The clouds had become denser. We had gone about half the way and were already somewhere over Ondava Verkhovyna, when an enemy fighter suddenly fell out of the torn clouds at us. There was a roar of an explosion, a crimson flame shot up – a shell landed in the left fuel tanks. A burst of fire burst into the cockpit and blinded me, but I found the strength to grab the parachute. I rushed into the general cabin. The flames spread like lightning. The burning floor collapsed under me, and my jumpsuit caught fire. But I managed to slip through the exit door.' The crew landed near the town of Yakubova Volya (north-west of Preshov) and managed to reach the positions of the Soviet partisan detachment.

The last transport planes flew to Slovakia on the night of 27–28 October. At that time, only one of the seven Li-2s was able to drop four bags of ammunition in an area still controlled by the rebels. This was the last rebel support mission. In total, the Soviet air force carried out about 2,000 flights to Slovakia, while 984 aircraft were able to land there.

For many participants in these events, everything ended tragically. On 3 November, the SS managed to capture most of the rebel leaders, including Generals Jan Golian and Rudolf Wiest. Both were later executed. Most of the employees of the American and British special services were also caught, sent to concentration camps and subsequently killed.

For Slovakia, everything ended in a complete disaster, and its entire territory, like neighbouring Hungary, was completely devastated. But the Slovak uprising is not as politicised and publicised as the Warsaw uprising, and it is very rarely remembered. At the same time, the Slovaks never accused the Russians of insufficient support and did not destroy the monuments erected in honour of the thousands of Soviet soldiers who died during the liberation of their country.

Chapter 13

# THE BALKANS: REVERSE BLITZKRIEG

On 24 August, immediately after the Red Army broke through the front in Romania, the German command ordered the urgent evacuation of troops from Crete and other islands of the Aegean Sea. This operation was called Anvil ('Unternehmen Amboss'). Later, due to the rapid advance of Soviet troops in the Balkans, it was decided to evacuate the whole of Greece.

The soldiers were transported from there by sea and by air. Initially, Ju 52s from I./TG4, II./TG4 and IV./TG1 were allocated for the air bridge, as well as Bv 138 and Do 24 seaplanes and flying boats, and Ju 52/3m See floatplanes from LTStaf-fel (See)1 and LTStaffel (See)3. Flights were carried out mainly at night or in bad weather and initially passed without major losses. But in early September, the Allies noticed an increase in German air and sea traffic in the Balkans and took action. Beaufighter night fighters from the RAF's 46 and 108 Squadrons began to actively operate along the entire route between mainland Greece and Crete. The RAF aircraft were based at Gambut air base in North Africa. They were equipped with modern radars and easily detected targets moving over the sea. This immediately led to heavy losses of transporters, especially the Ju 52.

With this in mind, flights began to be conducted only by single aircraft, without any mandatory tactics. Each crew had to choose the course, altitude and route independently. Some aircraft flew in a large arc over the Cyclades archipelago, the islands of Syros, Paros and Santorini, in order to keep their course as far as possible from the nearest Allied aviation bases. Such a route was safer, but it took strong nerves as this led to an overuse of fuel and there was a risk of an emergency landing on water. Others flew to Crete on the most direct course over the island of Milos, just hoping for luck and God's help. Some of the pilots tried to climb as high as possible so that in the event of an attack they could escape from the night fighter by a sharp dive, while others, on the contrary, pressed close to the water, hoping to avoid detection by radar. Both methods had their advantages and disadvantages. During a high-level flight, it was difficult for the crew to leave the downed plane or land on the water in the dark. But there was a better chance of reaching land. With low-level flight, it was easier to land a damaged plane on the water and escape on an inflatable boat, but there was almost no chance of reaching land on one engine.

By mid-September, the situation in the Balkans had become even more complicated. Bulgaria defected to the Allies, and soon the troops of the 3rd Ukrainian Front were concentrated in the western part of this country. By 15 September, units of the Soviet 17th Air Army of Lieutenant General Vladimir Sudets had relocated to airfields in the Sofia area. At that time, the compound consisted of about 1,000 aircraft (361 Il-2s, 357 fighters, 116 bombers, 105 Po-2-night bombers and 60 reconnaissance aircraft.

On 16 September, that is, less than a month after the collapse of Army Group South Ukraine, Soviet troops, together with the Bulgarians, launched an offensive against Macedonia and Serbia. One of the goals of the 3rd Ukrainian Front was to cut off the evacuation routes of the Wehrmacht from Greece. The next day, Soviet bombers began to raid the railway stations of Skopje and Niš, as well as railway bridges, tunnels and other structures.

On the afternoon of 19 September, thirty Douglas A-20s from the 244th Bomber Aviation Division, which took off from Vrazhevna airfield (near Sofia), raided the railway hub and the harbour of Thessaloniki. This was the first Soviet air attack on the territory of Greece. The pilots reported the sinking and damaging of twelve ships. The successful raid took place without losses, but seventeen bombers received various damage from anti-aircraft fire. Nevertheless, all of them were able to return safely to the base. This air attack came as a complete surprise to the Germans, and the Kriegsmarine suffered heavy losses. The torpedo boat *S-54* and the minesweepers *R-183, R-185, R-210, R-211, Alula, Otranto* and *Gallipolis* were sunk or severely damaged. They did not take any part in the evacuation of German troops from Greece, and all are listed as sunk or abandoned after the Germans left Thessaloniki.

A second air attack on Thessaloniki was planned for the next day, but for some reason it was cancelled. Instead, Douglas A-20s bombed the railway stations of Pristina, Raska and Mitrovica, dropping 496 high-explosive and 33 fragmentation bombs on them. On 21 September, the headquarters of the 17th Air Army again planned to raid Thessaloniki, but the mission was cancelled again. In the future, the Soviets refused to bomb Greek territory, probably for political reasons. In the following days, Il-2s constantly bombed and shelled the railway stations of Skopje, Mitrovica, Niš and Kraljevo.

On 30 September, the troops of the 3rd Ukrainian Front crossed the border of Yugoslavia and launched an offensive against Belgrade. All these events forced the German command to accelerate the evacuation of troops from the southern Balkans. In addition to the Red Army, the Bulgarian army and the RAF, the pro-communist People's Liberation Army of Greece (ELAS), which was supported by the Soviet Union, actively opposed the Germans. Until the summer of 1944, ELAS units operated using partisan methods, and during the German evacuation, their attacks became more open and bolder. It was also not calm for the Germans in Albania, where the local rebels also sharply intensified their activities.

Meanwhile, the German air bridge was being attacked more and more. Airfields in Greece were constantly bombed by British bombers, and transport planes were intercepted by night fighters. During September, air groups II./TG4 and IV./TG1 lost eighty aircraft. To compensate for this damage, the Germans had to allocate aircraft from recently disbanded aviation groups, industrial squadrons and aviation schools. Then they decided to involve bombers in the operation.

On 27 September, some of the crews from II. and III./KG27 received an order: to fly their He 111H-20s to Wiener Neustadt airfield in Austria the next morning to participate in a certain 'particularly important mission'. When the intrigued pilots arrived at this large air force base, a further goal was announced: to fly to Athens with an intermediate landing at Thessaloniki airfield. After arriving there, the crews were informed of their further task – the urgent evacuation of as many German soldiers from Crete as possible. In addition, the 2nd Staffel KG4, reinforced with additional crews, was involved in Operation Amboss.

The bombers intended for these missions had been thoroughly re-equipped. Two rows of seats were installed in the bomb bay, located opposite each other, which could accommodate eighteen passengers. In addition, the aircraft were equipped with an inflatable boat placed in the form of a package under the fuselage covering immediately behind the upper part of the cabin. From his seat, the crew commander could activate a mechanism that would open the compressed-air cylinder, with the inflatable boat inflating in a few seconds, opening the lid in the fuselage and poking out of the hatch. The five-man craft was attached with a safety rope, which was supposed to prevent premature drift of the boat and was easily detached. This elaborate design had one significant drawback – it was designed only to save the crew, not the passengers!

All flights were carried out in a hurry, as the Germans expected the landing of British troops at any moment as well as the capture of Belgrade by Soviet troops. In addition, the flights took place in the dark and clouds over the mountains, which often led to disasters. KG27 lost ten aircraft and nine aircrews in two weeks. These were the last missions in the long bloody path of this Kampfgeschwader. On 18 October, it was finally converted into fighter Jagdgeschwader KG(J)/27. Its protracted 'potato war' was over.

The Kriegsmarine also suffered heavy losses during this evacuation. For example, on 7 October, the British destroyers *Termagant* and *Tuscan* sank the destroyer *TA-37*, the anti-submarine ship *Uj-102 Brigitte* and the patrol ship *GK-32* south-west of Cassandra. On 12 October, aircraft from 809 Sqn FAA from the escort carrier *Stalker* sank twelve ships and vessels on the evacuation route at once, including the destroyer *TA-38*, two high-speed landing barges and three boats of the KFK type. A week later, planes from this aircraft carrier sank the *destroyer TA-18*. The total losses of the Kriegsmarine during the evacuation amounted to twenty-nine ships out of fifty-two that took part in this mission.

Meanwhile, on 12 October, the United Kingdom launched Operation Manna. The 4th Battalion of the 2nd Airborne Brigade parachuted into Megara airfield (50km west of Athens). The next day, six CG-4 Hadrian cargo gliders landed there, delivering jeeps and bulldozers to level the runway.

The culminating day in the fleeting Battle for the Balkans was 14 October, which became something of a reverse blitzkrieg for the Wehrmacht. On this day, British soldiers entered Athens, and the Red Army, together with Yugoslav partisans, entered Belgrade. By this time, the Germans had evacuated almost all their troops from Greece, as well as two-thirds of the 60,000-strong garrison of the Aegean Islands. These troops went to plug the next gaps in the crumbling front. Those who did not have time to be transported to the mainland were taken to the islands of Crete and Rhodes, which were declared by Hitler so-called 'core fortresses' ('Kern Festungen').

On 31 October, the Germans evacuated Thessaloniki shortly before the British got there. After that, the bombers from II./KG4 were among the last in the Luftwaffe to leave Greece. One of the last missions of this Kampfgeschwader in the Balkans was the evacuation of members of the puppet government of Albania led by Rexhep Mitrovica and his

German staff. On 17 November, Albanian rebels, with the support of the British, captured Tirana, and on 29 November the Germans and Albanians cooperating with them left Shkodra, their last stronghold in the north of the country.

By the end of 1944, the front line, which in January ran along the Dnieper and to the coast of Lake Ladoga, had moved to East Prussia, the Vistula, Slovakia, Hungary and Bosnia. Meanwhile, in October and November, the next epic battle was unfolding – for Budapest. But this is a completely different and separate story.

# CONCLUSION

Despite a series of major defeats at Kursk, Smolensk and on the Dnieper, the Germans still held vast territories of Russia. They still held positions near Leningrad and in the Crimea. Hitler said that the conquered space would allow him to keep the Red Army away from the borders of Germany and its allies for a long time. But in fact, 1944 brought the Germans continuous disappointments and catastrophes. In January, the Soviets launched a powerful offensive in the northern sector, then they consistently attacked the Germans in Ukraine, the Crimea, Belarus, and the Baltic States. Hitler's 'strategy' was to prohibit his generals from any retreat, delaying the adoption of 'unpleasant' decisions.

This made it easier for the Russians and led to the fact that German divisions constantly fell into pockets, which had to be supplied by air. Endless crisis situations forced the Wehrmacht to transfer its divisions from one sector of the front to another, plugging the gaps that had formed. Then the weakened sections of the defence collapsed, provoking more and more catastrophic defeats. The collapse that the German army experienced had no analogy in history. The front line moved to a distance of 500 to 1,000km, and more than 70 per cent of the available divisions were defeated, destroyed or captured. In nine months, military operations moved from the depths of Russia to the territory of European countries.

By 1944, the Russians had learned from the lessons that the Wehrmacht had given them in 1941 and 1942. The Red Army brilliantly mastered the tactics of blitzkrieg and learned how to conduct deep offensive operations. Just as German tanks had terrified Europe and Soviet Russia at the beginning of the war, now Russian tanks were terrifying Europe with the loud clang of their tracks.

By the beginning of 1944, there were 163 German divisions on the Eastern Front. The total number of German troops (including rear, auxiliary and volunteer units) numbered about 3 million men. The irretrievable losses of the Wehrmacht in the East this year amounted to about 2 million people, of whom 1.2 million died, and 760,000 more were captured. Thus, the German army lost two thirds of its soldiers in the battles described here. Of the eleven German armies (not counting Norway), eight survived the fighting in pockets, and some of them even found themselves in them twice. At least half of the armies were completely defeated. In order to plug the gaps in the defence, the German command had to send to the east most of the reserves, several divisions from Italy and almost all the troops evacuated from Crete and Greece in the autumn. It was perhaps the largest defeat of an armed forces in world history. The Russian blitzkrieg greatly facilitated the Allied landings in France and allowed them to quickly defeat the German armies in the West.

Of course, despite the successes, the Red Army was still not without many disadvantages. Often poorly trained and weakened divisions were rushed into battle, which were given unrealistic tasks. This led to large losses and an irrational waste of resources. From this book, it is clearly clear how Stalin differed from Hitler, and why Stalin ultimately won this war. Being a brutal dictator, Stalin nevertheless admitted his mistakes. After the first defeats at the beginning of the war, he stopped considering himself a genius, partially became disillusioned with Bolshevik ideals and even partially returned the almost destroyed Christian religion to the country. This flexibility eventually allowed the Red Army to gain the power it had demonstrated in 1944.

Hitler, on the other hand, never admitted his mistakes and never changed. Despite the terrible catastrophes that his orders led to, the Führer continued to consider himself a genius and a messenger of providence. Therefore, his 'strategy' had become predictable and uncomplicated.

In some countries, these events are called 'enslavement' or 'occupation'. The Soviet Union was accused of 'strangling the Warsaw and Slovak uprisings', of 'violating Polish sovereignty' and other atrocities. And Russians were attributed exclusively to villainous motives. But ordinary Russian soldiers, most of whom came from villages and provincial towns, were unaware of such political motives. Unlike the British and Americans, they came to Europe through completely destroyed and burned cities, having seen enough of the corpses of Russian women, old men and children. Many of them were very angry and went to the Third Reich to avenge the suffering and humiliation of their people. They believed that they were going on a campaign in order to liberate Europe from the Great Evil, and the memory of these events and the battles waged by their ancestors became sacred for several generations of Russians.

# REFERENCES AND SOURCES


Bartoszewski, Władysław T., *Dni Walczącej Stolicy: kronika Powstania Warszawskiego* (in Polish), Warsaw: Muzeum Powstania Warszawskiego; Świat Książki, 1984.

Bogatyrev S.V., Larintsev R.I., Ovcharenko A.V., *Enemy Navy Losses in the Black Sea Theater of Operations 1941–1944,* Kiev, 1998.

Craciunoiu, C. & Roba, J.-L., *'Stukisti'. Les Ju 87du Grupul 3 Picaij roumain (1943–1944),* Avions Hors-serie No. 52, 2021.

Glantz, David, *Red Storm Over the Balkans: The Failed Soviet Invasion of Romania,* Lawrence: University Press of Kansas, 2007.

Glantz, David; Orenstein, Harold S., *Belorussia 1944,* Routledge, 2004.

Glantz, David, *Soviet Military Deception in the Second World War,* Frank Cass, London, 1989.

Glantz David, *The Battle for Leningrad. 1941–1945,* Moscow: Astrel, 2008.

Gunderlach, K., *Chronik Kampfgeschwader 4 'General Wever',* Motorbuchverlag, 2013.

Grylev A., Vyrodov I., 'Loyalty to International Duty' (on the USSR's assistance to the Slovak National Uprising), *Military Historical Journal,* 1968, No. 10.

Hazard, M., *La Stukageschwader 2 'Immelman'. Tome II: septembre 1943–mai 1945*. Editions LELA Press, 2020.

Isaev, Alexey, *The 'Pocket' of Hube. The Proskurov-Chernivtsi Operation of 1944, Moscow,* Yauza, 2017.

Manstein E., *Lost Victories,* Moscow: AST; St Petersburg Terra Fantastica, 1999.

Precan, V., *Slovenské národné povstanie. Nemci a Slovensko 1944,* Dokumenty, Bratislava, 1970.

Waiss, W., *Chronik Kampgeschwader Nr.27 Boelcke. Teil 5: 01.01.1944–31.12.1944,* Helios, 2008.

## Archives

### Central archive of the Ministry of Defence of the Russian Federation

TSAMO RF, Foundation 217, Shap. Inventory 1221, Case 4991
TSAMO RF, Foundation 364, Shap. Inventory 0006278, Case 0112
TSAMO RF, Foundation 290, Shap. Inventory 0003284, Case 0703
TSAMO RF, Foundation 290, Shap. Inventory 0003284, Case 0690
TSAMO RF, Foundation 204, Shap. Inventory 89, Case 2324
TSAMO RF, Foundation 362, Shap. Inventory 0006169, Case 0189
TSAMO RF, Foundation 217, Shap. Inventory 1221, Case 5083
TSAMO RF, Foundation 20058, Shap. Inventory 1, Case 9
TSAMO RF, Foundation 20562, Shap. Inventory 1, Case 32
TSAMO RF, Foundation 332, Shap. Inventory 4948, Case 189
TSAMO RF, Foundation 332, Shap. Inventory 4948, Case 177
TSAMO RF, Foundation 332, Shap. Inventory 4948, Case 216
TSAMO RF, Foundation 332, Shap. Inventory 4948, Case 186
TSAMO RF, Foundation 332, Shap. Inventory 4948, Case 193
TSAMO RF, Foundation 236, Shap. Inventory 2673, Case 1090
TSAMO RF, Foundation 240, Shap. Inventory 2779, Case 1136
TSAMO RF, Foundation 240, Shap. Inventory 2779, Case 1146
TSAMO RF, Foundation 240, Shap. Inventory 2779, Case 1931
TSAMO RF, Foundation 243, Shap. Inventory 2900, Case 845
TSAMO RF, Foundation 243, Shap. Inventory 2900, Case 835
TSAMO RF, Foundation 243, Shap. Inventory 2900, Case 846
TSAMO RF, Foundation 243, Shap. Inventory 2900, Case 853
TSAMO RF, Foundation 243, Shap. Inventory 2900, Case 843
TSAMO RF, Foundation 244, Shap. Inventory 3000, Case 817
TSAMO RF, Foundation 244, Shap. Inventory 3000, Case 807
TSAMO RF, Foundation 244, Shap. Inventory 3000, Case 799
TSAMO RF, Foundation 244, Shap. Inventory 3000, Case 778
TSAMO RF, Foundation 233, Shap. Inventory 2356, Case 319
TSAMO RF, Foundation 241, Shap. Inventory 0002593, Case 0327
TSAMO RF, Foundation 241, Shap. Inventory 0002593, Case 0329
TSAMO RF, Foundation 241, Shap. Inventory 0002593, Case 0330
TSAMO RF, Foundation 13608, Shap. Inventory 20395, Case 58
TSAMO RF, Foundation 13608, Shap. Inventory 20395, Case 59
TSAMO RF, Foundation 13608, Shap. Inventory 20395, Case 60
TSAMO RF, Foundation 13608, Shap. Inventory 20395, Case 61
TSAMO RF, Foundation 13608, Shap. Inventory 20395, Case 62
TSAMO RF, Foundation 235, Shap. Inventory 2074, Case 846

TSAMO RF, Foundation 235, Shap. Inventory 2074, Case 847
TSAMO RF, Foundation 235, Shap. Inventory 2074, Case 848
TSAMO RF, Foundation 327, Shap. Inventory 0004999, Case 0221
TSAMO RF, Foundation 327, Shap. Inventory 0004999, Case 0233
TSAMO RF, Foundation 327, Shap. Inventory 0004999, Case 0219
TSAMO RF, Foundation 319, Shap. Inventory 0004798, Case 0268
TSAMO RF, Foundation 319, Shap. Inventory 0004798, Case 0266
TSAMO RF, Foundation 319, Shap. Inventory 0004798, Case 0270
TSAMO RF, Foundation 319, Shap. Inventory 0004798, Case 0265
TSAMO RF, Foundation 449, Shap. Inventory 9921, Case 141
TSAMO RF, Foundation 243, Shap. Inventory 0920263, Case 0015
TSAMO RF, Foundation 406, Shap. Inventory 9837, Case 815
TSAMO RF, Foundation 406, Shap. Inventory 9837, Case 814
TSAMO RF, Foundation 20215, Shap. Inventory 1, Case 29
TSAMO RF, Foundation 240, Shap. Inventory 2779, Case 869
TSAMO RF, Foundation 445, Shap. Inventory 9005, Case 218
TSAMO RF, Foundation 445, Shap. Inventory 9005, Case 241
TSAMO RF, Foundation 345, Shap. Inventory 5487, Case 219
TSAMO RF, Foundation 243, Shap. Inventory 2900, Case 935
TSAMO RF, Foundation 402, Shap. Inventory 9575, Case 521
TSAMO RF, Foundation 402, Shap. Inventory 9575, Case 528
TSAMO RF, Foundation 307, Shap. Inventory 4148, Case 280
TSAMO RF, Foundation 307, Shap. Inventory 4148, Case 279
TSAMO RF, Foundation 307, Shap. Inventory 4148, Case 280
TSAMO RF, Foundation 233, Shap. Inventory 2309, Case 18
TSAMO RF, Foundation 20502, Shap. Inventory 1, Case 84
TSAMO RF, Foundation 20502, Shap. Inventory 1, Case 68
TSAMO RF, Foundation 20502, Shap. Inventory 1, Case 63
TSAMO RF, Foundation 20502, Shap. Inventory 1, Case 65
TSAMO RF, Foundation 3443, Shap. Inventory 1, Case 77
TSAMO RF, Foundation 208, Shap. Inventory 2511, Case 80
TSAMO RF, Foundation 460, Shap. Inventory 5047, Case 545
TSAMO RF, Foundation 13607, Shap. Inventory 20368, Case 559
TSAMO RF, Foundation 13607, Shap. Inventory 20368, Case 553
TSAMO RF, Foundation 13607, Shap. Inventory 20368, Case 555
TSAMO RF, Foundation 299, Shap. Inventory 3070, Case 367
TSAMO RF, Foundation 299, Shap. Inventory 3070, Case 368
TSAMO RF, Foundation 3406, Shap. Inventory 1, Case 190
TSAMO RF, Foundation 299, Shap. Inventory 3070, Case 345
TSAMO RF, Foundation 320, Shap. Inventory 4522, Case 124
TSAMO RF, Foundation 320, Shap. Inventory 4522, Case 132
TSAMO RF, Foundation 320, Shap. Inventory 4522, Case 133

TSAMO RF, Foundation 3470, Shap. Inventory 1, Case 268
TSAMO RF, Foundation 3470, Shap. Inventory 1, Case 269
TSAMO RF, Foundation 3470, Shap. Inventory 1, Case 168
TSAMO RF, Foundation 323, Shap. Inventory 4756, Case 46
TSAMO RF, Foundation 846, Shap. Inventory 1, Case 8
TSAMO RF, Foundation 341, Shap. Inventory 1, Case 292
TSAMO RF, Foundation 341, Shap. Inventory 1, Case 293
TSAMO RF, Foundation 3409, Shap. Inventory 1, Case 3
TSAMO RF, Foundation 20545, Shap. Inventory 1, Case 26
TSAMO RF, Foundation 14361, Shap. Inventory 0443120c, Case 0001
TSAMO RF, Foundation 242, Shap. Inventory 2254, Case 152
TSAMO RF, Foundation 242, Shap. Inventory 2254, Case 162
TSAMO RF, Foundation 339, Shap. Inventory 5179, Case 18
TSAMO RF, Foundation 339, Shap. Inventory 5179, Case 18
TSAMO RF, Foundation 3465, Shap. Inventory 1, Case 450a
TSAMO RF, Foundation 20545, Shap. Inventory 1, Case 27

# INDEX